AUSTRALIA IMAGINED

AUSTRALIA IMAGINED

VIEWS FROM THE BRITISH PERIODICAL PRESS
1800–1900

Judith Johnston

with

Monica Anderson

University of Western Australia Press

First published in 2005 by
University of Western Australia Press
Crawley, Western Australia 6009
www.uwapress.uwa.edu.au

Publication of this book was made possible with funding assistance from the
Australian Academy of Humanities.

National Library of Australia
Cataloguing-in-Publication entry:

Australia imagined: views from the British periodical press 1800–1900.

  Bibliography.
  Includes index.
  ISBN 1 920694 45 5.

  1. Australia—History—19th century. 2. Australia—Foreign public opinion, British.
  3. Australia—Press coverage—Great Britain. I. Johnston, J. A. (Judith A.), 1947– .
  II. Anderson, Monica.

994

Consultant editor: Jean Dunn
Index by Anne Batt
Designed and typeset by Pages in Action, Melbourne
Typeset in 10/13pt Berkeley Book
Printed by BPA Print Group, Melbourne

CONTENTS

British Emigration

Letters Home

Colonial Life

Women

Men

The Chinese

Federation

Cartoons from *Punch*

EDITORIAL NOTE

The original spellings, punctuation and typesetting conventions have been retained, except on rare occasions when meaning is obscured and change has been silently instituted. The predominant use of single quote marks has been standardised. The very long paragraphs preferred by many nineteenth-century writers have occasionally been broken up a little, for the ease of today's readers.

The biographical notes preceding individual pieces are derived from the sources indicated in square brackets at the end of each piece, and cited in full in the Abbreviations. In the Introduction, the references in brackets are to the pages of this book.

An ellipsis (…) indicates that text has been omitted. Square brackets indicate editorial insertions. The varying use of '£' and 'L' to indicate pounds sterling has been standardised to '£'.

Conversions

1 mile	1.61 kilometres
1 acre	0.40 hectare
1 ounce	28.35 grams
1 pound (lb)	0.45 kilogram

Twelve pence (d.) made up one shilling (s.) and twenty shillings made up one pound.

ABBREVIATIONS

The following abbreviations of titles are used in the biographical notes preceding individual pieces.

ADB   *Australian Dictionary of Biography.*

ALB   *Australian Literature from its Beginnings to 1935*, E. Morris Miller. Melbourne: Melbourne University Press, 1940.

AWW   *Australian Women Writers: A Bibliographic Guide*, edited by Debra Adelaide. London: Pandora, 1988.

BALP   *Bibliography of Australian Literature Project: List of Australian Writers 1788–1992.* Canberra: National Centre for Australian Studies, 1995.

BR   *A Biographical Register 1788–1939: Notes from the Name Index of the Australian Dictionary of Biography*, edited by H. J. Gibbney and Ann G. Smith.

BWW   *The Oxford Guide to British Women Writers*, edited by Joanne Shattock. Oxford: Oxford University Press, 1993.

CDWB   *The Continuum Dictionary of Women's Biography*, edited by Jennifer S. Uglow. New York: Continuum, 1989.

DNB   *Dictionary of National Biography.*

GGW   *Great Grandmama's Weekly: A Celebration of The Girl's Own Paper 1880–1901*, Wendy Forrester. London: Lutterworth Press, 1980.

HW   *Household Words: A Weekly Journal 1850–1859: Conducted by Charles Dickens*, Anne Lohrli. Toronto: University of Toronto Press, 1973.

LCNUC *Library of Congress National Union Catalogue pre-1956 Imprints.*

LCVF   *Longman Companion to Victorian Fiction*, edited by John Sutherland. London: Longman, 1988.

NAP   *Nineteenth-Century Australian Periodicals: An Annotated Bibliography*, edited by Lurline Stuart. Sydney: Hale & Iremonger, 1979.

SG   *Several Generations*, N. J. B. Plomley. Sydney: Wentworth Books, 1971.

WDINP *Waterloo Directory of Irish Newspapers and Periodicals 1800–1900, Phase II.*

WI   *Wellesley Index to Victorian Periodicals 1824–1900.*

PREFACE

Inevitably, the task of selection for this book has meant both the omission of much fascinating material (the choice was almost boundless) and the abridgement of many pieces. For this we apologise, recognising how frustrating it can be to wonder just what omissions that ellipsis signals. However, every piece should be readily locatable for any interested reader, and accordingly we have provided full bibliographical detail. We have also included, as 'Further Reading' within the bibliography, a listing of every piece we found in which Australia is a dominant topic. And in our Introduction we refer to some of these. We trust that this list will prove a useful tool to researchers and to readers interested in the topic for its own sake.

Because of the vast amount of material available, we determined to range across as varied a set of journalistic genres as possible, including general articles, reviews of books, short stories, poetry, advice literature on emigration (often gendered), and leader articles on contemporary politics. The variations will reveal shifts and nuances and fissures that would not be obvious in a collection restricted to mainstream quarterly articles. For the same reason, we chose from a varied range of periodicals to ensure a disparate mix of political and social positions, a mix we consider to be essential. Topics within these genres include race, gender, nationhood and the various political domains, including home, space and place. We tried also to choose pieces which look at the various Australian colonies.

The categories that anchor our selection represent, in roughly chronological order, the key historical movements in the nineteenth-century settlement of Australia. And within those broad categories, the arrangement is chronological. 'Transportation' focuses on Australia's convict beginnings, while in 'Impressions' the British press reassesses the taint of convict settlement in terms of colonial development overcoming its dubious beginnings. 'The Aborigines' explores not so much frontier encounters as ruminations on the social, legal and political ramifications of land ownership and cultural integrity. 'British Emigration' reveals the press questioning and exploring the effects of large-scale emigration both on the home country and on the colonies, while 'Letters Home' offers the British reading public some sense of how individuals experienced migration. In 'Colonial

Life' the press normalises and domesticates the colonial experience to reassure British readers about this furthermost colonial destination, while in 'Women' and 'Men' the press speculates on just how national characteristics may change and shift. 'The Chinese' reveals anxieties about the possibility of disruption to the homogenised British colonial process, anxieties in part fostered by the eventual change from colonial dependency to colonial self-sufficiency, as explored in our final category, 'Federation'. We hope our readers will be struck, as we were, with the degree to which these pieces resonate with current issues in twenty-first century Australia.

We wish to acknowledge here, with our thanks, the financial support we have received for this project. The Menzies Foundation awarded Judith Johnston an Australian Bicentennial Fellowship in 1998, which enabled her to take up an Honorary Visiting Fellowship at the University of Leicester and there conduct the initial research for this book. A grant from The University of Western Australia brought the project to a significant pre-publishing stage, and the Vice Chancellor of The University of Western Australia, the Westerly Centre, UWA, and the Australian Academy of the Humanities provided publishing grants. We are most grateful to all three for this generosity and for the faith it demonstrates in this work.

For permission to use the material reproduced in this anthology we wish to thank Dr Andrew Lacey, University of Leicester Library, and Dr Toby Burrows, Reid Library, The University of Western Australia.

For their intellectual support for and interest in our project we wish to thank our colleagues in the Westerly Centre, The University of Western Australia, in particular Delys Bird, Tanya Dalziell, Kieran Dolin, Dennis Haskell, Tony Hughes-d'Aeth and Andrew Lynch. Kieran and Tony, and Victoria Burrows, read the Introduction in manuscript and offered their comments, which were much appreciated. Maureen de la Harpe, at University of Western Australia Press was ever-helpful in resolving the various minor problems and issues which arose, and Jean Dunn's editing insights are gratefully acknowledged.

Judith Johnston
Monica Anderson

INTRODUCTION

*Imagine these wide regions in the yet uncultivated parts of the earth
flourishing like our own, and possessed by people enjoying our institutions
and speaking our language.*
                                                    Quarterly Review, 1812, p. 355.

The typical Australian is an Englishman with a dash of sunshine in him.
                                                    Young Man, 1899, p. 180.

At the century's beginning, the author of our first epigraph employs the impera-
tive and demands of the *Quarterly's* readers that they *imagine* the impact of
wholesale emigration to the euphemistically described 'uncultivated parts of the
earth' (an apparently innocent phrase which helps so early in the nineteenth
century to establish the myth of *terra nullius* over the Australian continent). The
imperialist language ('flourishing', 'possessed') celebrates the prospect of the
spread of British culture and language across the world but conceals the anxious
wish to rid the country of its unproductive poor. The focus of our book is the
construction of European Australia within the pages of the nineteenth-century
British periodical press—of an antipodean site in relation to its superior island
opposite, Great Britain. Running counter to this narrative is the beginnings of
an independent 'Australian' political and cultural identity which, as our second
epigraph intimates, is nevertheless tied to ideas of Britishness and 'Home'.

Iain Chambers has argued that 'Britishness' 'can be displaced and condensed
in multiple identities, values, visions, ideas and criticisms that germinate,
pollinate and take root in the soil of civil society'.[1] We suggest that these displace-
ments and condensations occur, at the first level of discourse, in the diverse and
popular periodical press. In contributing to the formation of political and
cultural identity in Australia, they have inevitably affected the sense of identity
both of Indigenous people and of the colonisers themselves.

While it can be claimed that the British periodical press in the nineteenth
century was often an instrument of imperialist enterprises, it could be, and often
was, profoundly critical of Britain's colonial administration. And it gave space
to debates in which, later in the century, former British subjects (now calling
themselves 'Australian') participated eagerly. In part, we see this anthology as
elucidating the extent to which the press's emphasis on land and land ownership

played an important part in the construction of new settler identities. People saw themselves in a very new, often opportunistic and definitely economic relation to land, as the highly politicised concepts of ownership, possession, dispossession, appropriation, taming and familiarisation attest.[2] Thus, in our section on 'The Aboriginals' we have included articles which contest the stereotypical accounts, both negative and 'positive', which proliferated in the British periodical press across the nineteenth century; they question the colonial position on land rights in very strong terms indeed.

Greg Dening contends that culture is talk and that cultural identity is always grounded in talk and story.[3] We have sought to reassess the status of periodical press discourse, not as literary artefact, but as writing that contains these essential cultural elements of talk and story. As Dening elaborates in *Readings/Writings*, 'Cultural living in its bare bones is talk, talk translated into all sorts of symbols. That is its realism. We make all our relationships by talk, all our institutions, all our roles.'[4] Eliza Brown, an early settler of the Swan River colony, records that local Indigenous people designated writing as 'paper talk',[5] and we found this a usefully precise term when considering the periodical press. The press was so prolific, so all-encompassing, that it gave a particular voice to the talk and story of the British imperial project from which Australian political and cultural identity inevitably emerged.

Put simply, the articles in this anthology are British 'talk' about their Australian colony, a conversation between the British press and its readership about what is taking place 'out there'. But the conversation is overheard, because the periodicals are also purchased in Australia by the colonisers, and so speculations and conjectures about retaining an essentially British nationality are responded to in debates that move back and forth in the press.

We believe that there are advantages in this new and different perspective on the development of Australian national and cultural identity. Although often both ephemeral and contingent, the published material of the periodical press nevertheless delivers readings of a nascent Australian nation that are based as much on fictions and fantasies as on historical and political deliberations. The observant reader will note too that these articles address issues that remain the subjects of public debate within Australia today: water resources, the status of Indigenous people, immigration, the dominance of sport in the national psyche.

So how did the British press contribute to the shaping and formation of early versions of Australian identity? It did it by speculating on how emigration might change and alter the mindset of those who took ship, and on the effects that antipodean climate, geography, hardship and fortune might have both on emigrants and on the children born out of sight and sound of the British homeland.

The talk was focused, above all, on the ways in which the much-prized traits of British identity—honesty, integrity, courage, fortitude, and so on—might be transformed by the Australian experience. Sometimes the talk was positive and enthusiastic; sometimes negative and filled with foreboding. This was only natural when the effects of imperial expansion were being debated in a range of journals that represented both mainstream and radical points of view, and any number of shadings in between. So, despite the triumphal tone of our first epigraph, the press was not always so sanguine nor so enthusiastic about Australia as a colonial destination.

In 1825 Peregrine Bingham surveys the various destinations available to the prospective emigrant and the various reasons for emigrating. Interestingly, in this first discussion of the topic in the *Westminster Review*, Bingham makes two statements which are to be repeated over and over again throughout the century. The first is that anyone contemplating emigration must be industrious, hardworking, frugal. The second is that emigration grants independence to both emigrants and their children. While Bingham, we believe, considers only financial independence, over the century the word becomes linked variously to class, religion, politics, gender and, eventually, to independence from the 'mother' country itself. The two colonies Bingham names, New South Wales and Van Diemen's Land, have physical advantages such as climate, but he deems both to be disadvantaged morally, intellectually and politically. In particular, the presence of convict labour means that emigrants risk moral 'contamination' of their children. By contrast, Canada is 'free from this taint'.[6] This too is the burden of 'Emigration' by the editor of *Chambers' Edinburgh Journal*, who warns that emigrating to New South Wales and Van Diemen's Land must be deemed 'most improper' because both are 'crowded with a population formed of the offscourings of every town in England, Scotland, and Ireland—ruffians who break away in bands from their employers, and scour the settlements as freebooters'.[7]

Before the discovery of gold, the general tone regarding Australia in the British press is one of disparagement, due solely to the transportation of convicts. Even as late as 1849, at least according to William Smith O'Brien in 'Transportation as it now is' (p. 27), the colonies are 'nurseries of depravity' and the young nation is polluted at birth; Britain has indeed created a monster. The change of tone after the discovery of gold in 1850 is both dramatic and immediate, and can be readily located in an article from *Leisure Hour* entitled 'Australia I.—Its General Features and Resources' (p. 43). This article celebrates the escalation of free immigration to Australian shores, 'transferring thither our domestic habits, commercial enterprise, laws, institutions, language, literature, and religion', and confidently declares that the 'once penal country is admirably fitted for the nurture of great nations' after all.

Early in the century, the idea of Australia is occasionally dismissed with comic humour, epitomised by an article in the *Athenaeum* of 10 June 1829 entitled 'Literature of the Swan River' (p. 37). Its immediacy is quite startling when we note that the Swan River colonists arrived in Western Australia only in May the same year. With its unusual comic mode and intent, the article deliberately lampoons particular and readily recognisable colonialist imperatives, such as the push to produce arable and grazing land as quickly as possible, and concludes by employing these same colonialist truisms to the cultivation of literature:

> Wherever proper modes of culture have been adopted, and a skilful use has been made of the powers of machinery, every literary soil, however intractable at first, has at length been rendered productive, at a small expense of time and labour. The Committee, therefore, does not despair of seeing, in a few years, a plentiful crop of English plants, of every genus, adorning the banks of the Swan River; ... The Committee therefore recommend that the House should commence in the course of the next session, by sending out one metaphysician, two religious poets (that race being sickly), a reviewer, and a fashionable novelist.

Britain's imperialist culture is rarely mocked in precisely this way and certainly not later in the century when the failing empire is vociferously defended. The article specifically attacks the quality of Britain's contemporary literature and, by suggesting that Mr. A. K. Newman offers 'to settle four hundred novelists in the colony before next August', the comic possibilities throw into glaring relief the writer's belief that sub-standard literature is criminal in intent and that all purveyors of it should be transported. Moreover, there is an implicit critique of the British government's domestic policies, in which emigration and transportation are the too-easy solutions to over-population and working-class poverty. This position was adopted as consistently in the press as was the promotion of emigration. For instance, William Molesworth in the *London Review* derides the establishment of the first Australian colony as a cynical exercise by those who 'ruled England', and 'conceived the ideal of a community' at 'the antipodes of England':

> It was not difficult to find appropriate citizens; for the commission of a crime was a ready and sure index of an individual possessing some, at least, of the requisite moral qualifications. The gaols were swept of their inmates; the burglars, thieves, felons, and prostitutes of England were sent to form the first colony of civilized beings on the coasts of Australia, and to be the parent stock of a mighty nation. ... The real object was carefully concealed; whilst the scheme was represented under a feigned aspect, as a means of punishing crime, and clearing the country of its criminal population. Thus the sanction of the legislature was obtained, and the nation was deceived.[8]

As a contrast, sentiment is probably the most common mode in the poetry which appeared in the monthly magazines, as it was more generally. Emigration does appeal particularly to the sentimental, because it involves separation, both at a national and a domestic level ('Mother' as well as 'Mother England' is left behind), loss, exile and hardship. 'The Emigrant's Complaint', in which his spirit flies homeward only to discover the loss of his family, exemplifies the sentimentalising of separation and loss:

> I cannot stay; my heart is swelling;—
> My losses, graven on that stone,
> The dreary truth to me are telling—
> I stand in this wide world alone,
> With no kind voice to cheer me on;
> For all I loved are dead and gone.[9]

In a more symbolic style, 'The Landing of the Primrose' celebrates the arrival in Australia of a living primrose and records the crowds of homesick emigrants ('The felon and the free man') crowding the shore for a first glimpse:

> That precious thing—(Oh, wondrous!
> Oh, spell of potent power,
> From English earth transported!)—
> A little lowly flower.

This poem describes 'guilt-hardened' men reduced to tears, and blesses the wife of the ship's captain as the first to plant the primrose 'Upon the Exile's land!'.[10] By contrast, Richard Howitt's 'To a Small Australian Flower' (p. 132) celebrates instead the local Australian flora. Despite its being 'Held to be a noteless thing', Howitt's poem accords the flower a comparable value to that of the transported primrose, and indeed he considers transporting the plant back to England.

This notion of comparison between 'Home' and Australia is nowhere more profoundly carried through than in Catherine Helen Spence's 'An Australian's Impressions of England' (p. 50), which is reprinted here in full. The earliest idea of national identity in colonial Australia is sometimes attributed to the 1890s, and to the often misogynist articles published in the notorious *Bulletin*. Some three decades earlier, however, Spence helped to formulate, within specific limitations, a notion of Australian identity that embraced both men and women. Spence was Australia's first female political candidate, in the Federal Convention elections of 1897. When her name appeared on a list of the 'Ten Best Men', the printer said it could not be placed under such a heading and her name should be removed and replaced by that of a man. The party organizer replied, 'Not say she's one of the ten best men? Why she's the best man of the lot'.[11]

In her *Cornhill Magazine* article, Spence calls herself 'Australian' and writes about egalitarianism (with no sense of the term being gendered male, as it came to be later in the century). She is aware of woman's separate position, but does not tie it specifically to her ideas about national identity. When she talks about the Australian character, she means men *and* women. Spence also writes very precisely about what she sees as the difference between Australians and the English. Susan Martin has noted that, for white so-called 'Australians', any imagining of a national image was clearly framed by 'British understandings of nation'.[12] We think this is very much the case in the earlier decades of the nineteenth century and can best be located in Spence's article. She writes, for instance, of growing up 'at the antipodes'. By her deliberate use of that word, Spence is already signalling that Australia is diametrically opposite to Britain, not just geographically but socially and culturally as well. She believes this sense of oppositeness will grow and develop until Australia becomes a very distinct nation. She nevertheless affirms that 'we are still emphatically English', and tells her British readership that 'it will take several generations before we can have a distinct national character of our own'. It is notable that although Spence uses 'we' and 'our', she would not have conceived of Aboriginal people as forming a part of her imagined Australian citizenship.

In the 1890s the *Bulletin* and other Australian journals sought to develop that distinct national character about which Spence speaks. Unfortunately, the Australian they imagined never shifted beyond the categories of 'white' and 'male'. While she thinks it will take several generations, Spence's article does continually affirm her belief in the development of a distinctly Australian identity. For instance, she consistently uses phrases like 'We Australians' and 'your England' to express two very separate national identities. Of land, she writes that in 'England all land is private property, and is in few hands. In Australia a great proportion of the land is unappropriated, and held by Government in trust for the people':

> the careful cultivation of Britain, the utilization of every little bit of land (even the narrow ridges on the sides of the railways), the rarity of commons or waste land, gives us a painful impression. We feel cribbed and cabined and confined. Colonial children rarely like England; they do not like every place to be private property not to be trespassed over. There is no doubt that the concentration of all the landed property in the kingdom into few hands, appears a much greater evil to those who have grown up in such a country as Australia than to those who have all their lives seen nothing else.

Spence's words about land and property rights and trespass betray little, if any, awareness of Indigenous land rights.

The bulk of Spence's essay is about the contribution made by white women to the nation state, and celebrates the fact that hard physical labour and the many demands on their time makes Australian women stronger and more able than their English counterparts. At this precise historical moment, 1866, when agitation about the so-called 'Woman Question' is dominating the British periodicals, Spence believes that emigration and colonisation has for women been a liberating experience. Colonisation has freed them from the domestic sphere and in fact made the domestic a colonising tool. The presence of women and children consolidates the colonial project and completes the invasion. We think it is not surprising that colonising white women were the first to get the vote, in New Zealand in 1893 and in South Australia in 1896, because they were part of the broader public project of colonisation. More importantly, some of those who emigrated, like Spence, embraced the idea of an Australian identity eventually developing in direct opposition to British identity. However, Spence declares that the Australian has a 'quick though superficial intelligence', a description that qualifies and limits the 'Australian', and is suggestive of a still embryonic condition. Interestingly, 'quick though superficial' were the terms then most often used to describe and dismiss the intelligence of women.

Australia's embryonic condition is very apparent in the 1850 *Punch* cartoon 'Lord John Taking the Measure of the Colonies' by Richard Doyle (p. 136). Compared to other colonies named in the drawing, Australia is its central focus, a tall, callow youth fast outgrowing his garments. It was then a common belief, reiterated in any number of the articles we explored, that Australian youth grew too fast and ripened too soon, and for this reason would be 'less likely to have enduring physical fibre', as the author of 'Young Men in the Colonies' (p. 177) claims. The poem which accompanies the cartoon states that what is needed is a 'manlier style / Of clothing for the juvenile'.

The British press, naturally enough, retained, framed and occasionally contested the dominant ideologies of the day, most specifically those of gender, class and race. Gender ideologies are often intersected by class ones (the anxiety about the emigration of single, middle-class women for instance), and together they help construct the idea of a typical 'Australian' as a male, rather than a female, figure—although, as we later discuss, Punch also provides us with a female version, a 'Miss Australia'. Our categories 'Women' and 'Men' offer varied accounts of gendered experience in the Australian colonies and of the development of a specific Australian identity.

The 'typical' Australian, as developed in the press (and still surprisingly entrenched in the national psyche), is a white male figure most often categorised as the lone bushman: tough, taciturn, but with a heart of gold. He is defined very specifically as 'rural, unmarried, independent, drinking, smoking, nomadic anti-authoritarian'. This, as Susan Martin puts it, is a mere fantasy figure.[13] At the same time, 'independence' remains a common thread through so many of these articles. In William Jardine Smith's 'Wanted—A Career!' (p. 169), he remarks of the British male that at home 'a man walks in swaddling clothes', suggesting a moribund British nation.

In 1890 the author of 'Sydney in September' offers a much less complimentary but more mainstream contribution to the construction of the typical Australian male. It stands in contrast to the tough bushman so enthusiastically taken up at the time by the *Bulletin* and other local magazines. The following description, with its eugenics discourse, suggests that 'endurance' and 'staying power' are British characteristics being somehow bred out of young Australian men:

> these young Australians already differ somewhat in physical characteristics from their fathers. Australian-born youths are, for the most part, tall, slim, long-waisted, long-flanked, sloping-shouldered, frequently broad-chested but not deep, and somewhat narrow in the hips; a race manifestly formed for feats of agility, swiftness, and muscular grace rather than for those of endurance and staying power.[14]

Even as late as 1968 Craig McGregor was pointing out that the bushman is one of two leading myths about Australian society (the other being the larrikin) and suggesting that this is still how 'Australians' think of themselves.[15]

The bushman myth, then, is very persistent. It seems ridiculous when one considers the extent to which Australia was and is an intensely urban society and, what is more, it excludes so many other people—most women and Australians of non-British background, and all Aboriginals and Torres Strait Islanders. The bushman myth was in direct conflict with another prominent ideology in the nineteenth century, that of domestic values. So the ideal of the free-wheeling, unconstrained male is counter-balanced by the demands and responsibilities of the domesticated female. This might be defined, as Susan Martin does, as the rise of a masculinist culture.[16] This is not the 'Australian' of whom Spence was writing, but a late-century development in line with a masculinist push to counter the growing vociferousness of women's demands for greater equity—and, in Britain, for the right to vote, a right which their white colonial sisters were rapidly achieving. Thus masculinist culture was defined in opposition to the feminised one.

One woman who attempted to counter-balance the bushman myth was Louisa Lawson. Among many activities in Sydney, Lawson edited and published the *Dawn*, which appeared monthly for seventeen years, from 1888 to 1905. This is a remarkable achievement for any periodical and even more so for a radical paper. The *Dawn* focused on both public and domestic concerns. In 'The Australian Bush-woman' (p. 157), reprinted here in full, Lawson picks up the issue of the daily work of colonial women (both domestic and farming) that Spence had raised, and how this work contributes to the idea of nationhood. The article was first published in the Boston *Woman's Journal* in July 1889, and just a month later was republished in London in the *Englishwoman's Review*.

It is important to note at the outset that Louisa Lawson is far less concerned with the idea of national identity than she is with women's rights and the franchise for women. However, in this article it is clear that Lawson is contesting stereotyped ideas about women, and ideas about 'ideal' women, in favour of a feminist polemic that is far more vital to her political agenda. If she inadvertently contributes to the debate about national identity or even Australian types, that is merely coincidental to her more immediate feminist concerns. The very first thing Lawson states in 'The Australian Bush-woman' is that there are 471,000 women in New South Wales and 'about 471,000 different kinds of women'. In other words, at the outset Lawson wants to make a claim for individuality, for 'various stages of growth'. But she then agrees that she will sort her 'colonial sisters' into three categories: city women, country women, and bush-women. As bush-women are to be her subject, she describes them in some detail. They are, she says, 'grim, lonely, patient' and 'honest, hard-worked, silent, almost masculine'. She subsequently adds 'independent and taciturn' to the list.

Some of these words have been used to define the bushman: 'taciturn' is one, 'independent' is another. Superficially, therefore, that Australian type might almost apply to this particular group of women as well, women who are 'almost masculine'. But the bushman is 'lone', as opposed to 'lonely', and there is a world of difference between the two words. 'Lone' suggests that standing apart from the crowd or being solitary is a matter of choice; being 'lonely' is not a matter of choice, but of circumstance. As the *Macquarie Dictionary* puts it, 'lonely' means 'destitute of sympathetic or friendly companionship or relationships'. And this is why the very first word Louisa Lawson uses to describe bush-women is 'grim'. Physically, the bush-woman is 'thin, wiry, flat-chested and sunburned', the very antithesis of the fair, fresh-looking, well-built young woman who is introduced to Prince Alfred as 'Miss Australia' in *Punch*.

Lawson writes in praise of the 'self-abnegation' of these women, of the fact that they are 'self-neglectful'. She appears to celebrate their stoicism in the face of what she describes as 'ill-usage'. She writes that their husbands are 'indolent and neglectful' but not as a rule 'dissipated or brutal'. The picture she offers is far less appealing than the heroic stereotype so often promoted. She determinedly ends on a far more positive note, however, with a 'bright and promising story'. This new story, this bright promise, contributes indeed to a kind of national identity for the white Australian woman at least, a type sometimes referred to as 'the Australian Girl'. Lawson believes that the daughters of bush-women will be important to the country's future:

Take them all round, they are fine girls, always ready in an emergency, and capable of anything. Tough, healthy, and alert, they can cook or sew, do fancy-work or farm-work, dance, ride, tend cattle, keep a garden, break a colt. They are the stuff that a fine race is made of—these daughters of bushwomen. The men are more idle, and besides they have always the drink washing away their prospects; therefore we look to the girls for the future.

Her article ends with the prediction of a super female race: 'a race of splendid women, fit to obtain what their mothers never dreamed of—women's rights'.

According to Bernice McPherson, the developing notion of an Australian Girl was seen by some colonists as an improvement on the English middle-class model. Nevertheless, as McPherson clearly states, 'Australian colonial notions of femininity were drawn from middle-class English concepts of the feminine ideal'.[17] This clinging to the English ideal was counterbalanced by a burgeoning Australian ideal. Those who did cling to the old ways, Beverley Kingston argues, sought to construct a social hierarchy and standing for themselves at the very time when those hierarchies were under demolition.[18] Perhaps the concept of an Australian Girl who is vigorous and outgoing worked towards that demolition of old hierarchies and old ways.

The ideal of a young, virginal Australian femininity ties in very neatly with John Tenniel's 1868 cartoon for *Punch*, 'Our Australian Cousin' (p. 154), and accords with the idea that the country itself is 'young': socially, culturally and politically. Miss Australia is a shepherdess very much on the Arcadian model, with more than a hint of classical Graeco-Roman dress, decorated with what might be wattle blooms, or gold coins, and decked with armbands, bracelets and Greek-style sandals. She is taller than the prince, more stately and very dignified. The cartoon is accompanied by a letter to Australia from Britannia, who hears that her daughter is 'a fine handsome lass, with a bush of golden hair, blooming and buxom, who have [sic] not yet done growing—figure rather fuller than mine, but features much the same'. Note again that emphasis on family likeness, on youthfulness, and the need to finish growing. More significant, however, are Britannia's questions, which draw explicit and less than complimentary comparisons between the 'Old' country and the 'New', suggesting that in new places a more compassionate and humane society may develop:

Are your metropolitan streets as dirty as mine? In the bustling thoroughfares of Melbourne, or Sydney, or any other of your several capitals, do you take a human life nearly every other day in the year, as indifference and stupidity do in London? Are you old enough to have vested interests and a National Debt?

McPherson suggests that the image of the Australian Girl as young and pure was 'an ideal that was a complex mixture of the old world and the new', and that 'sections of the Australian population saw this ideal as an "improvement" on the English middle-class model'.[19] Our researches show that this concept was not confined to the Australian population, but emanates as well from the British press. This suggests that the values and attitudes that informed the image of the Australian Girl were recognised and accepted by significant numbers of people both at the margins and at the centre.

The characteristics that distinguish the Australian Girl from her British sister may be located in an issue that Catherine Helen Spence pointed out in the 1860s, and Louisa Lawson in the 1880s, namely that women in Australia had to do all kinds of domestic and outdoor work. In England it was not ladylike for middle-class women to work in paid employment outside the home, nor was it ladylike for them to do their own housework. In the Australian colonies, however, this rigid class divide had to be abandoned because there were simply not enough people to do the heavy, dirty work in the home. For working-class people who emigrated did so in part to abandon those rigid class divides and, in the parlance of the time, to 'better' themselves. As McPherson puts it, 'models of feminine behaviour' had to change to accommodate this situation.[20] William Thackeray captures this class issue to a nicety in 'Waiting at the Station' (p. 93), remarking that while a woman curtsies to him in London, 'when she gets into the Australian woods her back won't bend except to her labour'. As Lawson comments, 'any self-respecting girl would rather be independent'.

The issue of personal independence affected both men and women. In 'Young Men in the Colonies' (p. 177) we are told that 'England is gridironed with almost impossible social barriers'. And William Smeaton, in 'A Gallery of Australasian Singers' (p. 63), explores why Australian literature lacks 'quality' and offers as one explanation that in Australia 'Jack is as good as his master', so that poets must produce their lays as they go about their daily work. Financial independence and the breaking down of class and social barriers was reserved, however, for the European colonisers.

Racial injustice proved to be, and remains to a sorry extent, a more impassable barrier. Nowhere is this more apparent than in the long debates in the press about federation of the colonies. Every possible aspect is raised—trade, Chinese immigration, working-class men, the enfranchisement of women, trade union organisations, importation of slave labour into Queensland, education—with one notable exception. In the articles we explored, Indigenous people are rarely mentioned. Perhaps Edward Braddon in 'The Federation Movement in Australasia' (p. 214) demonstrates this silence best when he notes that the Australasian population is 'homogeneous', but parenthetically offers the exception: '(leaving out of consideration the few thousands of aboriginals in Australia, and the Maoris, who number about 40,000)'.

In 'Imperial Federation from an Australian Point of View', John Douglas considers that federation will 'at any rate give a common citizenship. Thenceforward the people of Australia will be Australians in a political as well as a geographical sense'.[21] He also warns that with independence will come specific responsibilities. In the same year, 1884, the politician Henry Parkes, also writing from Australia in 'Our growing Australian Empire' (p. 205), describes Australia in these terms:

> Here we have an imperfect picture of the Young England growing up in Australasia, which, in all the best characteristics of the race, is more English than Old England herself. ... The young man, full of hope and emulation, cannot continue to play his part before the world in the boy's jacket.

Parkes' words recall with uncanny exactitude Richard Doyle's cartoon for *Punch* of the youth so rapidly outgrowing his clothes. That Parkes sees the country in male terms is not surprising, despite the instances we have located in which Australia is a 'daughter' of the mother country. Julius Vogel, Premier of New Zealand, rejects the metaphor of 'mother country' outright:

> The use of the words 'mother country' has become so common that one can scarcely avoid the expression. It has been made the foundation of the hackneyed illustration that the colonies are children, and that when they arrive at years of maturity they are, of course, free to leave the parent home. Like many other metaphors it is sadly wanting in reason. The colonies are British territory won by great sacrifices and great enterprise in the past. They are unquestionably part of the Sovereignty or Empire, and no practice permits, or justifies, the submission of nations to disintegration unless under the coercion of dire necessity.[22]

Both men clung to the idea of empire, which was always going to be a white, masculinist ideal. But perhaps the last word at this point should be given to Robert Christison, writing from the British perspective for the *Westminster Review* in 1888. Even this late in the century, his position suggests little change:

> The population is British. Australians are intensely English; we wish them to remain so, because it is thought that the British Isles will require in the future additional strength from without, props with sure foundations to lean upon. To ensure England's safety, and to make progress towards a higher development, the time has arrived when a consolidation of the Empire, already begun by a few, should receive the due consideration of the many—when endeavours should be made to find vent for surplus capital at home, by developing her resources abroad, 'by sending labourers where they are crowded to where there are none,' by relieving the distressed, hungry, and unclad, by some State colonization scheme.
> This is England's duty, and this it should be her aim to achieve.[23]

The decisive declaration that 'Australians are intensely English' is no longer true, and perhaps never was. Those escaping class-bound, poverty-stricken lives often abandoned their Britishness with an eager embracing of lives that seemed to offer new dimensions. Others found adaptation more difficult, or with newly acquired wealth made themselves into versions of an Englishness they had either never known or never been permitted in the 'old' country. Either way, the 'new' country provided the freedom and independence to shift time-honoured barriers, a circumstance of which the British press was fully aware from the outset and which it considered and debated across the nineteenth century.

Today, the issue of national identity remains a fraught topic. People talk casually about the 'typical Australian' (or, even more oddly, about the 'real' Australian), but when pressed to describe such a person the limitations immediately become obvious. Don Bradman might be cited, or the soldiers who died at Gallipoli. Both represent a certain kind of national identity (gendered male) that might be termed positive, but in truth both are of an era that is now long past. In this extremely limited representation of the typical Australian, there is no place for Indigenous Australians, no place for female Australians, no place for Chinese Australians, nor for any of the great variety of other Australian immigrants. When critic Paul Byrnes, in reviewing the film *Oscar and Lucinda* in 'Too Big for its Book', describes the Australia it represents as 'the bastard offspring of Europe', he reflects some of the early anxieties of the British periodical press.[24] Hou Leong, in 'Photographic Essay: An Australian', in which he superimposes his own face over more familiar ones (Paul Hogan's as Crocodile Dundee, for instance), questions with keen-edged wit the stereotypical versions of national identity that dominate the Australian psyche.[25]

Lydia Miller, when delivering the fourth Barton Lecture in the centenary year of Australian Federation,[26] said that Australians are still not comfortable with who and what they are. Miller, a Guguelandji woman, works in Indigenous arts and is a member of the Cultural Network of the Australian National Commission for UNESCO. She used the terms 'we' and 'us' throughout her lecture, offering by this example a unity that is more often than not missing from public discourse. Australians, she declared, must achieve civic maturity. Australia will remain merely an imagined nation until reconciliation is achieved and until there is respect for Aboriginal and Torres Strait Islander heritage. Then, she told her audience, and only then, will Australia be a nation state:

> While we may wax lyrical about Australia as a nation, imbuing ourselves with a collective spirit about what it is to be 'Australian', it is ultimately Australia's conduct as a nation-state that will determine whether or not we have reached political and civic maturity and wisdom.[27]

In the British press this imagined nation, called by the continent's colonisers 'Australia', took slow shape across the nineteenth century. Now it is up to Australians themselves to imagine the kind of nation state Lydia Miller so eloquently proposes and to bring it into being.

Notes

1   Chambers, *Border Dialogues*, p. 15.
2   Seddon, *Landprints*, p. 21.
3   Dening, 'Endeavour and Hokule'a'.
4   Dening, *Readings/Writings*, p. 207.
5   Brown, *A Faithful Picture*, p. 39.
6   Bingham, 'On Emigration', pp. 462, 455, 457, 473.
7   'Emigration', p. 149.
8   Molesworth, 'New South Wales', p. 26. Incidentally, John Birmingham's review of *Sydney: An Oxford Anthology* in the *Australian's Review of Books*, June 2000, notes that Sydney is 'a city founded as a jail' and remarks 'how thin is the fourth estate's contribution'. His comment suggests the timeliness of this anthology, which brings the opinions of the fourth estate fully into view.
9   'L', 'The Emigrant's Complaint', p. 324.
10 Sutcliffe, 'The Landing of the Primrose', p. 303.
11 Thomson (ed.), *Catherine Helen Spence*, p. 467.
12 Martin, 'National Dress or National Trousers?', p. 92. See also David Malouf's illuminating essay, 'Made in England: Australia's British Inheritance', in which he writes that at the start Australia was a 'translated re-creation' of British society and culture; that it had gained a 'privileged place' in Britain's empire by the 1880s, but nevertheless was regarded by then as 'too "free" or to use Darwin's word, "ambitious"' (pp. 5, 22, 31).
13 Martin, 'National Dress or National Trousers?', p. 93.
14 'Sydney in September', pp. 112–13. An interesting pre-vision of European reaction to Australian troops who fought in the Boer War and the First World War.
15 Quoted in Kapferer, *Being All Equal*, p. 51.
16 Martin, 'National Dress or National Trousers?', p. 93.
17 McPherson, 'A Colonial Feminine Ideal', p. 12.
18 Kingston, 'The Lady and the Australian Girl', p. 41.
19 McPherson, 'A Colonial Feminine Ideal', p. 5.
20 McPherson, 'A Colonial Feminine Ideal', p. 12.
21 Douglas, 'Imperial Federation from an Australian Point of View', p. 856.
22 Vogel, 'Is it Open to the Colonies to Secede?', p. 902.
23 Christison, 'Independent Section. United Australia and Imperial Federation', pp. 342–3.
24 Byrnes, 'Too Big for its Books'.
25 Leong, 'Photographic Essay: An Australian', p. 116.
26 ABC Radio National, 4 March 2001.
27 Miller, 'Recognition of the Past … Reconciliation in the Future … Restitution Now', p. 154.

Works Cited

Bingham, Peregrine, 'On Emigration', *Westminster Review*, vol. 3, 1825, pp. 448–87.

Bird, Isabella. *Letters to Henrietta*, edited by Kay Chubbuck. London: John Murray, 2002.

Birmingham, John. Review of *Sydney: An Oxford Anthology*, in the *Australian's Review of Books*, June 2000, p. 23.

Brown, Eliza. *A Faithful Picture: The Letters of Eliza and Thomas Brown at York in the Swan River Colony 1841–1852*, edited by Peter Cowan. Fremantle: Fremantle Arts Centre Press, 1977.

Byrnes, Paul. 'Too Big for its Book', *Sydney Morning Herald*, 22 January 1998, p. 13.

Chambers, Iain. *Border Dialogues: Journeys in Postmodernity*. London: Routledge, 1990.

Christison, Robert. 'Independent Section. United Australia and Imperial Federation'. *Westminster Review*, vol. 130, 1888, pp. 335–48.

Dening, Greg. *Readings/Writings*. Melbourne: Melbourne University Press, 1998.

——'Endeavour and Hokule'a: The Theatre of Re-enactment and Cultural Identity'. Land, Place, Culture, Identity (seminar), Institute of Advanced Studies, The University of Western Australia, 3 May 2000.

Douglas, John. 'Imperial Federation from an Australian Point of View', *Nineteenth Century*, vol. 16, 1884, pp. 853–68.

'Emigration', *Chambers' Edinburgh Journal*, vol. 1, 1832, pp. 149–50.

'Inquiry into the Poor Laws', *Quarterly Review*, vol. 8, 1812, pp. 319–55.

Kapferer, Judith. *Being All Equal: Identity, Difference and Australian Cultural Practice*. Oxford: Berg, 1996.

Kingston, Beverley. 'The Lady and the Australian Girl: Some Thoughts on Nationalism and Class' in *Australian Women: New Feminist Perspectives*, edited by Norma Grieve and Ailsa Burns. Melbourne: Oxford University Press, 1986.

Knaplund, Paul. *The British Empire, 1815–1939*. New York: Howard Fertig, 1969 [1941].

L. 'The Emigrant's Complaint', *Howitt's Journal*, vol. 1, 1847, p. 324.

Leong, Hou. 'Photographic Essay: An Australian', *Asian and Pacific Inscriptions, Identities, Ethnicities, Nationalities*, edited by Suvendrini Perera. Melbourne: Meridian, 1995.

McPherson, Bernice. 'A Colonial Feminine Ideal: Femininity and Representation', *Journal of Australian Studies*, no. 42, 1994, pp. 5–17.

Malouf, David. 'Made in England: Australia's British Inheritance', *Quarterly Essay*, no. 12. Melbourne: Black Inc., 2003.

Martin, Susan K. 'National Dress or National Trousers?' in *Oxford Literary History of Australia*, edited by Bruce Bennett and Jennifer Strauss. Melbourne: Oxford University Press, 1998, ch. 5.

Miller, Lydia. Fourth Barton Lecture, ABC Radio National, 4 March 2001.

——'Recognition of the Past ... Reconciliation in the Future ... Restitution Now', *Unity and Diversity: A National Conversation: Barton Lectures*, edited by Helen Irving. Sydney: ABC Books, 2001.

Molesworth, William. 'New South Wales', *London Review*, vol. 30, 1835, pp. 25–47.

Seddon, George. *Landprints: Reflections on Place and Landscape*. Cambridge: Cambridge University Press, 1997.

Sutcliffe, Constance [Constance Eaglestone]. 'The Landing of the Primrose', *Ainsworth's Magazine*, vol. 1, 1842, pp. 303–4.

'Sydney in September', *Temple Bar*, vol. 90, 1890, pp. 111–17.

Thomson, Helen (ed.). *Catherine Helen Spence*. Brisbane: University of Queensland Press, 1987.

Vogel, Julius. 'Is it Open to the Colonies to Secede?', *Nineteenth Century*, vol. 26, 1889, pp. 897–911.

Transportation

SYDNEY SMITH ⎯⎯⎯⎯⎯⎯⎯⎯⎯⎯⎯⎯⎯⎯⎯⎯⎯⎯⎯⎯⎯

Sydney Smith (1771–1845), Anglican clergyman and journalist, founded the Edinburgh Review
*with Jeffrey Brougham. Subsequently he gained a considerable reputation in London as a preacher
and lecturer on moral philosophy. In 1831 Smith was appointed a canon of Saint Paul's Cathedral,
London, where he remained until his death. His published letters, speeches and sermons include a
collected* Works *published in 1840. [DNB; WI].*

This extract is from a review of Account of the English Colony of New South Wales. By
Lieutenant-Colonel Collins of the Royal Marines, *vol. II, London, Cadell & Davies.*

⎯⎯⎯⎯⎯⎯⎯⎯⎯⎯⎯⎯⎯⎯⎯⎯⎯⎯⎯⎯ from 'Collins's *Account of New South
Wales', Edinburgh Review*, vol. 2,
1803, pp. 30–42.

… But, however beneficial to the general interests of mankind the civilization of
barbarous countries may be considered to be, in this particular instance of it, the
interest of Great Britain would seem to have been very little consulted. With
fanciful schemes of universal good, we have no business to meddle. Why we
are to erect penitentiary houses and prisons at the distance of half the diameter
of the globe, and to incur the enormous expence of feeding and transporting
their inhabitants to, and at such a distance, it is extremely difficult to discover. It
certainly is not from any deficiency of barren islands near our own coast, nor of
uncultivated wastes in the interior; and if we were sufficiently fortunate to be
wanting in such species of accommodation, we might discover in Canada, or the
West Indies, or on the coast of Africa, a climate malignant enough, or a soil sufficiently sterile, to revenge all the injuries which have been inflicted on society by
pickpockets, larcenists, and petty felons.—Upon the foundation of a new colony,
and especially one peopled by criminals, there is a disposition in government
(where any circumstance in the commission of the crime affords the least
pretence for the commutation) to convert capital punishments into transportation; and by these means to hold forth a very dangerous, though certainly a very
unintentional encouragement to offences. And when the history of the colony
has been attentively perused in the parish of St Giles, the ancient avocation of
picking pockets will certainly not become more discreditable, from the knowledge, that it may eventually lead to the possession of a farm of a thousand acres

on the river Hawkesbury. Since the benevolent Howard attacked our prisons, incarceration has become not only healthy but elegant; and a county jail is precisely the place to which any pauper might wish to retire to gratify his taste for magnificence, as well as for comfort. Upon the same principle, there is some risk that transportation will be considered as one of the surest roads to honour, and to wealth; and that no felon will hear a verdict of '*not guilty*', without considering himself as cut off in the fairest career of prosperity. It is foolishly believed that the colony of Botany Bay unites our moral and commercial interests, and that we shall receive hereafter an ample equivalent, in bales of goods, for all the vices we export. Unfortunately, the expence we have incurred in founding the colony, will not retard the natural progress of its emancipation, or prevent the attacks of other nations, who will be as desirous of reaping the fruit, as if they had sown the seed. It is a colony, besides, began under every possible disadvantage: it is too distant to be long governed, or well defended: it is undertaken, not by the voluntary association of individuals, but by government, and by means of compulsory labour. A nation must, indeed, be redundant in capital, that will expend it where the hopes of a just return are so very small.

J. BETHEL _____

J. Bethel is a pseudonym for English-born Bryan Waller Procter (1787–1874), who published poetry as Barry Cornwall. Occasional playwright and prose contributor to annuals and periodicals, he practised law for a living. His books include A Sicilian Story *and* Mirandola *(1820),* The Flood of Thessaly *(1823) and* The Works of Ben Jonson with a Memoir of his Life and Writings *(1838). [DNB; WI]*

_____ 'The Farewell of the Convicts',
Fraser's Magazine, vol. 1, 1830,
pp. 727–8.

By the Author of 'The Rover's Song,' in our last Number.

> A BOAT is rowed along the sea,
> Full of souls as it may be;
> Their dress is coarse, their hair is shorn,
> And every squalid face forlorn
> Is full of sorrow, and hate, and scorn!
> What is't?—It is the CONVICT BOAT,
> That o'er the waves is forced to float,
> Bearing its wicked burden o'er

The ocean to a distant shore:
Man scowls upon it; but the sea
(The same with fettered as with free,)
Danceth beneath it heedlessly!

Slowly the boat is borne along,
Yet they who row are hard and strong,
    And well their oars keep time
To one who sings (and clanks his chain,
The better thus to hide his pain,)
    A bitter, banished rhyme!
He sings; and all his mates in woe,
Chaunt sullen chorus as they go!

The Farewell.
    1.
Row us on, a felon band,
    Farther out to sea,
Til we lose all sight of land,
    And *then*—we shall be free!
Row us on, and loose our fetters;
    Yeo! the boat makes way:
Let's say 'good bye' unto our betters,
    And, hey for a brighter day!

    Chorus.
Row us fast! row us fast!
Trial's o'er, and sentence past:
Here's a whistle for those who tried to blind us,
And a curse on all we leave behind us!

    2.
Farewell, juries,—jailers,—friends!
    (Traitors to the close.)
Here the felon's danger ends:
    Farewell, bloody foes!
Farewell, England! we are quitting
    Now thy dungeon doors:
Take our blessing, as we're flitting—
    'Curse upon thy shores!'

3.

Farewell, England!—honest nurse
    Of all our wants and sins!
What to thee's the felon's curse?
    What to thee who wins?
Murder thriveth in thy cities—
    Famine through thine isle:
One may cause a dozen ditties,
    But t'other scarce a smile.

4.

Farewell, England!—tender soil,
    Where babes who leave the breast
From morning unto midnight toil,
    That pride may be proudly drest!
Where he who's right and he who swerveth
    Meet at the goal the same,
Where no one hath what he deserveth,
    Not even in empty fame!

5.

So, fare thee well, our country dear!
    Our last wish, ere we go,
Is—May your heart be never clear
    From tax, not tithe, nor woe!
May they who sow e'er reap for others,
    The hundred for the one!
May friends grow false, and twin-born brothers
    Each hate his mother's son!

6.

May pains and forms still fence the place
    Where justice must be *bought*;
So he who's poor must hide his face,
    And he who thinks—his thought!
May Might o'er Right be crowned the winner,
    The head still o'er the heart,
And the saint be still so like the sinner,
    You'll not know them apart!

7.

May your traders grumble when bread is high,
      And your farmers when bread is low;
And your pauper brats, scarce two feet high,
      Learn more than your nobles know!
May your sick have foggy or frosty weather,
      And your convicts all short throats;
And your blood-covered bankers e'er hang together,
      And tempt ye with one pound notes!

8.

And so, with hunger in your jaws,
      And peril within your breast,
And a bar of gold, to guard your laws,
      For those who—*pay* the best:
Farewell to England's woe and weal!
… For our betters, so bold and blythe,
May they never want, when they want a meal,
      A PARSON TO TAKE THEIR TITHE!

The Author of the above rhymes, and the Editor, must beg to disclaim all identity with the Convicts, or their opinions:—And in order to avoid any further mistake, (his verses in the last Number, entitled 'The Rover's Song,' having been attributed to Mr. Barry Cornwall,) the author has consented to affix his name to the present production.

ANON. ————————————————————

————————————————— 'Comforts of Transportation',
                              Chambers' Edinburgh Journal, vol. 1,
                              1832, p. 32.

The following extract is explanatory of the 'comforts' enjoyed by convicts in Van Dieman's Land and New South Wales:—

'*Comfort* 1st.—As soon as he lands he is packed off sixty or seventy, or one hundred miles, into the interior, or he is placed in the prisoners' barracks,—of which it would be only necessary for an Hon. Member to see the inside to convince him it was no joke,—in either of which cases, if he has brought any trifles with him, he is sure to be relieved of them before the following day. If he does not lose his government clothing, he may consider himself fortunate; should he, however, do so, the following morning he may safely calculate upon.

'*Comfort* 2d.—In the shape of fifty lashes, or ten days' work on the tread mill, or in the chain gang.

'*Comfort* 3d.—If he be assigned to a master in the town, and happens to take a glass of grog after his long voyage, it is a great chance if he lodge not in the watch-house for the night, and take "fifty" before breakfast in the morning, by way of "comfort."

'*Comfort* 4th.—Travelling through a wild forest, without knowing his way, and surrounded, perhaps, by the hostile aborigines, who, so sure as they met, would kill him.

'*Comfort* 5th.—Should he lose his way, and escape starvation in the bush, probably a sound flogging for not having arrived sooner at his master's house.

'*Comfort* 6th.—Perpetual work, and no pay:—in many cases hard labour, hard living, hard words, and hard usage.

'We have hitherto spoken only of the reception met with by a well-disposed prisoner—one who wishes to reform. If he be in any way refractory, let the good people of England thoroughly understand, that he is sure of a most adequate reward. A short answer, when spoken to by his master or overseer, or a common soldier, or even a convict constable, is a crime punishable by flogging; getting tipsy, places him in the stocks; missing muster, may get him flogged, or into the chain-gang, where he works in irons on the roads. Should he commit any second offence, Macquarie Harbour, Port Macquarie, Norfolk Island, or Moreton Bay, is his fate, where every rigidity of discipline—nay, sometimes even cruelty— is exercised. The hardest of labour, and but one meal a day, of the coarsest food, is the lot of the man who goes to a penal settlement. To these places it does not take felony to send a prisoner; many have been removed there for very trivial offences. The gallant colonel, who wishes for places of horror and terror as receptacles for criminals, need not go far a-field; we can supply him with such places as would satisfy the most insatiate appetite for torturing and punishing. When men commit murder on purpose to be hanged, in preference to bearing the terrors of these places of secondary exile, it cannot be expected that they are in the enjoyment of much "comfort." This is no exposition tirade; nor is the statement made for our colonial readers; the facts are too well known here to require description. It is a true picture, intended for the eye of our numerous English readers.'

ANON. _____

*This extract is from a four-part series which includes: 'Account of the Country', pp. 124–5;
'Capabilities of Settlement', pp. 132–3; and 'Experiences of a Settler', pp. 149–51.*

_____ *from* 'Emigration to New South
Wales. Convict-System – Free
Settlers', *Chambers' Edinburgh
Journal*, vol. 7, 1838, pp. 142–3.

It has not been thought necessary in these articles to say any thing of the History
of New South Wales. Every body is aware that the colony was founded (1788) for
the reception of convicted criminals from Britain, and that, under the domina-
tion of a governor and council, it remains a penal settlement till the present
day. How one of the finest countries in the world should have been so long
devoted to this purpose, it would be out of place here to inquire; it is enough that
attention is called to the fact. According to the last reports, the whole population
of the colony amounted to 70,000 (now increased to upwards of 80,000), of
which 24,276 were convicts,* being at the rate of about one convict for every
two free persons; and of these free persons, of course, a considerable number
were either emancipated convicts or their immediate descendants. The unfortunate continuance of a headlong system of transporting criminals to New South
Wales, has had the most pernicious effects on the social condition of the settlers;
and, to aggravate the evil, there has ever been a very great disparity in the
number of individuals in the two sexes—as, for example, in 1833, the number of
males was 44,643, and of females 16,156, or nearly three to one. This last-men-
tioned evil, however, is in the course of rapid melioration, by the immigration of
respectable females to the colony.

So much has been lately published on the 'felonry' of New South Wales, with
representations of its vicious tendency, that we need not go into any details on
the subject. The writer of a work descriptive of the colony remarked, a few years
ago, that the free settlers deprecated the idea of government discontinuing to
send out convicts, and this statement not being repelled in the proper quarter,
there has ever since been a general feeling in Britain that the convict-system
should be continued in all its vigour, as a thing really necessary for the welfare of
the settlers.† From the statements which have been recently published, however,
it appears that, whatever may be the wishes of some persons respecting the
continuance of convict transportation on its present footing, with a view to

* Martin, p. 134.
† Martin corroborates this. He says, 'there are applications for five times the number of prisoners
that arrive in the colony.'—*History of Australasia*, p. 182.

procuring labourers or assistants on easy terms, a very strong desire is now manifested, both by the colonial government and by influential private colonists, for the incoming of free emigrants, both male and female, of respectable character, and who are able and willing to accept of employment at highly remunerating wages. The design is to encourage the settlement of a virtuous population, and thus gradually to overcome the evils produced by the lavish introduction of a population of an opposite quality. The home government has seconded these enlightened views; but whether it has at the same time resolved to restrain the transportation of convicts in future, in order to give the scheme of free settling the best chance of success, has not come within our knowledge. Possibly something of this kind is intended, for more rational opinions respecting the reformation and punishment of offenders are beginning to be entertained. Be this as it may, there is now a reasonable hope that the moral atmosphere of New South Wales will undergo a gradual and steady purification, and be therefore rendered congenial to the feelings and habits of respectable emigrants from the mother country; indeed, if we were not ourselves strongly impressed with this hope, and if we did not learn that very important improvements were at present taking place in the social condition of the colony at large, we certainly should not have said one word to induce emigrants to make this remote territory the land of their adoption.

Knowing the class of reckless beings who figure before our higher criminal courts, and who are for the greater part transported for their offences, one is very apt to imagine that the life which is led by free settlers among his convict servants must be one of constant misery; but in forming this idea, we should not be doing justice to human nature. It appears, that, although the convict-system has been in different respects injurious, the chief mischief has been confined in a great measure to Sydney and a few other places, and that in the country settlements it has not been productive of the disastrous consequences which one would readily suppose. The most conspicuous of its evils has been the divisions it has created in society, which are deeply to be lamented, for they, of course, retard the prosperity of the colony. Many of the emancipated convicts and their descendants are now men of considerable wealth and influence. ...

When convicts arrive in the colony, they are consigned to barracks for their reception, and are ready for disposal as servants to the settlers in all parts of the country. When disposed of to the settler, the convict is provided by him with the means of erecting a hut for himself, if no such accommodation exists at the settler's station. The convict receives no wages, but is provided with certain daily rations of food, clothing, bedding, and culinary utensils. The hours during which he is required to work are from six in the morning until six at night, with the allowance of an hour for breakfast and another for dinner. When a convict conducts himself with propriety for a certain length of time, and which is pro-portioned to the term of his sentence, he is entitled to claim from the colonial government what is called a ticket of leave, a sort of warrant or licence, which enables him to live where he pleases, and to employ himself in any legal way he may choose. This, of course, is recalled if he commits any new offence; and many advertisements are from time to time to be seen in the Sydney newspapers, intimating such recall, and naming the individuals. Though, while he conducts himself with propriety, the convict's peculiar condition in society is not obtruded upon him by any peculiar treatment, yet the slightest departure from this brings him immediately within the reach of the colonial laws. If refractory, or even merely insolent to the settler, his master, he may be taken before a magistrate, and either flogged, or sentenced to work for a certain period on a short allowance of food, in what are called the government chain-gangs, composed of convicts who had offended a second time, and are, as a punishment, worked in fetters. On the expiry of his original term of banishment, the convict becomes, in colonial phrase, an emancipist, and is then his own master.

WILLIAM SMITH O'BRIEN ⸻

William O'Brien (1803–64), parliamentarian and Irish nationalist, was found guilty of high treason on 7 October 1848 and sentenced to be hanged, drawn and quartered. Commuted to transportation for life, he took passage on the Swift *for Tasmania on 29 July 1849. He returned to Europe in 1854, having been granted a pardon on condition he never set foot in the United Kingdom. In 1856 he received an unconditional pardon and returned to Ireland. [DNB; WI].*

This extract is from a review of five government reports and two books on prison discipline and management, and transportation. See also Molesworth, 'New South Wales', in Further Reading.

⸻ *from* 'Transportation as it now is',
Edinburgh Review, vol. 90, 1849,
pp. 1–39.

… In Great Britain alone more than three thousand criminals are annually sen-tenced to transportation. In dealing with such a mass of crime, we are evidently engaged in a task of no ordinary magnitude; and on the judicious prosecution of which the gravest interests of the nation, domestic and colonial, are involved.

… The system of transportation and assignment of convicts was in force until 1840; and had been tried chiefly in New South Wales. Under its operation, the colony was found to have sunk into so deplorable a state of demoralisation, that the principle of assignment was in consequence abandoned, and the stream of transportation directed elsewhere. The next two years were a period of transition from one system to another. ... and in 1843 [Sir Robert Peel's government] established at Van Diemen's Land the 'probation' system. ... In 1846 the probation system was found to have been attended with such shocking consequences, that it was deemed absolutely necessary to suspend for two years transportation to Van Diemen's Land. ...

So appalling was the exposure of the effects produced in the Australian colonies by our system of transportation, that those on whom the chief responsibility rested hesitated respecting its renewal; and it became necessary gravely to consider, whether it was desirable or even justifiable that it should be resumed. Was it the practice which was defective,—or was the principle unsound? On what grounds, it was asked, does England assume the singular privilege of establishing colonies to be deluged and drowned with the flood of her own wickedness? What right has any country to turn even a wilderness into a school of sin,—to create, even at the Antipodes, huge nurseries of depravity,—to pollute a young nation from its very birth, and to saturate with its own corruption the sources whence countless generations are to spring? These doubts are not to be removed by showing that the colonies may have no right to remonstrate: it signifies little whether they oppose or are participators in the guilt—if guilt it be. The questions will be asked, and the answers must be given, with reference to higher and more enduring considerations than the pleasure or the profit of England, or the material prosperity of her colonies.

... On a review, then, of the present system of transportation,—and availing ourselves of the additional information afforded by the experience of the last two years—we are confirmed in the opinion we have already expressed, that all the changes made have been in the right direction. We wanted to check crime by *severe* punishment, and we have secured every sort of punishment which was formerly inflicted,—imprisonment, hard labour, and expatriation,—and they are now indissolubly combined: the first so severe in character as to reach the point at which the powers of human endurance fail; and the second so conducted that there is no necessary limit to it, except the duration of the sentence. We wanted a *certain* punishment; since transportation, as formerly managed, had its prizes as well as blanks—and the prizes generally fell to the most vicious. We have now a fixed amount of suffering which must be endured by all, but which may be indefinitely prolonged by misconduct. We wanted an *equal* punishment; and we have reduced inequality to the lowest point,—The inequality of individual constitutions and positions, physically, mentally, morally, and socially: and these we no longer aggravate by superadding the excessive inequality arising out of assignment. We wanted a system of transportation which should rid our country of its criminals. Formerly all the seven years' convicts, forming one-half of the whole number, were, at the end of about four years, turned loose again upon society in England: now all but those disqualified by sickness or infirmity are sent to a distant land.

So much for transportation as a punishment,—as a means of protecting society against criminals by terror, restraint, removal: now let us look at it, with regard to reformation. Once a convict ship conveyed to the mind the deepest impression of every thing that was depraved and dangerous; now a superintendent, having landed 292 convicts, can say, that 300 emigrants would not have behaved so well—that the black box was in the hold, the irons out of sight, and that he would be happy to take out 300 more such, without a guard. Once a criminal described the fatal pollution of a penal settlement in these memorable words, which drew tears from a judge; and which we trust will never be forgotten:—'Let a man be what he will, when he comes here he is soon as bad as the rest—a man's heart is taken from him—and there is given to him the heart of a beast.' Now the desk of the chaplain at Pentonville is filled with letters from the convicts to him, full of gratitude and thanks, and kind wishes, and promises of steadiness, and exhortations, with money for their relatives, and good reports of each other. Formerly our system of transportation produced in New South Wales such a state of crime, that, when the veil was raised by Sir W. Molesworth's committee in 1837, the people of England stood aghast at the sight of the monster they had created; and, for very shame, the system was abandoned. ...

One thing is clear. Either our convicts must be kept at home, or they must be sent abroad; and they cannot be sent abroad if the hesitation of our colonies to receive them is stimulated into resistance by declamation at home. We may not again, after our eyes have been opened by the lessons we have learned in New South Wales and Van Diemen's Land, repeat the frightful experiments of purely penal colonies; neither may we refuse due weight to a deliberate and general expression of the wish of any of our dependencies. We must satisfy them that we will not arbitrarily overbear their sense of what is right, and their perception of their own interest. We must appeal to these feelings, and enlist them on our side, if we would hope to establish a system of transportation which shall last. Happily in this instance (is it ever otherwise?) our highest duty is also our wisest policy. We have a living mass of crime pressing upon us at home, corrupting the community and consuming its substance. While, if we endeavour to remove it in the way we have hitherto done, every colony rises against us; and the evil of a temporary suspension of transportation, which we have already felt more than once, may, by incautious measures, become a chronic disease. In this dilemma, urged by a sense of our Christian duty, we are asked at last to attempt to purify and elevate our criminal population. In some degree we have already done so; and there is good reason to believe that, by extended and persevering efforts, we may do so to a very great extent. Our colonies, treated with just consideration, now appear prepared to examine the question dispassionately. In case the early stages of our new penal system should succeed in reforming our criminals up to a certain point, there can be little doubt, we think, of the success of the latter stages. Criminals, whose presence might still have constituted a formidable social danger in their former home, may under these circumstances be safely admitted by countries in the condition of our colonies—where they would be rapidly absorbed into a new and industrious population, without provoking either scandal or alarm.

ANON. ————————————————————

———————————————— 'Botany Bay Theatricals', *Working Man's Friend, and Family Instructor*, vol. 2, 1852, p. 323.

BOTANY BAY THEATRICALS.—Some years ago, one of the male convicts in Botany Bay wrote a farce, which was acted with great applause in the theatre, Port Jackson. Barrington the noted pick-pocket, furnished the prologue, which ended with these two well-known lines:—

> 'True patriots we, for be it understood,
> We *left* our country for our *country's good*.'

Impressions

SYDNEY SMITH

See biographical note on p. 19.

This extract is from a review of A Statistical, Historical and Political Description of the Colony of New South Wales, and its dependent Settlements in Van Diemen's Land *by* W. C. Wentworth *(1819);* Letter to Viscount Sidmouth on the Transportation Laws, the State of the Hulks, and of the Colonies of New South Wales *by* Henry Grey Bennet *(1819); and* O'Hara's History of New South Wales *(1818).*

_____ *from* 'Botany Bay', *Edinburgh Review,*
vol. 32, 1819, pp. 28–48.

This land of convicts and kangaroos is beginning to rise into a very fine and flourishing settlement:—And great indeed must be the natural resources, and splendid the endowments of that land that has been able to survive the system of neglect and oppression experienced from the mother country, and the series of ignorant and absurd Governors that have been selected for the administration of its affairs.

But mankind live and flourish not only in spite of storms and tempests, but (which could not have been anticipated previous to experience) in spite of Colonial Secretaries expressly paid to watch over their interests. The supineness and profligacy of public officers cannot always overcome the amazing energy with which human beings pursue their happiness, nor the sagacity with which they determine on the means by which that end is to be promoted. Be it our care, however, to record, for the future inhabitants of Australasia, the political sufferings of their larcenous forefathers; and let them appreciate, as they ought, that energy which founded a mighty empire in spite of the afflicting blunders and marvellous cacaeconomy [evil economy] of their government.

... The Governors of Botany Bay have taken the liberty of imposing what taxes they deemed proper, without any other authority than their own; and it seemed very frivolous and vexatious, not to allow this small effusion of despotism in so remote a corner of the globe:—but it was noticed by the Opposition in the House of Commons, and reluctantly confessed and given up by the Administration. This great portion of the earth begins civil life with noble principles of freedom:

May God grant to its inhabitants that wisdom and courage which are necessary for the preservation of so great a good!

Mr Wentworth enumerates, among the evils to which the colony is subjected, that clause in the last settlement of the East India Company's charter, which prevents vessels of less than 300 tuns burden from navigating the Indian Seas; a restriction, from which the Cape of Good Hope has been lately liberated, and which ought, in the same manner, to be removed from New South Wales, where there cannot be, for many years to come, sufficient capital to build vessels of so large a burden. ...

The means which Mr Wentworth proposes for improving the condition of Botany Bay, are—Trial by Jury—Colonial Assemblies, with whom the right of taxation should rest—the establishment of distilleries, and the exclusion of foreign spirits—alteration of duties, so as to place New South Wales upon the same footing as other colonies—removal of the restriction to navigate the Indian Seas in vessels of a small burthen—improvements in the Courts of Justice—encouragement for the growth of hemp, flax, tobacco and wine; and, if a colonial assembly cannot be granted, that there should be no taxation without the authority of Parliament.

In general, we agree with Mr Wentworth in his statement of evils, and in the remedies he has proposed for them. Many of the restrictions upon the commerce of New South Wales are so absurd, that they require only to be stated in Parliament to be corrected. The fertility of the colony so far exceeds its increase of population, and the difficulty of finding a market for corn is so great,—or rather the impossibility so clear,—that the measure of encouraging domestic distilleries ought to be had recourse to. The colony, with a soil fit for every thing, must, as Mr Wentworth proposes, grow other things besides corn,—and excite that market in the interior which it does not enjoy from without. The want of demand, indeed, for the excess of corn, will soon effect this without the intervention of Government. Government, we believe, have already given up the right of taxation without the sanction of Parliament; and there is an end probably, by this time, to that grievance. A Council and a Colonial Secretary, they have also expressed their willingness to concede.

Of Trial by Jury, and a Colonial Assembly, we confess that we have great doubts. At some future time they must come, and ought to come. The only question is, Is the colony fit for such institutions at present? Are there a sufficient number of respectable persons to serve that office in the various settlements? If the English law is to be followed exactly—to compose a jury of twelve persons, a panel of forty-eight must be summoned. Could forty-eight intelligent, unconvicted men, be found in every settlement of New South Wales? or must they not be fetched from great distances, at an enormous expense and inconvenience? Is such an institution calculated for so very young a colony? A good government is an excellent thing;

but it is not the first in the order of human wants. The first want is to subsist; the next, to subsist in freedom and comfort; first to live at all, then to live well.

A Parliament is still a greater demand upon the wisdom and intelligence and opulence of a colony, than Trial by Jury. Among the twenty thousand inhabitants of New South Wales, are there ten persons out of the employ of Government, whose wisdom and prudence could reasonably be expected to advance the interests of the colony, without embroiling it with the mother country? Who has leisure, in such a state of affairs, to attend such a Parliament? Where wisdom and conduct are so rare, every man of character, we will venture to say, has, like strolling players in a barn, six or seven important parts to perform. Mr Macarthur, who, from his character and understanding, would probably be among the first persons elected to the colonial legislature, besides being a very spirited agricul-turist, is, we have no doubt, justice of the peace, curator and director of a thou-sand plans, charities, and associations, to which his presence is essentially necessary. If he could be cut into as many pieces as a tree is into planks, all his subdivisions would be eminently useful. When a member of Parliament, and what is called a really respectable country gentleman, sets off to attend his duty in our Parliament, such diminution of intelligence as is produced by his absence, is (God knows) easily supplied; but in a colony of 20,000 persons, it is impos-sible this should be the case. Some time hence, the institution of a Colonial Assembly will be a very wise and proper measure, and so clearly called for, that the most profligate members of Administration will neither be able to ridicule nor refuse it. At present we are afraid that a Botany Bay parliament would give rise to jokes; and jokes at present have a great agency in human affairs.

Mr Bennet concerns himself with the settlement of New Holland, as it is a school for criminals; and, upon this subject, has written a very humane, enlight-ened, and vigorous pamphlet. The objections made to this settlement by Mr Bennet are, in the first place, its enormous expense. The colony of New South Wales, from 1788 to 1815 inclusive, has cost this country the enormous sum of £3,465,983. In the evidence before the Transportation Committee, the annual expense of each convict from 1791 to 1797, is calculated at £33 9s. 5¾d. per annum, and the profits of his labour are stated to be £20. The price paid for the transport of convicts has been, on an average, £37 exclusive of food and clothing. It appears, however, says Mr Bennet, by an account laid before Parliament, that in the year 1814, £109,746 were paid for the transport, food and clothing of 1016 convicts, which will make the cost amount to about £108 per man. In 1812, the expenses of the colony were £176,000; in 1813, £235,000; in 1814, £231,362; but in 1815 they had fallen to £150,000.

The cruelty and neglect in the transportation of convicts, has been very great—and in this way a punishment inflicted which it never was in the contem-plation of law to enact. During the first eight years, according to Mr Bennet's statements, one-tenth of the convicts died on the passage; on the arrival of three of the ships, 200 sick were landed, 281 persons having died on board:—These instances, however, of criminal inattention to the health of the convicts, no longer take place; and it is mentioned rather as an history of what is past, than a censure upon any existing evil.

In addition to the expense of Botany Bay, Mr Bennet contends that it wants the very essence of punishment, terror;—that the common people do not dread it;—that instead of preventing crimes, it rather excites the people to their commission, by the hopes it affords of bettering their condition in a new country. ...

It is a scandalous injustice in this colony, that persons transported for seven years, have no power of returning when that period is expired. A strong active man may sometimes work his passage home; but what is an old man or an aged female to do? Suppose a convict were to be confined in prison for seven years, and then told he might get out if he could climb over the walls, or break open the locks, what in general will be his chance of liberation? But no lock nor doors can be as secure a means of detention as the distance of Botany Bay. This is a downright trick and fraud in the administration of criminal justice. A poor wretch who is banished from his country for seven years, should be furnished with the means of returning to his country when these seven years are expired.—If it is intended he should never return, his sentence should have been banishment for life.

The most serious charge against the colony, as a place for transportation, and an experiment in criminal justice, is the extreme profligacy of manners which prevails there, and the total want of reformation among the convicts. Upon this subject, except in the regular letters, officially varnished and filled with fraudulent beatitudes for the public eye, there is, and there can be but one opinion. New South Wales is a sink of wickedness, in which the great majority of convicts of both sexes become infinitely more depraved than at the period of their arrival. How, as Mr Bennet very justly observes, can it be otherwise? The felon transported to the American plantations, became an insulated rogue among honest men. He lived for years in the family of some industrious planter, without seeing a picklock, or indulging in pleasant dialogues on the delicious burglaries of his youth. He imperceptibly glided into honest habits, and lost not only the tact for pockets, but the wish to investigate their contents. But in Botany Bay, the felon, as soon as he gets out of the ship, meets with his ancient trull, with the footpad of his heart, the convict of his affections,—the man whose hand he has often met in the same gentleman's pocket—the being whom he would chuse from the whole world to take to the road, or to disentangle the locks of Bramah. It is impossible that vice should not become more intense in such society. ...

Thus much for Botany Bay. As a mere colony, it is too distant and too expensive; and, in future, will of course involve us in many of those just and necessary wars, which deprive Englishmen so rapidly of their comforts, and make England scarcely worth living in. If considered as a place of reform for criminals, its distance, expense, and the society to which it dooms the objects of the experiment, are insuperable objections to it. It is in vain to say, that the honest people in New South Wales will soon bear a greater proportion to the rogues, and the contamination of bad society will be less fatal: This only proves that it may be a good place for reform hereafter, not that it is a good one now. One of the principal reasons for peopling Botany Bay at all, was, that it would be an admirable receptacle, and a school of reform, for our convicts. It turns out, that for the first half century, it will make them worse than they were before, and that, after that period, they may probably begin to improve. A marsh, to be sure, may be drained and cultivated; but no man who has his choice, would select it in the mean time for his dwelling-place. ...

... Upon the subject of emigration to Botany Bay, Mr Wentworth observes, 1*st*, that any respectable person emigrating to that colony, receives as much land gratis as would cost him £400 in the United States; 2*dly*, he is allowed as many servants as he may require, at one-third of the wages paid for labour in America; 3*dly*, himself and family are victualled at the expense of Government for six months. He calculates that a man, wife, and two children, with an allowance of five tons for themselves and baggage, could emigrate to Botany Bay for £100, including every expense, provided a whole ship could be freighted; and that a single man could be taken out thither for £30. These points are worthy of serious attention to those who are shedding their country.

ANON.

Reference is made to Francis Jeffrey (1773–1850), editor and literary critic; Robert Montgomery (1807–55), poet; James Mill (1773–1836), philosopher and historian; and Henry Colburn (d.1855), publisher. The author of The Disowned *is Bulwer Lytton.*

'Literature of the Swan River',
Athenaeum, 10 June 1829, pp. 361–2.

REPORT OF THE COMMITTEE OF THE HOUSE OF COMMONS, APPOINTED TO CONSIDER THE EXPEDIENCY OF ESTABLISHING A SWAN RIVER LITERATURE. (NOT YET PRESENTED, BUT KINDLY COMMUNICATED TO 'THE ATHENAEUM,' BY THE CHAIRMAN, MR. ALDERMAN WOOD.)

In pursuance of the directions which they have received from your Honourable House, the Committee for considering the most practicable means of effecting a settlement on the banks of the Swan River, have occupied themselves during the present Session in considering the expediency of establishing a literature in this infant colony. The result of their investigations they have now the honour to lay before the House.

The valuable evidence of Peter M'Culloch, esq., contained in page 4 of the Appendix, convinced the Committee of the following truths: that the principal circumstance which checks the free growth of a literature in an old country, is the fictitious value attached to works which have been long in the market, though those works cannot have been benefited by any of the improvements which have recently been introduced into the manufacture—that it is obviously advantageous, when a country is rapidly advancing, that it should have a literature which keeps pace with its advancement, and, consequently, which changes its character every few years—that this never, however, will happen, so long as an old literature exists, most men habitually preferring that to which they are accustomed—that, consequently, it would be desirable to devise means for preventing, if possible, the establishment of an old literature, for which attempt a colony obviously offers the greatest facilities—that the chief cause of works continuing to live after it is for the interest of the public that they should die and make way for new ones, is the quantity of time and thought that has been expended on their production—that, consequently, the less of time and thought that is spent upon their production, the more chance is there of their answering the purpose intended; and, to express the whole in the form of a simple proposition,—THAT IN LITERATURE THE FINENESS OF THE ARTICLE, INSTEAD OF VARYING DIRECTLY AS HAS BEEN SUPPOSED, VARIES INVERSELY AS THE INFERIORITY OF THE MATERIAL EMPLOYED IN ITS PRODUCTION.

After listening to this beautiful application of the principles of science to a subject which had not previously been brought within their sphere, the Committee proceeded to their next duty. It was to ascertain *firstly*, which branches of literature could be most easily accommodated to Mr. M'Culloch's principles, and which, consequently, it was most desirable to introduce into the new settlement; and, *secondly*, to ascertain what class of settlers would be likely to undertake this office.

Keeping these two objects in sight, the Committee proceeded to examine several gentlemen whose acquaintance and personal connection with literature entitled their opinions to weight and deference. They would particularly call the attention of the House to the evidence of Mr. Jeffry (pp.9–16 of the Appendix,) who asserted as his conclusion from the experience of thirty years, that the value of a review depended almost entirely upon the exclusion of all study and speculation from it. The Committee cannot resist making a short extract.

Examination of Mr. Jeffry.

'You mentioned that the practice of reviewing had been very much improved of late years. Have those improvements tended to diminish the quantity of labour employed in the production?

'Most materially, though persons not in the secret are self-importantly proclaiming the reverse, to our infinite amusement. They fancy that the increase of subjects and the length of the articles, is a decisive on their side, whereas we know that the increase of subject has been accompanied by a much more than proportionable increase of common forms, and that the length of the articles is an admirable security that they are never read.

'You talk of common forms, what are they?

'Forms for beginning articles, such as, 1st. The Solemn; as for instance, "No one who contemplates the vast events which have been altering the condition of the old and new continents during the last twenty-five years, with the eye of a statesman and the spirit of a philosopher, can," &c. 2. The Abrupt; viz., "This is a mighty pleasant book." 3. The Common-place; as, "The nineteenth century is, unquestionably, an age of invention." 4. The Facetious; as, "A friend of ours was wandering one day near his seat in the West of England," &c. 5. The Polite; as, "We think the author of this book a very good-natured, easy, gentleman-like man." 6. The Impertinent; as, "This wont do;" with about twenty others, which it would tire the Committee to mention. Then, also, there are forms of conclusion. 1. The Eloquent, called more commonly in "The Edinburgh Review," "the Holy Alliance paragraph," chiefly used after very dull articles. 2. The Tremendous, generally a quotation from Fox or Grattan. 3. The Propitiatory, wherein an author is called a man of talents, and an honest man, at the end of an article written to prove that no one could have written his book who was not a fool and a knave. 4. The Saucy, the invention of which belongs to my lively young friend who writes about Macchiavelli and the Catholic Question. 5.—But I will not trouble the Committee any further.

'How do you furnish the middles of articles?

'The greater part from the public accounts and reports of the House of Commons, a good many from the reports of the Society for the Diffusion of Useful Knowledge, a few with quotations, and a great part of the remainder from old numbers of the Review.

'Do you exclude original articles altogether, then?

'Not entirely; there are one or two boys on the establishment who are proud of their skill in turning sentences, and therefore do not make use of those that are for each case made and provided. But they waste their time egregiously.

'You think that a Quarterly Swan-River Review might be published, which would not consume any portion of the settlers' thoughts which will be needed for other purposes?

'If the editor understands his business, certainly.'

The next person whom the Committee examined was Mr. Robert Montgomery, whose answers were throughout clear, straightforward, and satisfactory. (See

Appendix, pp.50–54.) He was decisive as to the possibility of raising a poem on Noah's Ark in the course of the voyage, of its going through several editions, and of its not being remembered at the end of the twelve-month.

The Committee must also particularly request the House to peruse the evidence of Mr. A. K. Newman, (pp. 216–219, of the Appendix,) who offered to contract, upon terms which the Committee must confess were exceedingly reasonable, to settle four hundred novelists in the colony before next August. For many reasons, the Committee were disposed to urge the adoption of the proposal, especially as Mr. Newman deposed that he was able to show by tables in his possession, that the writers for the Minerva Press contributed more to increase the population of England than any other body, country curates alone excepted. But they were deterred from coming to a final resolution, by Mr. Newman intimating that he could not answer for the continuance of these meritorious individuals in health, unless the House would undertake to provide them with an atmosphere like that to which they have been accustomed in Paternoster-row and Drury-lane.

The next witness was Mr. Mill the author of several works on history, philosophy, and political economy. His evidence is too important to be abridged. The Committee give it in his own words.

Mr. Mill examined.

'You are a political economist, Mr. Mill?

'I am.

'Do you agree in a principle which has been just enunciated to the Committee by one of your class, that books are better in proportion to the smallness of the time and thought spent in raising them?

'Every objection affects an argument either to a material or to an immaterial extent. To know whether my objection to this proposition would affect the conclusion founded upon it in the one way or the other, I must know what the conclusion is.

'You do object to the proposition, then, to a certain extent?

'So far as this, that I believe works have been written upon which a great portion of time and thought has been bestowed, which, nevertheless, possess a high value.

'Could you favour us with an instance?

'A recent work published by Messrs. Longman, Hurst, and Co., and entitled "An Analysis of the Phenomena of the Human Mind."

'Do you think it is generally desirable that books of such a description should be written?

'The necessity existed, but it has ceased. The book is written. Henceforth no work on the human mind will not cost its producer more time and trouble than is necessary merely to write down his ideas.

'Supposing, then, it were proposed to found a school of Metaphysics on the banks of the Swan River, do you imagine this object might be accomplished without departing from the principle of Mr. M'Culloch's proposition?

'Certainly; I could point out to the Committee ten young gentlemen of my own acquaintance, who, by means of the formulae provided in the book I have mentioned, would be able to establish the school and to write all the necessary treatises for it without spending a single thought.

'Without spending a single thought?

'I adhere to my words.

'What security would there be for their adhering to this economical principle?

'The security of an axiom which is as undoubted as any thing can be in moral science, as it has been generalized from a series of extensive observations, that the quantity of subject-matter consumed by any individual may equal or fall short of, but cannot exceed, the quantity of the same subject-matter possessed by that individual.'

The force of this clear, decisive and satisfactory evidence, was not shaken in the minds of the Committee by the counter testimony of a gentleman from Highgate, who entertained them for the space of six hours, with an account of the course and study of reflection necessary to the preparation of a work on the 'Elements of Discourse,' which, he observed, was intended as a metaphysical primer or horn-book, from which a student possessed of a hard head, a willing heart, a clear conscience, a good memory, and strong book-mindedness, might, by the application of all his faculties, acquire a knowledge of the alphabet of the science. The Committee think it would be decidedly inexpedient to send out this gentleman or any of his disciples to the new settlement. As much of his evidence as could be reported by the Clerk of the Committee will be found in the Appendix. (pp. 96–204.)

Abundantly confirmatory of the principal facts deposed to by Mr. Mill, was the testimony of the 'Author of the Disowned.' The following extract from the evidence of this important witness, will set the question in a very clear light.

Examination of the 'Author of the Disowned.'

'In the course of the last winter, Sir, you published a metaphysical novel?

'I did—a metaphysico-fashionable novel.

'The metaphysics of which gave, as the Committee has been informed, universal satisfaction.

'If universal means merely of or belonging to the visible universe, I may say that it gave more than universal pleasure; for not only did it perfectly satisfy myself and the Lady Patronesses, but also a large body of bipeds, existing, for the most part, "*extra flammantia mœnia mundi*," on the north side of Oxford-street, and in the dark caverns of Westminster; and there called, as I learn from a dweller in those solitudes, who has described them particularly in the last "Edinburgh Review," Utilitarians or Benthamites.

'You mentioned, Sir, in a former part of your examination, that you were occupied nearly two months in the composition of the four volumes?

'I believe the MSS. did lie upon my table for nearly that time.

'Can you inform the Committee how large a portion of that two months was spent in preparing the metaphysics of the work?

'The press was delayed nearly a week by the dilatoriness of one of the parties.

'To what parties do you refer?

'A document which I have in my pocket will explain. I must beg leave to mention, that it was given to me this morning by my publisher, and that, being somewhat pressed for time, I unconsciously thrust it into my waistcoat. It is an offence which I never was guilty of before, and I trust the Committee will not betray me. The document is as follows:

DEAR SIR,—You remember that in our original negotiation respecting 'The Disowned,' it was agreed that the charge for procuring the metaphysics, which I undertook, should not be included in the price of the copyright. I now beg leave to forward for your perusal the inclosed bill, which I have received from the different persons who took part in providing them.—I am, Sir, &c. &c.

H. COLBURN.

BILL.

To selecting metaphysical opinions from 'The Westminster Review,' at the rate of 4s. for every 100,	£2	1	6
To finding authorities for the same, at the rate of 2s. for the name of every ancient philosopher—1s. for all philosophers previous to Hobbes—and 6d. for all since,	3	2	1
To washing, dressing, and making gentlemanly, the opinions taken from 'The Westminster Review,' as per former item. (This, being a delicate business, was undertaken by my own shopman.)	21	0	0
To fitting the same to the character of Mr. Mordaunt,	4	5	0
	£30	8	7

'This, I understand, is much above the ordinary rate; and I learn from a person at the Bar, with whom I have the misfortune to be acquainted, that, if the bill were taxed in the Court of Chancery, it would be reduced to one-third of its present amount.'

The portions of the evidence to which the Committee has referred, are sufficient, they submit, to prove the feasibility of the scheme for introducing literature
into the new settlement. By comparing them with the other parts of the evidence
contained in the appendix, it will be seen also, that some kinds of literature
possess a decided superiority over others in the facility of their production, yet
that there is none which, under proper management, may not be suitable for the
present purpose. Wherever proper modes of culture have been adopted, and
a skilful use has been made of the powers of machinery, every literary soil,
however intractable at first, has at length been rendered productive, at a small
expense of time and labour. The Committee, therefore, does not despair of
seeing, in a few years, a plentiful crop of English plants, of every genus, adorning
the banks of the Swan River; and, by their periodical decline, making room for
fresh flowers to spring out of a soil, upon which the animal matter they leave
behind them has operated as a rich and fertilising manure. All things, however,
must proceed gradually; and every great practical scheme should be preceded by
one which is merely experimental. The Committee therefore recommend that the
House should commence in the course of the next session, by sending out one
metaphysician, two religious poets (that race being sickly), a reviewer, and a
fashionable novelist. As it is desirable that all obstructions should be removed
which can impede the suggested, or any future, emigration of persons of this
description, the Committee would further recommend the repeal or modification
of that clause in the original charter of the colony which provides that no
convicts shall be allowed to settle in it.

ANON. _____

*This extract is from a five-part series which includes: II. Its Gold-Fields, pp. 513–17; III. Its
Agricultural and Pastoral Life, pp. 529–33; IV. Emigrants and Emigration, pp. 545–50; V. New
South Wales and Victoria, pp. 561–5.*

'Australia. I—Its General Features
and Resources', *Leisure Hour*, vol.1,
1852, pp. 497–501.

Persons of mature age can well remember the time when Australia, the 'great
south land', was invested with no pleasing associations, and would have been
regarded as the last spot on the surface of the globe to be voluntarily selected as
a home. Thought recoiled from it as a vast natural jail, expressly adapted by
its position at the antipodes, as well as by irreclaimable sterility and physical
incongruities, to receive the outcasts of society, whose crimes demanded their

separation from the orderly part of the human race, and justified exile to a desolate region. The lapse of a few years has wrought a wonderful change in popular sentiment. It has been found that the once penal country is admirably fitted for the nurture of great nations, being provided with resources for the sustenance of millions in comfort. A population of free immigrants has rapidly poured in, to occupy rich grass-lands, and fertile grain-soil, transferring thither our domestic habits, commercial enterprise, laws, institutions, language, literature, and religion; and the struggle is now intense on the part of thousands of our well-conducted, manual-labour classes to reach the shore, owing to the recent discovery of its gold-fields, and the excessive demand for labour which has been consequently created.

There previously existed a great general demand for the able-bodied of both sexes, to engage in various departments of industry, and develop the productive resources of the island-continent. Large sums are at the disposal of the home government, chiefly the produce of land sales, remitted by the colonists themselves, for the despatch of healthy emigrants of good character from the mother country, to meet a pressing want for additional hands. But the detection of the precious metal in large quantities having caused a pell-mell rush of the already settled population to the auriferous sites, abandoning all ordinary occupations for gold-digging, there is instant employment at good wages to be found for the strong arm and willing mind, positive ruin hanging over the great staple interests of these colonies unless their labour-market is supplied. But independently of the recently changed condition of society in Australia, it is not going too far to say, that no part of the world presents a fairer opening to persons intending to emigrate, with a view to devote themselves to a course of regular industry.

As multitudes are, therefore, now employing an hour of leisure in turning their thoughts to this region as a future home; and thinking that they may do so with advantage to themselves and the mother country, we devote a few pages of the 'LEISURE HOUR' to the task of offering them some information and assistance. Let it not be understood for a moment that we encourage the idea of leaving the shores of England, in the expectation of cheaply obtaining wealth by 'prospecting' for gold in the river-basin of the Murray. We would rather discourage the thought to the best of our ability. Experience confirms the statement, that where gold-seeking is a source of sudden emolument, the success is very commonly and speedily negatived to the individual by the mad spendthrift spirit which it elicits, while in a great number of cases no adequate compensation is obtained for hard toil, and in not a few, wretchedness and demoralization are items of evil added to the sting of disappointment. It is to those alone we address ourselves, who look forward to the service of the flockmaster and grazier, or to prosecuting avocations abroad kindred to those with which they are familiar at home.

Australia—remarkable for its great extent (containing a territorial area nearly equal to that of Europe), its singularly regular conformation, and recent discovery—comprises at present the four following colonies:—

	Founded.	Population, last Census	Capitals and Principal Ports.
NEW SOUTH WALES	1788	180,000	Sydney, Moreton Bay.
VICTORIA, LATE PORT PHILIP	1836	78,000	Melbourne, Geelong, Portland Bay.
SOUTH AUSTRALIA	1836	67,000	Adelaide, Port Adelaide, Port Lincoln.
WEST AUSTRALIA, OR SWAN RIVER	1829	4,600	Perth, King George's Sound.

The progress of these settlements, the last excepted, is without a parallel in history. Sydney, after an existence of sixty years, had nearly 40,000 inhabitants; Adelaide and Melbourne, in the space of sixteen years, had each grouped an estimated population of 25,000 persons; while at the time of the American revolution, after a period of more than a century and a half, Boston only possessed 18,000 inhabitants, and neither Philadelphia nor New York at all equalled the size of Sydney.

It is not easy in a few brief paragraphs to reply to the natural inquiry of the intending emigrant, 'What kind of country is Australia?' But, referring exclusively to the settled districts, we will offer some general observations upon the subject, which, though necessarily imperfect, may not be unsatisfactory either to the outward-bound passenger, or the stay-at-home crowd.

Australia is, then, eminently a land of *contrarieties*; a kind of miniature world, in many respects turned upside down; and novelties will often arrest attention, till the new settler has become accustomed to his change of place. Situated in the southern hemisphere, nearly opposite to the position of Great Britain in the northern, the seasons are of course the reverse of our own, midsummer falling in January, and midwinter in July. The spring months are September, October, and November; the summer, December, January, and February; the autumn, March, April, and May; and the winter, June, July, and August. The sun, which is southerly to us, is northerly to our brethren at the antipodes. They have reverse conditions likewise with reference to the temperature of the breeze, the north wind being hot, and the south wind cold. Both in botany and zoology, nature exhibits a thousand singular arrangements, many of which have no parallel elsewhere. Its trees, which are entitled to rank as evergreens, from not periodically casting their leaves, are more generally ever browns. Owing to scanty foliage, the majority afford little shade, except when they are very closely grouped, which is an exception in the distribution of the ligneous vegetation; and for the same reason, along with the peculiar pale tint of the leaves, the forests are never sombre scenes. Some bear fruits like cherries, with the stones attached to the outside. Others yield what seem delicious-looking pears, but are really pieces of hard wood. There are trees which have leaf-stalks performing the office of leaves, while in other cases the leaves seem twisted out of their proper position, being vertical, or presenting their edges towards the stem, so that both surfaces have the same relation to the light. Nettles of an arborescent stature, from fifteen to twenty feet high, are not uncommon. Native flowers have seldom any odour. Parasitical plants are found growing in the ground, an exception to the almost universal law of the vegetable kingdom, that true parasites are incapable of taking root in the earth. The animal creation is correspondingly peculiar. ... The characteristic animals are furnished with pouches in which to stow their young, and move by enormous leaps, outstripping the gallop of the horse. Wild quadrupeds are, however, few, both as to species and individuals. All are of the pacific class, the indigenous dog excepted, which is only an object of annoyance to the shepherd and danger to the flocks, at the outskirts of the settlements. There are various tribes of honey bees, but none of them have stings. Birds of beautiful plumage abound, but songsters are wanting. Swans are black; eagles, white. The cuckoo utters its note at night; the owl screeches by day.

In a region of such extent—the distance from Sydney to Perth corresponding to that between Edinburgh and Constantinople—there are, of course, large tracts unavailable for the support of civilized man, consisting of peat swamps, saline marshes, rocky hills, stony and sandy plains, either absolutely sterile, or productive only of 'scrub'—the colonial term for a species of stunted, unprofitable brushwood. But there still remains millions of unoccupied acres of the greatest fertility, adapted for the growth of grain; and more especially for the sustenance of flocks and herds, which may be multiplied for centuries, without fear of overtaking the natural provision for them. For miles and miles, the character of the country has been often compared to the park scenery around the seat of an English noble. Trees of interesting appearance occur solitarily, not more than three or four to the acre, or form small clumps; sheep whitely dotting the landscape, of which there are not far short of twenty millions at present on the pastures of Australia, yielding the finest wool, and placing it at the head of wool-growing lands. ... Abundant crops of wheat, barley and maize are raised, with ordinary garden vegetables. Though possessing not a single native species of edible fruit, save the cranberry and a few other berry-bearing plants of no importance, the introduced vine and orange thrive, and almost all exotics succeed, except those which require a colder climate, as the apple, gooseberry, and currant, with oats among the cereals. Yet not more there than here does nature supersede the necessity for stern exertion on the part of man, nor can a competence be secured, and distress be avoided, without a due amount of labour. Let no one, contemplating a settlement within its bounds, dream of a land flowing with milk and honey, in the sense of riches being acquired, or a comfortable subsistence being gained, apart from pertinacious effort. A more immediate and ample return for toil is its prime and only recommendation to the emigrant. The application and thrift which at home scarcely avail to ward off beggary, may there be confidently expected to place him in easy circumstances; but beggary will still be his neighbour, if the maxims of industry and economy are neglected, while little sympathy in distress will be awarded him abroad, owing to the well-founded presumption, that he is pinched as the consequence of his own indolence or folly.

The climate of all the coasts and colonies is remarkable for its dryness. Owing to this circumstance, and the absence of towering mountains covered with perpetual snows, there are no vast rivers comparable to those which are found in other great regions of the globe, and permanent waters are generally scarce. The streams, though subject to extraordinary floods from heavy rains in winter, are largely reduced in summer through drought, and commonly either lose their continuity, becoming a series of detached ponds, or are converted into stony highways. This deficient irrigation adapts the country more for pastoral than agricultural purposes, while, except in favoured spots, it renders the herbage scanty, as compared with that of our own fields, and necessitates extensive 'runs' out of all proportion to the number of cattle and sheep which are pastured on them. But the long-continued droughts, which threatened the colony of New South Wales with destruction while its area was contracted, have since been ascertained to be but partial visitations, and have not been experienced in South Australia or Victoria. It is to the dryness of the atmosphere that the superior quality of the Australian wool is attributed. In winter thin ice is formed; but snow is very rarely seen, except in the upland districts.

In summer, the temperature rises high, and the range of the thermometer is often excessive in the course of a few hours; but the greatest solar heat has no relaxing or debilitating effect upon the constitution, and the rapid interchange of heat and cold is endured without inconvenience. The only atmospheric annoyance is the hot wind, which occasionally blows in summer from the unexplored interior, and seems to indicate in that direction the existence of vast sandy deserts, which, baking beneath a tropical sun, give a fierce temperature to the breeze that passes over them. Volumes of impalpable dust, and gritty particles of some size, are raised, and swept along by this blast from the central fiery furnace. The sky, though clear of clouds, assumes, consequently, a hazy aspect, through which the sun glows like a ball of copper, while the haze magnifies the glaring orb. Exposed objects, as the handles of doors, sometimes become so hot as to be almost painful to grasp. Though excessively disagreeable, there is nothing immediately injurious in the hot wind. If necessary, journeying and out-of-doors labour may generally be prosecuted without danger, in the very teeth of it, while annoyance is avoided by keeping at home, with doors and windows closely fastened. The visitation is over in about two days, and is terminated by a cool breeze from the south, after a short but occasionally a very sharp contest.

It is a consideration of prime importance to the emigrant, that the ordinary Australian climate is in a high degree genial to the senses, exhilarating to the mind, and conducive to health and longevity. This is the uniform testimony of experience. Through the greater part of the year, the sky is beautifully bright and the air balmy. The dry, pure, elastic atmosphere gives a buoyancy to the spirits, seldom known in our fog-breathing country; and owing to the same cause, exposure at night, 'bushing it under a gum-tree, with a saddle for a pillow,' is attended with no ill effects. Acute inflammatory disorders are rare. Endemic diseases, fevers, or agues, are seldom or never met with, from the general absence of marsh exhalations. The prevalent complaints to which new settlers are specially liable, are ophthalmia and dysentery. The former arises from the reflection of the solar glare; the latter is usually brought on by injudicious diet; but both appear generally in mild forms, where strictly temperate habits are observed. It has been repeatedly stated, that individuals in middle or advanced life, even after the decay of the animal system has commenced, have acquired new vigour on proceeding to Australia, like trees transplanted to a more congenial soil, and have apparently received an addition to what might have been deemed in their case the ordinary term of existence. From some unknown reason, but doubtless climatic, birth is given to children by parents at a more advanced stage of life, and the young increase in stature more rapidly than in England.

Opinions in favour of the mineral wealth of this great island were expressed by the naturalists who accompanied the early navigators to its coasts, and were subsequently repeated by scientific explorers of the interior. The experience of the last ten years has strikingly illustrated their sagacity of observation. Coal occurs in abundance in various parts of New South Wales, and also at the Swan River, while copper, iron, and lead are products of South Australia. ... The discovery of gold in the neighbouring colonies, now an all-absorbing pursuit, suspending largely all other branches of industry, will form the subject of a separate notice.

At a period when numbers are on the eve of embarking for the Australian ports, to be followed by a greater crowd, we are unwilling to close this paper without some remarks of an immediately practical nature. The voyage, a distance of some 16,000 miles by ship's course, is of course a formidable enterprise, though really a very safe and easy trip compared with the shorter adventure of the Pilgrim Fathers, in a crazy bark across the channel of the Atlantic. Good vessels usually accomplish the passage in about ninety-five days; but the emigrant should calculate upon an interval of four months, and arrange accordingly; while, to guard against casualties, ships carry provisions and water for a still longer period. … It is of little consequence at what period of the year an emigrant sails; but if he contemplates the manual labour of pastoral life, August has its advantages, as he will then arrive about the commencement of the Australian harvest, when also the settlers come down to the ports from the interior with their wool, and make their arrangements of the ensuing season. But the present extraordinary demand for labourers renders the employment of able hands certain at any time. By sailing in the interval from November to March, the advantage is secured of arriving in the cool part of the Australian year.

The length of the voyage necessarily renders the cost of transport high. Respectable parties of moderate means, neither ample nor stinted, may secure a comfortable passage, with provisions on a liberal scale, by from £20 to £25. Steerage passages range from £15 to £18. Families are taken at reduced prices, according to number and age. Free passages are granted by the government to a limited number of agricultural labourers and domestic servants, subject to certain restrictions;* and the emigration of others belonging to the impoverished class is aided by societies established for the purpose.† Those who pay for their own passage should never deal with ship-agents, but with principals, and satisfy themselves as to the respectability of the party with whom they treat. … In a sea-worthy ship, and with a competent commander, there is little danger to be apprehended, beyond the casualties to which in other forms we are liable by land; and with reference to the sense of confinement, much will depend upon the habits of the passenger. He cannot do better than judiciously divide his time during the transit, occupying himself as much as possible with acquiring useful knowledge respecting the country to which he is going, resolutely beforehand turning a deaf ear to sundry advertisements with which the newspapers are rife. One now before us announces, that 'emigrants will find pleasure during the voyage, and profit upon their arrival, by taking out a cornopean at 35s. or a flute at 25s.' We advise all who are open to such seductions, to stay at home; and those who sail away from us, should learn how to stitch and use tools on their passage, so as to be their own tailors and carpenters when settled in Australia.

---

* Office, No. 9 Park-street, Westminster.
† Family Colonization Loan Society: Office, No. 3, Charlton-crescent, Islington.

CATHERINE HELEN SPENCE _____

Catherine Spence (1825–1910), Scottish-born novelist, journalist and feminist political reformer,
emigrated in 1839 with her family to the new colony of South Australia. The first of her several
novels, Clara Morison, *was published in London in 1854. Always interested in political reform, in*
particular in extending the franchise, she published an influential pamphlet, A Plea for Pure
Democracy, *in 1861. She travelled to Britain in 1865–66 and became a full-time journalist with the*
South Australian Register *in 1878. In no small part due to her activities, white women in South*
Australia achieved the right to vote in 1896. [ADB]

_____ 'An Australian's Impressions of
England', *Cornhill Magazine*, vol. 13,
1866, pp. 110–20.

It is always interesting and often very useful to English readers to hear the opinions of intelligent foreigners with regard to their country and their society; and
perhaps the first impressions of an Australian colonist, after twenty-five years'
absence from Britain, may be worth a little attention. Those who, like myself,
have left a provincial part of the mother-country when very young, and have
grown up at the antipodes, must have as few preconceived ideas about England
as any foreigner. Our knowledge has been hitherto derived from books and
newspapers, or from conversations with new-comers or friends who have been
on a visit to England, and is necessarily very incomplete; but at the same time we
are of the old stock, born in Britain, and with a love and reverence for it greater
than any American can possibly have. No spirit of rivalry or antagonism has ever
arisen in any of the Australian colonies to prevent us from taking the kindliest
view of the mother-country. Although our political institutions are different, and
our social distinctions less marked, we are still emphatically English; and it will
take several generations before we can have a distinct national character of our
own.

It may be asked what there can be to strike us as new or strange if we are so
English in character? The character may be the same, but the circumstances are
so different under which we have grown up, that we cannot help being surprised
at much that we see and hear. In our case, we have an enormous territory
sparsely peopled by an agricultural, pastoral, and mining population, with here
and there a town or city built on the sea-coast for the sake of imports and
exports, and here and there a township close to a gold field or a copper mine; and
in the other case you have a small country dotted over with large and populous
towns, connected together by a network of railways, and crowded with industrious workmen. With us we only produce the raw material, and all our efforts are
directed towards producing it with the smallest amount of labour. With you all

invention is on the stretch to make as much out of the raw material as possible, by labour and by machinery. In England all land is private property, and is in few hands. In Australia a great proportion of the land is unappropriated, and held by Government in trust for the people; and those portions of it which are sold are in many hands, and often transferred. In England you have enormous wealth side by side with great want. In Australia labour and the rewards of labour are more equally divided. With you the suffrage is limited, with us it is all but universal. Here you have a State church and many Dissenters; in Australia, or at least in that part of Australia in which I have grown up, there is no endowment whatever given by the State to any religious denomination. Our climate is hot and dry, with no winter snows and no summer rains; our vegetation is different, our landscape scenery is different. So that, I think, it must be acknowledged that however English in character and feeling a colonist may be, he is likely to see much that will strike him as new when he visits England virtually for the first time in his life.

And the first thing that strikes him forcibly is the magnitude of the towns and cities, especially the enormous extent and population of London—not the first day or the second, but after living in it for a week or two, and seeing the miles of streets closely built and crowded with people in every direction. He, accustomed to think a great deal about the carriage of goods and about road difficulties, can scarcely conceive how such masses of people can possibly obtain their daily supplies of food and fuel, even by the bewildering number of railways that radiate from the great metropolis. He sees little signs of manufactures, and he wonders how these millions can get a living. Do they live off each other, or off the country in general? Do foreigners, colonists, and provincials all flock to London to be fleeced, that the city population may be supported? He feels as if England must be small indeed, to necessitate men to leave the healthful, breezy country, to crowd into the streets and courts and alleys of London, Manchester, Birmingham, and Glasgow. The contrast between the wealth and the poverty of England strikes him with a strange feeling of awe when he compares the hideous slums of London with the miles of streets in which no one can live on an income of less than a thousand, two thousand, five thousand pounds a year; or when, 'in the season,' he contrasts the splendid equipages, the beautiful horses, the liveried servants, the perfectly appointed equestrians, the idle gentlemen, and the handsome and elegantly-dressed ladies in Hyde Park, with the ragged beggars whom he meets at every street-corner. And yet, painful as this is, how pleasant to an Australian home on a visit is London and London society. For the first time in his life he is at leisure to see everything and to enjoy everything; and for the first time in his life he finds other people who are as idle as himself, and with whom he can visit or travel, or merely saunter about London. It is only in London that one can find company in idleness or pleasure-seeking. In all the great manufacturing towns life is as busy and rather more anxious than it is in Australia or the United States; and in small provincial towns there is too much exclusiveness for Australians to penetrate into society when on a short visit.

The great beauty of the English landscape, its undulations, its softness, its wonderful variety of mountain, wood, and shore, impresses most favourably a visitor from our far south land. Its perpetual verdure contrasts with our pastures scorched up for many summer months. The exquisite changes in the tints of the foliage of your forest-trees—from those of spring, when the young leaves are 'some very red, and some a glad light green,' as your oldest descriptive poet expresses it, to the luxuriant greenery of summer, and then to the mellow and russet tints of autumn—are always full of interest to eyes long accustomed to evergreen trees, almost all of one genus, with long narrow pointed leaves. We have, nevertheless, many very handsome trees, and I think the first impression we have of your English trees is, that they are very small compared with ours; and if we land, as I did, in the end of winter, the leaflessness is painfully cheerless. They also strike us as different from ours in having been planted and cared for by the hand of man, for our forest-trees do not shoot up straight to the light, or throw out their branches symmetrically, as yours do; but as we watch the development of the first bud into the tender leaf and the full foliage and the autumn decay, these varieties seem to compensate for the months in which there is not a leaf on the trees. The variety of foliage, too, in the beech, the oak, the elm, the ash, the pine, the birch, the chestnut, the lime, and the various firs and pines, makes us desire that we could add as many varieties to our gum-trees and wattles, and our stringy-bark forests. Although no country of equal extent has such a variety of natural scenery as Great Britain, had she trusted merely to her indigenous trees, the landscape of to-day would have much less beauty, and the gardens would have shown a very different list of fruit-trees. We Australians have imported and cultivated, with even greater success than in Europe, the vine, the orange, the peach, nectarine, plum, apricot, apple and pear, the fig, the almond, the olive, the loquat, the mulberry, and the cherry-tree, and under certain favouring conditions, we can grow the strawberry, the raspberry, and the English currant; so that though nature gives us scarcely one edible fruit in all the vast island of Australia, it is the very paradise of fruit through the cultivation of what we can import. And I hope that we shall add your forest-trees to ours with as much success.

To our eyes, accustomed to great stretches of plain and great ranges of hills, the undulations, the valleys, the small mountain ranges, the narrow belts of trees planted for shelter, or by way of ornament, the green hedgerows interspersed with occasional trees, the beauty of the numerous rivers and of their banks, the great extent of sea-shore, with all the various aspects of the coast—sandy, shingly, or rocky, and often green to the water's edge, give us constant and great enjoyment. Above all things, we admire your rivers, your lakes, and your mountain streams. Even the recent exceptionally hot and dry summer is moist compared to what I have been accustomed to; and it is a curious coincidence that the last Australian summer has been the longest and the driest known for very many years. Engaged in a perpetual warfare with the dryness of our climate, with a long summer, frequently rainless for many months together even in our most favoured districts, and in the interior sometimes rainless for eighteen months at a time, and with our water-courses often quite dried up in summer, and our rivers frequently lost in sandy plains before reaching the sea, we turn to your perennial streams with an admiration you can scarcely understand. In all landscapes, whether on canvas or in nature, we prefer those where there is fresh water to be seen. The sense of utility intensifies the sense of beauty.

But, on the other hand, the careful cultivation of Britain, the utilization of every little bit of land (even the narrow ridges on the sides of the railways), the rarity of commons or waste land, gives us a painful impression. We feel cribbed and cabined and confined. Colonial children rarely like England; they do not like every place to be private property not to be trespassed over. There is no doubt that the concentration of all the landed property in the kingdom into few hands, appears a much greater evil to those who have grown up in such a country as Australia than to those who have all their lives seen nothing else. Although I am not so much of a Radical as to suggest a division of property, I must say that I think every facility should be given to the transfer of land, and that some step should be taken to prevent the inheritance of colossal fortunes. In no country should there be any limit placed to what a man may acquire by industry and abstinence, but as to what he may inherit, I think a line may be drawn. Is it really for the benefit of a country, or for the good of the individual, that a fortune of two or three millions should be left to one man, or even to two or three?

In your England an agricultural labourer, working from the earliest days, when he is worth sixpence a week to frighten the crows, till he is worn out at sixty, earns in all his life about £800, or at the utmost, £1,000. This is the money-worth of his life's work. There are proprietors and millionaires who have as much as that for every day of their lives without doing anything in the world for it, or, at least, without needing to do anything. No doubt, under such a system, England has grown up a very great country; science and art and invention and literature have all been encouraged, but the question arises, would it not have been a greater country and a happier country if there had not been such an enormous disparity of conditions?

This state of things cannot but strike a colonist more forcibly than it strikes a foreigner, for most Europeans have grown up under a similar system, and in many old countries the contrast between the two ends of society is as marked as in England. The wealth of England is certainly a surprising thing to any stranger; but I believe that continental visitors are most impressed with the great numbers and great importance of the middle class,—those with incomes of between five hundred and fifteen hundred a year, while we are most surprised at the large landed proprietors and the commercial millionaires. The middle class, and especially the 'upper middle' class, is a most valuable element in the population; all the more so because it is a fluctuating element, a class which it is comparatively easy to rise to or to fall from. There are very few landed estates of that value in England, and that small number is on the decrease, so that the income I speak of is derived generally from business or from stock or funded property, which is easily transferred. When such an income comes to be divided amongst a man's family, they must either work to supplement it, or fall in social position and let others rise. If it is derived from a salary, of course it stops with a man's life, and unless the family have a business or a salary of their own they must fall. This is and will be the position of all our upper classes in Australia, for though there is no hindrance to making wills in any way, neither law nor custom favours the rights of primogeniture either for land or for personal property, and land is as easily transferred as Bank stock. We are likely to have few large fortunes and many moderate ones, and it is to be hoped that the labouring classes will, in the earlier days of the colonies, become habituated to a standard of comfort that they will not willingly fall from. I should be sorry to see the working man and his family worse fed, worse clothed, or worse lodged than he is at present in Australia, and I should hope that the opportunities of rising from his class will continue to be as frequent as now, and be a permanent spur to legitimate ambition—not one chance in ten thousand, but something a great deal more attainable than that. It is the high rate of profits rather than the high rate of wages that has been such a boon to the working classes in our country, for all savings could be easily invested in land or in building societies, so as to produce from ten to twenty per cent.; so that the inducement to save was much greater than here, where savings-banks' interest is very small, and where co-operation is still but imperfectly understood. The thing that astonishes us is how working people in Britain can bring up a family and save anything for old age, and there is no doubt that to do it they must practise a minute economy that is most creditable to them.

With us, all our ingenuity is directed to the economy of labour; with you, though you certainly do multiply your hands marvellously by the employment of machinery in manufactories, in all your rural pursuits the efforts of the farmer are directed towards the economy of land. To this end he is lavish of labour and of capital. Perhaps in no country in the world is there so great an extent of land cultivated with so few hands employed in it as in the colony of South Australia, which is the granary of the south land. There are four acres under tillage for every man, woman, and child in the colony—and not a sixth part of the male population engaged in it; making about one adult male for eighty acres of land. The crops are what would be called very short, but it is better for us to have half crops than to bestow double labour on them; and with the reaping machine to take our wheat off the ground, with cheap land, and with a market for our surplus grain in the adjoining colonies, the farmer finds that an average crop of fourteen bushels per acre pays him very well.

By-and-by as the world advances, and our population increases, we must change our tactics, and bestow more careful cultivation on our land, particularly as, though we have great extent of territory, we have limitations as to arable land. In the vast interior of Australia there are tracts which may feed flocks and herds, with, on the whole, tolerable success, but which can never be available for agriculture, for there is no certainty of rains. In some seasons the tropical rains from the north extend so far south, and in some seasons the winter rains from the Southern Ocean extend so far north, but in many years Central Australia has no rain at all.

The quantity of enclosed land under pasture in England strikes an Australian as enormous, and proves to him, without any reference to statistics, that a very large proportion of the grain supplied for feeding the people must come from abroad. It is right and natural that it should be so. If England is the workshop of the world, if there are manufactured for other nations those articles of utility, comfort, and luxury which they cannot as well fabricate for themselves, it is a natural consequence that these work-people should draw their food from foreign countries. Britain has a population far beyond what she can feed, let her strain all the resources of scientific agriculture to the utmost. To me there appears something perilous in the position. I do not say that my alarm is well grounded, but it is natural for an inhabitant of a great food-exporting country to feel so. Observing the intense anxiety felt by the inhabitants of the Midland counties about the supplies of coal, and hearing the calculations that are often made as to how long it will hold out at the present enormous rate of consumption, I could not help concluding that upon this hinged, in an enormous degree, the present pre-eminence of Britain, and that a very large number of the superabundant population are in fact living upon this coal, and on what can be made of it. Science may probably discover a new heat-generator before the coal is worked out, but it is not likely that the new parent of force will be so exclusively English as its coal-mines. It may be one in which our Australian inferiority is not so marked, and consequently make us more favourably situated for manufactures than we are now. This may not come till long after our day, but I am so much accustomed to look forward a few generations for the future of our own colony, that the old habit clings to me; and wherever I turn I see so many instances of the economy of land, so many proofs of its enormous money-value, so much care taken of it, and of all that can be supposed to increase its productive powers, that it is impossible for me to overlook that greatest of all distinctions between the new country and the old.

Perhaps nothing on the surface of society strikes a colonist more than the number of old people whom he meets. In travelling about in various ways, in public gatherings for any purpose, and in general visiting society, the number of grey heads is remarkable. It is not because England, as compared with Australia, is more conducive to longevity (though I believe that will be found to be the case, in a great measure, when our colonies are old enough to draw the comparison fairly), but because our colonies as a rule were settled and reinforced by young people, and thirty years is too short a period for our old people to appear numerous.

And the next thing that strikes a stranger like myself, who goes a good deal about, and visits both his own friends and relatives and colonial friends' friends, is the extraordinary varieties of society he meets with in England. I think on the whole that this is the most remarkable feature in England. I do not speak of business life, I believe that is the same all over the world; a merchant in London may do more business, but he conducts it on the same principle as one in Sydney, or Paris, or New York. Shopkeeping is the same thing here as at the antipodes, and the learned professions are conducted after the same fashion; but I speak of the family life, the social life, the life which men and women lead together and which women lead by themselves, and where we see the characters, the tastes, and the hobbies that do not come out in the shop, the office, or the factory.

The extent of this variety is rarely seen by foreigners, or by American travellers. As a rule, those who are able to write books on England, have already attained some celebrity, and in virtue of this, they go from one circle where people of literary or scientific eminence associate to another of the same sort, and very rarely meet with the average commonplace Englishman or Englishwoman, who nevertheless is a most important element in the country. They perhaps neglect to describe such of them as they do see; they naturally wish to note only what is distinguished and uncommon, and their book gains in piquancy while it loses a little in absolute fidelity. Then, again, a clever writer is apt to be lionized, and treated with apparently frank hospitality, but yet with real reserve.

But though a colonist of long standing, I have not been long enough away to have no home in England, and my relations have not forgotten me, so that I have them to visit; and we make a practice of visiting our friends' friends, and will go a good deal out of our way to take a parcel, or a message, or a full, true, and particular account of friends long settled in Australia, with children growing up about them, to the loving relatives whom they left in the old country. All the reserve which is said to be a national characteristic (though I must say I have seen none of it), melts away like snow in sunshine before such an introduction. We get to the heart of the family at once. They wish us to see as much as they can show us of their daily life, that we may carry back as faithful a picture as we bring; and even their fixed conviction that everything is, and must be, better in England than in Australia, makes them more frank.

You enter one circle, and you are in the heart of that large world known as the religious world. You see it in the books on the table, you hear it in the conversation; and the visitors and the engagements of the family are all of one class.

You enter another, and you are in the scientific world. Papa's spare hours are devoted to the prosecution of some branch of science, or some invention which is dearer to him than his daily work. Some part, often a very large part, of his family sympathizes with him and works with him; and he surrounds himself with those books and men who are congenial to his researches.

You go to another, and find a number of people living for society—in town going out four or five nights a week, besides doing a good deal in the way of luncheon-parties and flower-show fêtes, and, as a general rule, going everywhere to see and to be seen; and in the country, unable to exist without the aid of picnics, water parties, croquêt parties, and volunteer reviews.

You may next, through a letter of introduction, drop into the very heart of all sorts of philanthropic movements, and there you meet with a variety of people each with his or her panacea for the existing evils of society. One says, Educate the people; another, Wash them and give them decent homes; another says, Give votes to the people, and raise them so that they will educate and provide for themselves. One works for children, another labours in prisons, a third visits workhouses. Here we see a man spending his life, or all of it that he can spare from the earning of his own living, in the education of poor children on a principle of his own; there a woman giving all her life to the reformation of juvenile criminals, and another to the relief and assistance of distressed governesses. The more this class of workers do, the more they appear to disclose that needs to be done; and one feels doubtful whether such great evils can be combated altogether by the noble efforts of so active a body of volunteers, and whether a little Government legislation would not enable them to work with more benefit to the world. But if anything could tempt me to remain in England, it is that I, too, might aid a little in such work.

The class I speak of now is most antagonistic to that passed last under review; they entertain a great mutual contempt of each other. The society girls and the society gentlemen despise the active philanthropists as being ill-dressed, strong-minded, and most fatiguing; they are sure that they have dreadful quarrels amongst themselves, and that the women are, or are to be, all old maids. The philanthropists, on the other hand, despise the objectless, frivolous existence, pity the restlessness, and cannot even see the prettiness of the fluttering butterflies. And yet they are very pretty: their dress costs them more thought than anything else in the world, and certainly costs their parents a great deal of money; but it is pretty after all. If they quarrel among themselves, which I have no doubt they do as much as the strong-minded ladies do, it is a matter of less concern to the world in general, and so it is not heard of.

Your next visit may be to quiet people, who are a world to themselves. You see there simple domestic life, and hear nothing about gay parties, or science, or politics, or progress, or woman's rights, or religious movements in whatever direction. You would scarcely think that any public events took place at all; for though Paterfamilias reads the newspaper, he never talks of it. Mamma looks after her servants, who give her a good deal of trouble; the girls do fancy-work, have each a friend—the sweetest girl in the world—and are very glad to play a game of croquêt with any one; and the young men are far more tiresome than the girls, inasmuch as a lack of ideas in them is more intolerable in the sex which has had the greater advantages.

Again, you may meet with a circle of people who are devoted to art, who are great admirers of some kinds of poetry, and who have travelled a great deal. In such a circle an Australian feels his deficiencies very much. He has no picture-galleries at home; he does not know what to admire or how to express his admiration, and often makes distressing blunders in the opinion he gives. Though he may have taken long bush rides, and made narrow escapes from death by thirst or starvation, he has not travelled in their sense of the word, for he has not seen any antiquities, or stood on any world-renowned height to view a classical land.

Again, your next acquaintance may be among that intelligent public for whom authors write their books, and to whom discoverers and inventors address themselves; not the average Englishman, but one far above him; the man whom superficial thinkers call commonplace, but in reality the man who keeps commonplace people from stifling everything that is new and original. He does not himself write or invent, but his apprehension is quick, his judgment calm and clear, and the opinions which Smith, Brown, and Jones would never adopt from books, partly because they do not read them and partly because they cannot understand them, they are often forced to accept, because a sensible man like Robinson offers them in a palatable form, and in quantities which they can swallow and digest at once. Such men as Robinson (good men of business, who provide for their families, and do a little charitable work unostentatiously) never come before the public in any way, so that we cannot ascertain how numerous they are in Britain. We can only guess that they are on the increase, by observing that a new idea makes more rapid way now than formerly. The author of a book or an essay, who tries to popularize ideas, either of his own or of some greater mind, by writing as clearly and as brilliantly as possible, and introducing familiar illustrations, in hopes of reaching Smith, Brown, Jones, and Robinson by it, fancies when his opinion is received, his discovery accepted, or his suggestions adopted, that he has reached them all; whereas he has only convinced Robinson, and through him he influences the others. Those who write are apt to magnify their office, and have great facilities for doing so; but, for my part, I feel we cannot be grateful enough, and England cannot be grateful enough, to the intelligent reader. We need him everywhere; in town he is valuable, but in provincial society he is invaluable. It is supposed that the essence of provincialism is the exaggerated idea people have of their own importance, and the intense interest they take in their neighbours' affairs, and that you can escape these things in a city; but the provincial mind can be provincial even in London, and only exchanges its curiosity about the events of the village or the neighbourhood for curiosity as to the affairs of its own set, which to that class of minds is the world. The domestic arrangements, the love affairs, and the money matters of other people, can be as interesting in London as at Land's End. An engagement entered into or broken off, or a last will and testament, perhaps, furnishes a topic of conversation for a longer time in the country, but it can be dwelt upon very sufficiently anywhere. I used to fancy that we, in Australia, thought too much about money, and made it too much our object of existence, but I believe conversation runs more on money in England than with us. The manner in which young people speak of *unearned* money—of what may be left by relations, or what may be gained by an advantageous marriage, and not of what can be earned by industry, or saved by economy, strikes me painfully. There is a sadly worldly tone in the manner in which the sacred subjects of death and marriage are discussed. In a new country, like ours, girls very rarely have any money, and young men are generally the architects of their own fortunes; marriage takes place at an earlier age, and need not be so very carefully weighed beforehand as it must be in England. We have here and there an old maid, but the mass of our women are wives and mothers, and too full of domestic duties, either to have the high cultivation or the desire for a wider field, which we see so general among middle-class educated English-women.

But I have not space to enumerate all the various phases which English society offers. There is the political world, where one really hears about parties, and divisions, and patronage, and Government influence. There is the literary world, where one would fancy people were only born for the purpose of reading books, and where there is as much interest felt in the affairs of the set, as in the provinces one sees taken in those of the parish. There is the sporting world, which comes out strong in conversation at certain times of the year. There is the agricultural world, the manufacturing world, with its one employer, and its thousands of operatives. There are Englishmen, whose business and associations are with foreign countries, and there are foreigners whose business is all with English.

In each of the circles which I mention, a colonist feels the limitation of his stock of general information. His own life is various, but its very variety prevents him from carrying out any branch to the perfection which he sees in England. Although he may observe, read, and reflect a good deal, he has not had either the leisure or the opportunities to enable him to cope with those who have made one thing the study of their lives. But if we can appreciate and admire the thoroughness of the leaders of English intellect in all its departments, we may get some credit with them for our quick though superficial intelligence, and our adaptability to circumstances. The definite daily work, for instance, which our colonial women have to do, if it prevents them from being devoted to literature, to art, or to philanthropy, brings out an amount of common sense and consideration for others which is too apt to be wanting among the many thousands in England who have no taste strong enough to become a pursuit, and who on leaving school find that there is nothing for them to do. I certainly think that the position of the larger proportion of unmarried women in the United Kingdom is a most unenviable one, and I would submit for many generations to the discomfort of having a short supply of domestic servants in Australia, rather than take from our middle-class women their present multifarious occupations, until some other or better career is opened to them.

One consequence of our high wages is, that we do not see anywhere the exquisite finish and completeness in our domestic arrangements that you have in England. We have some very handsome and well-furnished houses in Australia, but it is the little details, the little conveniences, the many arrangements made that the family should be saved any avoidable trouble or annoyance that must strongly impress a colonist. I think it is very likely that we in Australia will have a taste for sumptuous furniture and appointments and equipages, but I do not think we can ever come up to the old country in the little details which give completeness. From our wealthy class not being a permanent class, we are never likely to have the old-established magnificence, the collections of pictures handed down from father to son, and added to by each generation, the ancestral woods, the beautifully-kept pleasure-grounds; so that, to see these things, our young Australians must visit Europe, and, in the visit, let us hope that they will learn somewhat beyond pleasing the eye.

I, gathering my ideas of England hitherto almost exclusively from books, have had to rectify and modify many of them on closer knowledge. I do not see, for instance, that England is filled by tuft-hunters and match-makers, by worldly parents and calculating children. There is a good deal more regard paid to appearances and to position, and, as I think, a more concentrated love of money here than in the colonies; but I believe these things are rather on the wane than on the increase. The real goodness of England is not to be seen in a superficial glance through what is called society, but in the homes of the people. I am satisfied that English society is sound at the core, and that it is neither heartless nor altogether conventional.

From the liberal manner in which the opinions and customs of other nations are now considered, and from the great patience with which I have often been listened to when talking about the affairs of an obscure and distant colony, I am convinced that England is losing her insular character, and that, to quote Chaucer again, 'gladly will she learn and gladly teach.' This openness of character will, in time, root out old national jealousies, and it will still more endear the old country to the far outshoots who are already sufficiently disposed to be proud of their descent.

ISABELLA LUCY BIRD [MRS BISHOP] _____

Isabella Bird (1831–1904), English-born travel-writer, journeyed to Australia, New Zealand, Hawaii and the Rocky Mountains in 1871. Her Australian travels were serialised in Leisure Hour, *published by the Religious Tract Society. She told her sister 'I think the Australian colonies must be more prosaic than any others. Such hideous country. Such hideous leafage and the golden calf the one deity' (Bird, Letters to Henrietta, p. 86). She preferred more exotic locations, later visiting Japan, Malaysia, Tibet, India, Persia, Kurdistan, Korea and China, and was appointed the first female Fellow of the Royal Geographical Society in 1892. [BWW; Isabella Bird,* Letters to Henrietta, *edited by Kay Chubbuck, London, John Murray, 2002].*

This extract is from a nine-part series which includes: II. pp. 87–92; III. pp. 149–52; IV. pp. 183–6; V. pp. 218–20; VI. pp. 249–51; VII. pp. 314–18; VIII. pp. 413–16; IX. pp. 469–72. See also p. 171 below.

_____ *from* 'Australia Felix: Impressions of
Victoria. I', *Leisure Hour*, vol. 26,
1877, pp. 39–44.

… Warehouses, works, docks, railways, tramways, and shipping offices lined the shore in the neighbourhood of the pier, but beyond, villages of villas, half-hidden among the sombre-tinted woods, fringed the bay as far as the eye could reach;

and above all, piled on several hills, with the spires of churches and the high roofs of public buildings emphasizing the masses of street architecture, rose the great capital of Australia Felix, the child of gold and wool, not thirty-eight summers old. ... The piled-up city, the blue waters of the bay, the green woods of the Yarra, were bathed in a violet light, and the Dandenong Hills lay in violet masses against the sky; yet it was early afternoon, usually the most colourless hour of the day! This was un-English, and so was the blueness of the sky, which looked far higher than our own, the intensity of the sunshine, and the carnival of rich colour which the sunset brought with it. Un-English, too, and the better growth of a free-hearted land of abundance, were the lavish hospitalities from which there was no escape, and the alacrity of unbought civility which seemed to take a stranger at once under its cordial guardianship. But the faces and voices on the pier were English; the great ships which lay along both its sides bore familiar names; the steam-cranes at work were familiar sights; the train waiting at the station was on the English model; and after 17,000 miles of ocean travel Victoria was 'home!'

... In the Golden Land wealth and culture are not always wedded, so some, even of the Collins Street shops, minister to bad taste and extravagance by costly freaks, decidedly 'loud,' in dress and ornament; but one cannot but be impressed by the number of windows which contain articles in quiet good taste only, at prices hardly in excess of those at home, with the excellence of the print and philosophical instrument shops, and the number and size of the booksellers' shops, one or two of which look like public libraries rather than retail stores, and are as well supplied with standard literature and with the newest books in all departments as any in London.

Bourke Street, which runs parallel with Collins Street, is less aristocratic, and consequently more amusing. It is far less handsome and expensive, but busier and more colonial looking. There are cheap shops, cheap auctions, cheap restaurants, and third-rate amusements. There, late on any afternoon, are to be seen staring red boxes, with leather curtains, suspended by stout leather straps above wheels whose thick coat of mud tells of miry ways in the not distant 'bush.' ... When the boxes disgorge their contents, one may see a daintily dressed girl, or showy matron in velvet and jewellery, from 'up the country,' whose travelling companions have been an unsuccessful digger in fustian and jack-boots, who has brought nothing from the auriferous region but mud and empty pockets; a stockman, shaggy and bearded, with rusty spurs and miry boots; a Chinaman or two, ... and the inevitable colonial loafer, or 'bummer,' who travels by every coach, train, and steamer. In Bourke Street one also sees stockmen's horses, with bush saddles, hitched to posts, black, aboriginal men and women, ox teams, and many other suggestions of a life not yet flattened into complete conventionality.

WILLIAM HENRY OLIPHANT SMEATON _____

William Smeaton (1856–1914), Scottish-born teacher, novelist and journalist, emigrated to New Zealand in 1878, moved to Australia in 1883 and returned to Scotland in 1893. He wrote on Australian life and literature for the British periodical press during the 1890s, and edited English texts and collections of English verse and prose. Oliphant exploited his Australian experiences in novels of adventure such as By Adverse Winds *(1895),* The Treasure Cave of the Blue Mountains *(1898), a juvenile adventure story, and* A Mystery of the Pacific *(1898). [ALB; LCVF]*

_____ *from* 'A Gallery of Australasian Singers. Alfred Domett; Adam Lindsay Gordon; James Brunton Stephens; Henry Kendal; Thomas Bracken; George Essex Evans; Miss Jennings Carmichael', *Westminster Review,* vol. 144, 1895, pp. 477–503.

… To the critic making a detailed study of Australasian literature, the fact is borne home that the harvest is rather one of promise for the future than of satisfactory quality for the present. In no department is the fact more apparent than in poetry. The causes are not far to seek. In the mass of Antipodean verse, from Charles Harpur, 'the grey forefather of Australian song,' to J. B. O'Hara and Miss Jennings Carmichael, certain outstanding elements impress themselves on the mind of the student—(1) the absence of any markedly original note in the great Australasian choir, and the extent to which the singers of the South have been influenced by the leading voices in England and America; (2) the essentially objective character of the poetry, and the surpassing love of Nature, under all the manifold and glorious phases wherein she reveals herself beneath the Southern Cross, that inspires the Australasian poets almost without exception; (3) the poverty of metrical *repertoire*, in a comparative sense, exhibited by Antipodean singers, with the exception of Domett and Stephens, as though they feared to venture outside the well-beaten track of familiar, nay, even of hackneyed rhythms, lest, in the parlance of their own land, they might 'get bushed' in the devious tangle of unaccustomed measures.

Why should such be the case? A prime principle in political philosophy, familiar to students of Comte, Maine, and the two Mills, affirms that during the earlier stages of 'nation-making,' intellectual progress and development naturally remain in abeyance. The late Walter Bagehot, in his suggestive study, *Physics and Politics*, remarks: 'Long ages of dreary monotony are the first facts in the history of human communities;' and further: 'Better and higher graces of humanity are impediments and encumbrances in the early period, that in the later era are among the greatest helps and benefits.' Australian literature, and especially its poetry, furnishes an illustration of the principle. The fact that the Muse of the Antipodes has not yet wholly cut her leading-strings and abandoned an almost slavish imitation of English and American models, results from the circumstance that hitherto the mass of the inhabitants has been too busily engaged in 'nation-making' to permit primarily of the enjoyment of those years of widely diffused liberal education indispensable to the creation of the literary taste and 'atmosphere' of culture; and, secondarily, of that patient, studious development of the imaginative faculty, and of the cultivation of its 'voice' in metrical expression which learned leisure and the existence of a literary class *in se* tends to foster. This, then, is one of the reasons why an Australasian poetic literature more distinctively original than what meets us to-day has not been produced.

Further, the fact must be remembered that the conditions of life have not in the past been favourable to such a result. Australasia is the land of labour and of manual toil, the Paradise of the working man, the Sahara of the scholar—a land where Jack is as good as his master, where the labourer of to-day may be the lawgiver of to-morrow, and where each man, from the millionaire to the miner, has literally, not metaphorically, to earn his bread by the sweat of his brow. Her singers, therefore, have had but little leisure wherein 'to don their chaplets and singing-robes,' as Horace says in his noble ode to Tyndaris. They must even voice their lays amidst their daily toil, or, figuratively speaking, in their shirt-sleeves, pouring forth their music, with generally but little elaboration or revision, in the white heat of enthusiasm, and in the glad consciousness of existence. For of life under these sunny skies of the great Southern continent, and amidst its soft, balmy zephyrs blowing off the blue Pacific, we may write, in the words of Wordsworth's noble sonnet on the French Revolution:

> Bliss *is* it in that dawn to be alive,
> But to be young *is* very heaven!

In fact, the Australasian poet in many respects revives the old Greek conception of his office as the 'doer' ... or the 'maker' (an analogous use of the term occurring in the Scottish poet, William Dunbar's 'Lament for the Makars'), uniting in himself the duties of the sturdy colonist, the political organiser or reformer, and the singer!

This circumstance it is which saliently affects both the spirit and the *technique* of Australasian poetry. The conditions under which it is largely produced, as well as the social atmosphere of busy toil, wherein the singers of the Antipodes live, move, and have their being, exercise a powerful moulding and modifying influence upon the body of the work achieved. Hence, with all its faults of lack of originality and the like, its character is essentially a poetry of action, exhibiting at times a virile vitality, a Pindaric energy, and a rapidity of epic movement, akin in kind, though of course not in degree, to that 'Homeric swiftness' so prominent an attribute of the *Iliad*.

Another cause of the fact why a more distinctively original native poetry and a metrical structure more highly developed does not exist in the Australasia of to-day, is to be traced to the circumstance that in the Antipodes there is no large leisured class whose wealth places them beyond the necessity of a fight with fortune—no hereditary lords of the soil, to whom for generations culture and learning, politics and social reform, have constituted definite aims in life to be pursued *con amore*, without a divided allegiance having to be shared with what the Germans term the *Brodwissenschaften*—the Bread and Butter Sciences. In Australasia, alas! the *Brodwissenschaften* engross the major portion of the native singers' time. The Muse in the Antipodes to her votaries is passing fair in very sooth, but, alack! she is almost entirely destitute of that 'one thing needful' in these grossly material latter days—the almighty dollar! However willing she may be, she cannot recompense those who tender her their heart's service with the vulgar but necessary means of life. The singer under the Southern Cross, though content with little, and quite as ready as his brethren elsewhere to shout 'my mind to me a kingdom is,' must have 'something' to keep body and soul together. His best energies, therefore, are too often devoted to labouring among the sheepcotes of Admetus, when he should have been singing on the sunny slopes of Parnassus.

To this lack of learned leisure I largely attribute the mimetic quality in Australasian verse. Many English critics and readers complain of the lack of local colouring and topical distinctiveness therein, and the charge is not unwarranted. To allow the spirit of his own beautiful surroundings slowly and subtly to permeate through the very inmost fibres of his being, the Australasian poet has literally not the time. While he communed with Nature amid her lonely and lovely beauties, far from the ken of men, he would be unpleasantly reminded of the wants of his own 'nature,' which craved sustenance as well as sublimation. Yet it is this very lack of intimate communing with his own world around him which has caused the Antipodean singer, when describing some scene peculiarly colonial in character, to allow, involuntarily, perhaps, a note to break in from one or other of the great English or American poets—from Wordsworth, Tennyson, or Swinburne, from Longfellow, Lowell, or Whittier.

The growth of an original poetic temperament in Australasia has thus been stunted, alike as regards 'creative efforts' among the poets themselves, and in 'appreciative sympathy' among the great mass of the people. The influence of each on the other is correlative. What is so rarely produced will not commend itself to the main body of colonial readers; what is unwonted or distasteful to those readers, whose time for all mental cultivation is so limited, will not be largely produced. And thus the poetic sense of the inhabitants of Australasia, never having enjoyed favouring circumstances for development along natural or original lines, remains to-day little better than a weakling and a gnome. The struggle for existence in a new country, whose very immensity serves to dwarf prospects of success, however promising, by overshadowing achievement with what remains to be achieved, has been so severe, that intellectual effort is rated as of secondary importance to pastoral, commercial, or political enterprise. Hence the wool-king, the Mount Morgan or Broken Hill mining millionaire, the successful party leader, are the present objects of the average Australasian's worship. There is something tangible about their exploits; while the labours of a Kendall, a Gordon, or a Brunton Stephens, by their mysterious impalpableness, represent no correlative value in £ s. d.—the one standard of appraisement keenly appreciable by all Australasians.

Finally, though perhaps the most potent reason of all, in accounting for the lack of a more distinctively original native poetry, and a more highly developed metrical structure, as well as for the comparative want of appreciation of poetry in Australasia, must be cited the excessively sport-loving character of the people. Not that a love of sport in moderation is antagonistic to high intellectual development. Greece with her Olympic, Nemean, and Isthmian games, and the high honours accorded to the victors in the several contests, would disprove any such position. But in the colonies sport simply takes precedence of all else, the climate—so favourable during nine months of the year for all kinds of out-of-doors exercises—materially conducing thereto. Australasians, in truth, take all manner of athletic exercises as seriously as an Englishman takes politics.

CLARKE HUSTON IRWIN _____

Clarke Irwin (1858–1934), Irish cleric, wrote and edited various publications produced by the Presbyterian Church of Ireland including Daybreak; a Juvenile Missionary Magazine (1888); Presbyterian Churchman (1890–91) and Temperance Year Book (1896–1909). He published other religious works, including A History of Presbyterianism in Dublin and the South and West of Ireland (1890). [LCNUC; WDINP]

'Australian Sketches' is a seven-part series which includes: 'Aspects of Social Life', pp. 183–7; 'Politics and Public Men', pp. 256–60; 'The Education Systems', pp. 320–3; 'Churches and Mission Work', pp. 392–7; 'Literature', pp. 520–2; 'The English Language in Australia', pp. 652–5.

_____ *from* **'Australian Sketches: The Romance of Early Exploration'**, *Leisure Hour*, **vol. 47, 1898, pp. 107–11.**

… I fear it must be admitted that the average Englishman's knowledge of Australian history is not much larger than that of my friend, who on most subjects is particularly well-informed. Australia, to many residents in the British Isles, is associated chiefly with thoughts of convicts, of gold-diggings, and frozen mutton—perhaps also I should add, of broken banks! Yet the early discovery, and subsequent exploration, of the Australian continent contain pages as romantic as any chapter of British history. Under the Southern Cross, without any of the blare of trumpets or glamour of battle, deeds of heroism and endurance have been performed which are fit to rank among the noblest annals of the British race.

… One of the most famous names in the early exploration of Australia is that of Sturt, whose name is perpetuated in Sturt Street, Ballarat, and Sturt County, South Australia. Sturt was a captain in the 39th Regiment. Interested, as many then were, in finding where the rivers (such as the Macquarie, Lachlan, Murrumbidgee, etc.) which seemed to flow into the interior emptied themselves, he determined, if possible, to solve the problem for himself. So far as one great river is concerned, he succeeded nobly. Leaving Sydney in 1829, with a small party of men, he embarked in a whaleboat on the rapid Murrumbidgee, and was borne on its waters till they emptied into the larger river, which he then named the Murray. How he made his way down this river, encountering hostile tribes of blacks, and disarming their suspicion and opposition by his kindliness, till, after a journey of 2,000 miles, he traced the Murray to the sea near what is now the city of Adelaide in South Australia, will ever remain one of the great events of Australian history. He left Sydney in the beginning of November, and did not reach the mouth of the Murray till February 9, 1830.

But it was on the return journey that Sturt's powers of endurance and those of his comrades were taxed to the utmost. The tea which they had brought with them was soon exhausted, and presently their daily fare was bread and water. Heroically they toiled at the oars, but the strain was too much for some of them. They all became haggard and emaciated. Sometimes they actually fell asleep at the oars. One of them completely broke down and began to talk incoherently. At last they reached Sydney, on May 26, after an absence of almost eight months. They laboured, and now others have entered into their labours. The river Murray now plays an important part in connecting the wheat-growing and wool-producing districts with the great centres of trade. Nor must I forget that it is a familiar name on election platforms in the colony of Victoria, whose northern boundary it mainly forms. When a political orator wants to wax eloquent over the iniquities of the other side, he is sure to say that the people are being roused 'from the Murray to the sea!'

… The limits of this paper forbid anything more than the mention of Sir George Grey, who, as Captain Grey, went out with Mr. Darwin on the *Beagle*, and explored the north-western coast of Australia in 1837 and 1838; of Stuart, who in 1862 crossed the continent from Adelaide to Port Darwin, and thus prepared the way for the telegraph line which connects Australia with the cable from England; or of Cunningham, Mitchell and Leichhardt and others, down to the 'Horn expedition' from Adelaide in 1895, which penetrated into unknown regions of the interior, and should be fruitful in scientific results.

The globe-trotter who thinks Australia uninteresting because it has no ancient ruins, should at least remember that the century of its connection with England has been no unworthy chapter in the history of the British Empire.

The Aboriginals

JAMES AUGUSTUS ST JOHN _____

James St John (1801–75), traveller and journalist, wrote predominantly for the Foreign Quarterly
Review *but also for* Bentley's Magazine, *the* Cornhill, *the* Dublin University Magazine,
Edinburgh Review *and others. His books include* The Education of the People *(1858). [WI]*

This extract is from a review of The Picture of Australia: exhibiting New Holland, Van Diemen's
Land, and all the Settlements, from the first at Sydney to the last at the Swan River, *London,
1829. The review begins, 'New Holland is one of those countries about which a great deal has been
written and very little is known' (p. 166).*

_____ *from* 'Aboriginal Natives of
Australia', *Westminster Review*,
vol. 12, 1830, pp. 166–86.

... The greater number of those writers who, in their reasonings on human
nature, have had occasion to allude to the aboriginal inhabitants of Australia,
appear to have delighted in representing them as the last link in the chain of
humanity.

M. Bory de St. Vincent, who delivers his opinions in a very decisive tone,
appears to dwell with peculiar satisfaction on the disgusting picture of these poor
savages which his fancy has produced. Their retreating forehead, their distended
nostrils, their hideously prominent lips, which constitute something like a snout,
give them, in his opinion, a striking resemblance to the mandrill ape; and nature
having refused them the further point of resemblance which wrinkles and a
peculiar colour would furnish, they have been at the pains to supply the defect
by art. Their eye-brows are thick and projecting; their mustachios thickest on the
middle of the lip; their hair is black, but neither crisp nor woolly, generally falling
in large masses, something resembling curls. It never, he says, grows very long.
The beard seems to be scanty, though the whiskers are bushy enough. This
writer allows, however, that they possess fine dark eyes not expressive of ferocity.
The ear, though large, is well formed. The body is stout, and well proportioned;
but the arms, thighs, and legs, both in men and women, are unnaturally slender.
They are accordingly weak, in comparison with Europeans. The women are not
much wider across the loins than the men; though their breasts, which grow long
with age, are at first large, firm, and hemispherical.

This description of their physical form, however, is much nearer the truth than that which follows of their moral condition. It is here that the genuine resemblance to the brute is found. Aristotle imagined that man could not exist in total ignorance of the social state; but M. Bory de St. Vincent is of a quite different opinion. Here, he says, are human beings without religion, without laws, without arts, living in pairs, entirely ignorant of the first principles of society. To add still more to their brutality, they are utterly destitute of modesty, have no clothing, no habitation, not even a tent to defend their bodies against the inclemency of the seasons, to which they expose themselves with the most stupid resignation. Nature itself seems to have condemned them to perpetual wretchedness, having bestowed upon them a country which produces no eatable fruit, no nutritive root, no animal which can be domesticated.

... M. Lesson, who is in general a better-informed writer than the preceding, agrees with Bory de St. Vincent in describing these miserable negroes as buried in the most profound ignorance and wretchedness, and in a state of moral degradation which almost places them on a level with the brute. He does not, however, assert that they live like the inferior animals in pairs, ignorant of all ideas of society; but remarks that they are collected into small tribes, which have no communication with each other. It is difficult to understand precisely what he means by 'communication.' These little tribes are sometimes at peace, and sometimes at war, with each other; and this, we imagine, is to have some kind of communication. Besides, it is ascertained that many of these tribes speak the same language; and that persons living in the vicinity of each other, and speaking the same language, should have no manner of communication, is difficult to be conceived.

... M. Lesson observes that of all the social habits of their white neighbours they only adopt such as are vicious and degrading; for example, the habit of drinking. But is not this the case with the poor and the miserable, even in the most polished countries of Europe? If we blame these wild men for not adopting virtues of which we fear they catch but few glimpses among the colonists, what are we to say of the canaille of Europe, who, amid all the blaze of science and civilization, refuse to be philosophers, and remain obstinately and blindly attached to vice and misery? According to his mode of reasoning the body of every nation in Europe are still savages, ignorance and vice being every where more prevalent than knowledge and virtue. The pleasures of the senses are the most intelligible of all pleasures; and in the hands of a man of a capacity for legislation the love of the Australian for these pleasures might be converted into a means of civilizing him.

But the most absurd accusation of all is to come. M. Lesson charges these poor creatures with immodesty, because they go entirely naked without shame. But were our first parents immodest in Paradise? Are our children immodest, because, if not prevented, they would run about, as they do in Hindoostan, in the same state? The immodesty is in the writer's own mind. The connexion between the idea of modesty and the idea of clothing is arbitrary; and if the naked savage perform no indecent action, he may be regarded as at least equal in point of modesty to a Parisian whether in breeches or petticoats. Besides, it is well known that among many nations highly civilized, nakedness is sometimes regarded as a sign of purity. The ascetics of Hindoostan, who profess an extraordinary degree of virtue, go entirely unclad. The ancient Greeks represented many of their Gods and Goddesses naked; and civilized ladies, of unimpeachable virtue, view these statues without a blush. To a truly modest mind, as Livia finely remarked to Augustus, a naked human being, whether male or female, is but a statue.

To contrast, in some measure, with the accounts of the above writers, with whom Mr. Malthus exactly agrees, we shall now present the reader with Mr. Dawson's description of the manners and character of these people. On many points he concurs with the writers whose opinions we have been detailing. He observes, for example, that both in men and women the arms, the thighs and the legs are too slender for the body; but he saw no corpulent persons in the country. … The Australian when first born is of a bright copper-colour, and if he afterwards grows darker, the change is rather attributable to the oil, soot, and ochre, with which he incessantly daubs himself, than to the effects of climate. The beard is short and curly, but very thick. As this appendage, however, is rather regarded as a nuisance than an ornament, the Australian contrives with a burning stick to shave himself, on particular occasions. When he is fortunate enough to procure a European to operate with a razor upon his chin, he conceives himself, like the Turcoman chief in Hajji Baba, to be in possession of supreme felicity, and grins from ear to ear with inexpressible gratitude. In fact had M. Lesson but once beheld one of these chocolate-coloured Australians under the hands of a skilful barber, he would no longer have despaired of their civilization. The cheek bones are high, as in the Tartar race, and the whole visage has a square cast, like that of the Mongols.

Though they appear to have made but little progress in the arts of life, they are not, as M. Bory de St. Vincent imagines, insensible to the advantages of a comfortable hut; but on the contrary, whenever the inclemency of the weather renders shelter desirable, they erect very neat little dwellings with poles and twigs, the door of which is always on the lee side. On that side also the fire is kindled, that the wind may bear the smoke away from the hut. They are, moreover, extremely particular in the choice of their food; never eat any thing raw or tainted; and select the purest water to drink. They are, however, a voracious people; generally drink ardent spirits, in the neighbourhood of the colonies; and, consequently perhaps, are remarkably short-lived.

The women, as among all other nations, are smaller than the men. M. Lesson asserts that they are still uglier and more disgusting; but this is not the fact. On the contrary, among the young women, Mr. Dawson saw many that were very pretty, and, except that their limbs were somewhat too slender, particularly well formed. Their bosoms were full and handsome, their waists small, and the breadth across the loins corresponding with the development of the form above.

Instead of the extraordinary lasciviousness attributed to them by M. Viery, the women of Australia exhibit a remarkable fidelity to their husbands, and, as might be inferred from that circumstance, are fond and affectionate mothers. Adultery is punished with excessive severity. The first act of courtship, savage as it seems, is generally a mere ceremony, to which the women submit not unwillingly. The savage has no time for long courtship, and knocks his mistress down, and carries her off by force, that her virtue may appear unimpeachable, and her resistance great. After this cruel ceremony, she is not generally ill-treated. Mr. Dawson, in fact, observes that the Australians seldom or never make use of any thing which is given to them, without sharing it to the last morsel with their wives. Accordingly, when the husband dies, he is long and deeply lamented by his wife, who would not, in such a state of society, affect or feel grief for a tyrant.

ANON. ⎯⎯⎯⎯⎯⎯⎯⎯⎯⎯⎯⎯⎯⎯⎯⎯⎯⎯⎯⎯⎯⎯

⎯⎯⎯⎯⎯⎯⎯⎯⎯⎯⎯⎯⎯⎯⎯ 'The Natives of Swan-River',
Saturday Magazine, vol. 8, 1836,
pp. 29–30.

Every authentic piece of information connected with this increasing settlement is valuable. The following fact, which is related in a simple and artless manner, by one who lives near the spot where it occurred, sets the disposition of the natives in a very pleasing light. The affecting calamity which two of them were the means, under Providence, of remedying, seems to have called forth such tenderness and active zeal on their parts as would have done honour to any human being, however well instructed. Indeed, judging from this statement, we cannot but feel that the character of the natives, (who are well styled, at present, the most abject of human creatures,) presents a good ground in which to plant the truths of our holy Religion.

About half-past seven o'clock on the evening of the 11th of December, 1834, it was reported to Mr. Norcott, that one of Mr. Hale's children, a boy, between five and six years of age, was missing, and that he had not been seen since one o'clock on that day, when his brother left him on the beach, looking at some soldiers who were fishing there. The natural conclusion was, that the child had mistaken his path on returning home, and had wandered into the bush. Immediate search was made, conceiving that he could not have gone far from the settlement, and was kept up for two hours, indeed till the darkness of the night compelled the party to relinquish all hope of finding him.

At four o'clock the next morning Mr. Norcott, accompanied by Corporal Blyth, of the 21st regiment, Smith of the police, and the two natives, Migo and Molly-Dobbin, who are now attached to the mounted police corps, set out to renew the search, fully calculating upon finding the little boy in less than an hour. They soon came upon the track where he had been the preceding day, and pursued it for some distance to the northward, when it was lost by all but the natives, who, notwithstanding the wind had been blowing very fresh, and had rendered the trace imperceptible to an unpractised eye, still continued to follow them up along the beach for about four miles, when they intimated that he had turned into the bush; here they still followed him into an almost impenetrable thicket, through which they said he must have crawled on his hands and knees. Their progress was now very slow, in consequence of the thick bush, and the difficulty of perceiving the track on the loose sand; but the acuteness of the natives, who are certainly most astonishingly gifted, led them through it; and in about an hour's time they regained the beach; the boy having made a circuit inland of about 400 yards.

The track was now more strongly marked, and was perceptible to the whole party, continuing so over a space of about five miles, occasionally in and out of the bush. At the end of about nine miles further, the natives were quite at a fault, owing to his having left the beach and entered a thicket, which it was with difficulty they could push themselves through; they, however, persevered, and delighted the party by every now and then crying out, 'Me meyal geena!' meaning, 'I see the footmarks.' Mr. Norcott, who was on horseback, finding great difficulty in passing through the scrub, took a position on a high hill, overlooking the untiring progress of the natives in the hollow below. They were then making their way through a perfect mass of matted bush; and Mr. Norcott informs us, such was the apparent difficulty in tracking the child, that he was about to despair of success, when, to his astonishment, they held up a cap, which was known to belong to the boy. This circumstance cheered them in their pursuit, and about half an hour afterwards the track directed them again to the beach. They proceeded until they reached the sand-cliffs, about ten or twelve miles from Clarence; one native continuing to walk a little way in the bush, in order to be certain that the boy had not crossed or left the beach, and the other remaining with the party on the beach. Here it was ascertained that he had again taken to the bush, and they found no difficulty in tracking him until they came to an elevated spot where the wind had entirely effaced the marks of his feet. This was a most anxious moment, as even the natives seemed to be doubtful whether they would again discover the track. Migo, however, descended the hill, persisting in search along the plains inland, and, after having made a circuit of about half a mile, was once more so fortunate to fall in with the track; but, notwithstanding they had found it, they were sorely perplexed to retain it, and were kept near the spot for two hours, off and on, losing and again discovering it.

The party had nearly given up all hope of seeing the child, when Molly-Dobbin pointed out the track on the side of a deep ravine. They were then about 600 yards from the beach. The natives then went down into the ravine and commenced hallooing, thinking the child might be asleep in the bush, and still persevered in pressing through the thickest scrub, and the most difficult country to penetrate through which they had yet passed; and observing by the tracks, that the child had evidently been there within a very short period, they journeyed on with a better hope of obtaining their object, and restoring the lost child to his afflicted parents. No sooner were these feelings of gratification excited at viewing the recent footsteps, than, at a distance of about 300 yards, the child was seen lying on the beach, its little legs washed by the surf, and apparently in a state of insensibility. Mr. Norcott galloped up to him, and calling his name, the boy instantly jumped up. Another hour, and probably the child would have perished, as the waves were rapidly gaining on him.

The joy and delight of the two natives is described to have been beyond conception; and their steady perseverance, Mr. Norcott says, was beyond any thing he could have anticipated from them: when it is considered that they walked a distance of nearly twenty-two miles, with their eyes, for ten hours, constantly fixed upon the ground, and at the same time evincing the most intense anxiety to be instrumental in rescuing the child from its impending fate, we cannot but esteem the act, and highly applaud the noble disposition of these two savages.

Mr. Norcott took the child up, and placing him on his horse before him, the party made the nearest road home, where they arrived at nine o'clock at night, having been a distance of thirty-nine miles, after being out seventeen hours without the slightest refreshment.

It is surprising that the child should have got so far, in the manner he must have been frequently compelled to force himself through the bush. He is not three feet high. His clothes were much torn, and his body was covered with scratches and bruises.

(FROM THE WESTERN AUSTRALIAN OF JAN. 3, 1835)

ANON. _____

This extract is from a review of two works, P. E. de Strzelecki's, Physical Description of New South Wales and Van Diemen's Land, accompanied by a Geological Map, and Diagrams and Figures of the Organic Remains (1845) and E. J. Eyre's, Journals of Expeditions of Discovery into Central Australia, and overland from Adelaide to King George's Sound, in the year 1840–1, sent by the Colonists of South Australia, with sanction and support of the Government, including an Account of the Manners and Customs of the Aborigines, and the state of their relations with Europeans (1845).

_____ from 'Australia', North British
Review, vol. 4, 1845–46,
pp. 281–312.

… One of the most revolting and disgraceful sophisms by which private cupidity has successfully deluded the British Government into measures for the interests of a few individuals, under the pretext of a principle of public law and right, sanctioned by reason and religion, is that the native uncivilized inhabitants of a country, the wild aborigines, are not the rightful owners of the land of their nativity, the land which they merely live upon, but do not cultivate; that the foreign colonists, who intrude into, settle on, and cultivate this land, become, *ipso facto*, the legitimate owners, and may expel the aborigines who do not cultivate it, but merely live upon it by hunting, fishing, and gathering the roots, fruits, and spontaneous products of the soil; and may do so justly, by the law of God and man. The natives have no rights of property, according to this sophism, in the soil of their native land, because they do not plough, sow, and reap, and make it available for a civilized subsistence. On this new principle in the moral code, our encroachments on the natives of New Zealand, the grants by our Government to speculating land-companies on the Exchange of London, of land of which the natives had a distinct appropriation among themselves by tribes, and proprietary rights which no individual of a tribe had a power to alienate— our deportation of all the natives of Van Diemen's Land whom we had not starved or massacred, to Flinders Island in Bass Strait, where the miserable remnant of the people we tore from their native home are perishing from the face of the earth—the American aggressions on, and occupation of, the hunting territories of the Indian tribes, and the French razzias [hostile incursions or raids] in Africa for the purpose of establishing civilized agricultural colonies in a land now only occupied or overrun by the wandering Arab tribes and their flocks, may all be justified,—all are deeds equally conformable to this law of nature and of nations, that the more civilized may, as matter of right, seize on the land which the less civilized do not use and cultivate.

It is reasoned thus; and this reasoning is unblushingly avowed and acted upon by our land speculators who receive, and by our colonial department which grants, allotments of land in Australia and New Zealand. The earth, it is piously observed, was given by its Creator to man to live on, to use and cultivate, so as to produce a civilized subsistence for the human race in the highest moral and Christian state which human nature here on earth can attain; therefore, if a wild uncivilized race of natives in a country merely wander over its surface, living on its spontaneous productions, the wild fruits, game, fish, without cultivating the land, and raising a more abundant and civilized subsistence out of it, they may be justly, legitimately, and on right principle before God and man, driven out, and dispossessed by those who can cultivate the land, and bring it by their industry to the use for which it was intended by the Creator, the abode of civilized Christian men. Now the premises here are right, but the conclusion is wrong. The earth is no doubt given to man for his support, and in a civilized, rather than in a savage state; but are we to conclude from this that we are to despoil, expel, or massacre our fellow-men who are in a savage state, instead of reclaiming, and enlightening, and civilizing them, if we can, and letting them alone if we cannot? The use and cultivation of the land are but relative terms. The savage who merely hunts over it, uses it for his subsistence as well as the farmer who ploughs and sows every foot of it. It is but in the quantity of subsistence derived from a given area of land, that the savage native and the civilized colonist differ as to the use of it; and if the use, the productive use, be the basis of proprietary right, what right would landholders in a civilized country, in England for instance, have to their estates, if it could be demonstrated that others, for example their tenants, understood and could practice agriculture, or the productive cultivation of land, much better, and therefore had a better right to the property of the land, since they could produce more subsistence for man from it?

Civilization itself is but a relative term, and can confer no legitimate right on man in one state, to appropriate to themselves what is not their own, but the neglected property of men in another state. On a jury we would hold it to be no excuse for a thief, that the man whose pocket he had picked was drunk, or blind, or an idiot. Our colonial department not only admits the excuse, but acts upon it. The right of our Government to the land which it has granted in Australia to emigration companies or individual settlers, stands upon no better grounds, socially, morally, or religiously considered, than this sophism affords. The principle and the practice of our colonization in Australia and New Zealand will be the indelible blot on British history in the nineteenth century. It can only be accounted for from the want of a permanent Board or Head for colonial affairs. By the rapid succession of colonial ministers on every political change in the Cabinet, a new man is placed for a year or two in charge of affairs to which the study and experience of a life time are required, and he must of necessity depend on men he has found in permanent subordinate situations in the colonial department, who may be sufficiently faithful, exact in the routine of business, and well informed, but are not responsible for the advice they give, and are in the position which in this country always, and justly, is loaded with the public distrust and dislike, that of secret unseen advisers—not of a public board acting under the eye of the public. It may be doubted if advisers bred in the routine of the Colonial Office are above the views of the petty colonial policy of times of a lower moral standard in national acts, than that which the present generation applies to public men and measures.

It would be ridiculous to assert that the public responsible men, the Cabinet Ministers, who, on each change of administration, take the important charge of colonial affairs, are self-acting in their office, judge from their own knowledge, have weighed the information laid before them, deliberately by themselves, colony by colony, case by case, interest by interest, without trusting to the opinion of irresponsible officials under them, who in reality manage the colonial affairs of the empire under their name and responsibility. It would require the lifetime of the oldest, and the abilities of the ablest, of the public men who, in the course of thirty years, have held the department of colonial affairs, to understand, and satisfactorily to their own consciousness of the trust, to manage the complicated interests of our colonial empire; yet there are at present four public men living, none of them very aged, Sir George Murray, Lord Glenelg, Lord John Russell, and Lord Stanley, who have held the office of minister of the colonies. With such a brief tenure of office, with the unavoidable ignorance of the peculiar local interests and circumstances of the business in the department to which they have been appointed by chance in the distribution of office, and with the drawbacks on their time and minds, of parliamentary business, party discussions, ministerial meetings, cabinet councils, and white-bait dinners, it would be unjust to throw upon the individual ministers the faults of the system and position in which they are placed. They are not to blame for continuing to act on the system which their predecessors acted upon, and the principles of which they have not had the time to examine, before they are called upon to sanction it by renewed acts. In this way we must account for the unprincipled aggressions on the property of the natives in Australia, permitted under each succeeding minister of colonial affairs, although each individually would have cut off his right hand rather than have given, knowingly and deliberately, his official sanction to such atrocious violations of justice and humanity.

'It has generally been imagined,' says Mr. Eyre, 'but with great injustice, as well as incorrectness, that the natives have no idea of property in land, or of proprietary rights connected with it. Nothing can be farther from the truth than this assumption, although men of high character and standing, and who are otherwise benevolently inclined towards the natives, have distinctly denied this right, and maintained that the natives were not entitled to have any choice of land reserved for them out of their own possessions, and in their respective districts.

'In the public journals of the colonies, the question has often been discussed, and the same unjust assertion put forth. A single quotation will be sufficient to illustrate the spirit prevailing upon this point. It is from a letter on the subject, published in the *South Australian Register* of 1st August 1840:—"It would be difficult to define what conceivable proprietary rights were ever enjoyed by the miserable savages of South Australia, who never cultivated an inch of the soil, and whose ideas never extended beyond obtaining a sufficiency of white chalk and red ochre wherewith to bedaub their bodies at their filthy corroberies." Many similar proofs might be given of the general feeling entertained respecting the rights of the aborigines, arising out of their original possession of the soil. It is a feeling, however, that can only have originated in an entire ignorance of the habits, customs, and ideas of this people. As far as my own observation has extended, I have found that particular districts, having a radius, perhaps, of from ten to twenty miles, or, in other cases, varying according to local circumstances, are considered generally as being the property and hunting-grounds of the tribes that frequent them. These districts are again parcelled out among the individual members of the tribe. Every male has some portion of land, of which he can point out the distinct boundaries. These properties are subdivided by a father among his own sons during his own lifetime, and descend almost in hereditary succession. A man can dispose of, or barter, his land to others; but a female never inherits, nor has primogeniture among the sons any peculiar rights or advantages. Tribes can only come into each other's districts by permission or invitation.'

Here are surely well-established proprietary rights, which, in common honesty, ought to have been respected by our Colonial administration. But to Mr. Eyre's testimony we add Captain Grey's, whose travels in Western Australia are well known, and whose subsequent appointment to the high situation of Governor-resident in South Australia is a proof that our Colonial Department reposed the fullest confidence in his opinions and information.

'Landed property does not belong to a tribe, or to several families, but to a single male; and the limits of his property are so accurately defined, that every native knows those of his own land, and can point out the various objects which mark his boundary.'

But here is testimony still more minute and satisfactory as to the state of proprietary rights to land among the natives, from Dr. Lang, the Principal of Sydney College, New South Wales, whose situation and character are equally beyond undue bias or prejudice, and whose long personal acquaintance with the state of the natives and colonists makes him more able, perhaps, than any man, to give correct information.

'You ask,' he says, 'whether the aborigines of the Australian continent trace any idea of property in land? I beg to answer most decidedly in the affirmative. It is well known that these aborigines in no instance cultivate the soil, but subsist entirely by hunting and fishing, and on wild roots they find in certain localities, especially the common fern, with occasionally a little wild honey; indigenous fruits being exceedingly rare. The whole race is divided into tribes, more or less numerous, and designated from the localities they inhabit; for, although universally a wandering race with respect to places of habitation, their wanderings are circumscribed by certain well-defined limits. In short, every tribe has its own district, the boundaries of which are well known to the natives generally; and within that district all the wild animals are considered as much the property of the tribe inhabiting, or rather ranging, on its whole extent, as the flocks of sheep, and herds of cattle, that have been introduced into the country by adventurous Europeans, are held, by European law and usage, to be the property of their respective owners. In fact, as the country is occupied chiefly for pastoral purposes, the difference between the aboriginal and European ideas of property on the soil is more imaginary than real, the native grass affording subsistence to the kangaroos of the natives, as well as to the wild cattle of the Europeans, and the only difference, indeed, being that the former are not branded with a particular mark like the latter, and are somewhat wilder and more difficult to catch.'

After saying that the intrusion of a stranger of another tribe, on the land of any tribe, is resented, and a cause of war among the natives, just as such an intrusion is punished as a trespass by the European settlers, Dr. Lang goes on to say—

'But particular districts are not merely the property of particular tribes; particular sections, or portions, of those districts are universally recognized by the natives as the property of individual members of these tribes.'

It can scarcely be maintained, in the face of such testimony as that of M. De Strzelecki, Mr. Eyre, Captain Grey, and Principal Lang, all disinterested observers, long resident (Mr. Eyre for twelve years) among the natives, that these aborigines have no sense of proprietary rights in land. The right and use, according to their social condition, are evidently as well understood, distinctly appropriated, and exclusively exercised by the natives of Australia, as by the inhabitants of any English village, or of any Highland parish, over a common pasture to which they have an exclusive right. If the natives even had no sense of proprietary rights, we did not thereby acquire an honest right to the property which from ignorance they neglected. The total abandonment, by our successive Colonial administrations at home, of the plain principles of justice and humanity, by sanctioning the occupation of the land of Australia without any claim of conquest, cession, or purchase, and without any provision for the starving tribes turned out of their land and means of subsistence, has, naturally enough, produced in the colonists an equal abandonment of all principles of justice and humanity in their treatment of, and dealings with, the natives. ...

...We speak of the razzias of the French in Africa. Three men only are accountable for them; not a nation. Louis Philippe, Guizot, and Marshall Bugeaud, are alone accountable, to God and to posterity, for the deeds there perpetrated, or allowed. The perpetrators are but the military machinery in their hands. But who are accountable for the razzia in Van Diemen's Land? for the razzias now permitted in Australia? We employ no soldiery. We lay the flattering unction to our souls that we do not cut the throats of the natives; we do not shoot them, except it be one by one on every pretext the savage stock-keeper can find—we only kill them by hunger and disease—we only take their land, water, hunting-grounds, fishings, fuel, and leave them to perish gradually, to be extinguished in a few years by famine, misery, infanticide, and hardships in the desert, by intemperance and venereal diseases in the towns, and by the extension of English law, with its conventional offences and punishments, to people in a savage state. ...

ANON. _____

This piece is from the column 'Progress of the Truth' describing Christian Missions in various parts of the world.

_____ **'Moravian Mission to the Aborigines',**
Quiver, vol. 1, 1861, p. 182.

A report recently presented at Melbourne says: 'The brethren, Revs. Spieseke and Hagenauer, have continued their work unremittingly at their station, Ebenezer. About 150 blacks may be considered as coming from time to time under direct instruction, whilst twice that number are more or less under their influence in the surrounding districts. The signs of spiritual life in some of the natives have been unquestionable, whilst the minds of all usually resident at the station may be said to have received an impulse for good, since their present behaviour will contrast very favourably with their conduct in former days, and also with the behaviour of those blacks who only occasionally visit the missionaries. One of the missionaries writes:—'Our station has been the continual gathering-place of the surrounding blacks; in fact, they call it their home.' And again:—'There is a great difference here between last year and this, and the acknowledgment of sin amongst a good many blacks proves the working of the Spirit of God. Our chapel is progressing. The little tower is finished, and the bells sound pleasantly through this wilderness.'

EDITH SIMCOX ⎯⎯⎯⎯⎯⎯⎯⎯⎯⎯⎯⎯⎯⎯⎯⎯⎯⎯⎯⎯

Edith Simcox (1844–1901), English writer and social commentator, wrote reviews and articles on art, literature, history, moral philosophy, economics, education, women's suffrage, and trade for the Academy, Fraser's Magazine *and the* Nineteenth Century, *as well as for the* Times *and the* Manchester Guardian. *[BWW]*

The extract is from a review of W. B. Spencer and F. J. Gillen, The Native Tribes of Central Australia *(1899) and E. M. Curr,* The Australian Race *(1886–87).*

⎯⎯⎯⎯⎯⎯⎯⎯⎯⎯⎯⎯⎯⎯⎯⎯⎯⎯ **from 'The Native Australian Family',** ***Nineteenth Century*, vol. 46, 1899, pp. 51–64.**

… It remains for us to ask whether there are any real circumstances, past or present, which may help to interpret the seemingly meaningless elaboration of Australian family custom, and to illustrate the spirit in which the customary law is carried out and obeyed. In every camp there is a meeting-ground set apart for the social converse of men, and no woman must intrude on this spot, even when the men are absent. There is also a woman's camp or meeting-place, where the children, young girls and widows, or other unattached women—such as betrothed girls, whose destined husbands are at a distance—camp together. Boys who have passed the first initiatory ceremony, usually performed between the age of ten or twelve, are told by their elders that in future they must not play with the women and girls as they have done hitherto, but they must go to the men's camp. Married men and their wives occupy the same *gundi*, or hut shelter, so that the separate camps for youths and men, girls and children, show us the most primitive form of an organisation that became famous in ancient Crete and Sparta, and is familiar to ethnologists from the surviving examples in three continents, the commonest token of it being the presence of a common village hall, where strangers are received and the single men of the village live and sleep. In the course of the next great initiation ceremony—of circumcision—the future mother-in-law of the youth initiated hands him a fire-stick, telling him, as she does so, always to hold fast to his own fire—'in other words, not to interfere with women assigned to other men.' And that this is not a mere counsel of perfection remote from the realities of life appears from the statement that the most contemptuous and opprobrious term of reproach to a man is *eturka*—one who marries unlawfully (*i.e.* out of his proper class) or is in any way excessively addicted to female society. A strange man is in no case allowed to approach the hearth of a married woman.

Women of one division are allowed to speak to men of the other and to meet them in camp, and they may speak to and receive visits from women of their own division and from their husband's half of his division, if he is away. The remaining half of the husband's division (the family of his wife's mother) is *mura*, and may neither speak nor approach. 'Even now a man or woman *mura* to each other will make a detour of half a mile rather than go within distinguishing distance of each other's features.' In food-hunting expeditions men and women keep in companies apart, and at the mysteries the appearances of the women are strictly regulated and confined to the scenes in which it is supposed appropriate for them to take part.

A strict separation of the sexes in common life is by no means peculiar to Australians. In a classic account of the golden age of Chinese society (circ. 1000 B.C.) in the Confucian Book of Odes, it is cited as an indication of the general good behaviour that 'men and women would avoid one another on the road,' and we know that in general upon the narrow African footways it is the duty of a woman to efface herself in the bush if she sees a man approaching, while if she omits to do so and is carried off she would be supposed to have invited her fate. According to Miss Kingsley, in Western Africa a charge of so-called adultery may be brought and a heavy fine inflicted 'merely for brushing against a woman in a crowded market-place or bush path, or raising a hand in defence against a virago.' Confucius discourses upon the exogamy rules of China in a chapter called 'Concerning Dykes.' Civilised man defines a savage, white or black, as a being with whom the present impulse is uncontrollable; and the sort of dykes that are required to restrain the savage do not take the form of a threatened penalty by way of deterrent, but of a material impediment by way of prevention. As soon as savage moralists had arrived at the conception of the marriage tie as respectable, they thought—not so very unwisely—that the safest way to ensure its being respected was to keep every man and woman out of the way of temptation or opportunity to outrage it; and for this purpose the polysyllabic dykes ... were reared, high, wide and fashionable. The taboo of parents-in-law lends itself too easily to a venerable type of joke, but we may perhaps feel more respectfully towards the Australian legislator—who has blundered into a system that tends to unite old women and young men, and conversely—if our ethnological researches have happened to touch on those Russian districts where it is usual for little girls to be betrothed to men who live *ad interim* with their mothers-in-law.

The hypothesis adopted by Westermarck, that primitive man was monogamous, like the anthropoid apes, is as little susceptible of direct proof as any other, though it taxes the imagination less severely than some. But different sections of the human race develop on somewhat different lines, and as we clearly cannot place our modern conception of relationships among the 'innate ideas' of the race, while human law, as a rule, presupposes the existence of the offence it forbids, we must suppose that before exogamous rules were invented some associated groups intermarried without restriction: a cave and a one-roomed city tenement have identical social disadvantages, which operating without restraint throughout a small community, or a number of communities, would easily cause tragedies and disasters of a quite different order from any supposed consequences of the marriage of first cousins. Given an obvious practical necessity for a system that will keep potential wives and husbands apart up to the time of marriage, and keep their families apart afterwards, the Australian customs are far from unsuitable to their purpose. The elders of the tribes may well have had reason to agree with Hans Breitmann, 'Vood mit vood soon makes a vire,' and they appear accordingly to have thought it expedient to arrange that no boys and girls who were at liberty to marry should be, in popular phrase, 'brought up together.' On this view, the exogamous races are those which have had the temperament that leads to the trial of unsatisfactory experiments in sexual lawlessness, against which their more or less elaborate marriage regulations are a reaction: but there does not appear to be any place in a theory, which takes account of all the authentic facts, for the conception of an intermediate or transitional stage of regulated disorder, *i.e.* one in which the exceptions of Australia were the rule.

No attempt has been made above to enumerate all the supplementary regulations whereby people are made *Ipmunna* or *Mura tualcha* to each other, and in divers ways kept from contracting marriages which the mere rules of class division might in some cases allow, though they would be contrary to the spirit of the legislation as a whole. Where, as is no doubt often the case, the regulation goes beyond what any rational purpose could require, we must allow something for the love of regulating for its own sake, which is one characteristic of primitive man. The Australian has something of the child and a great deal of the schoolboy in his composition. His mysteries give the impression of a set of Winchester 'notions' elaborated by grown men who had nothing else to do, and the irrational part of this marriage law might be brought into something the same category of law-loving foolishness. But in Australia, as elsewhere, the law usually defines a rule of conduct slightly above, instead of considerably below, the spontaneous conduct of the average man.

British Emigration

WILLIAM MAGINN (ATTR.) _____

*William Maginn (1793–1842), Irish writer and journalist, in 1830 established the highly successful
Fraser's Magazine, for which he wrote satires and parodies both in verse and prose. An alcoholic, he
became destitute and was sent to a debtors' prison in 1837. [DNB; LCVF]*

_____ *from* 'The Desperate System. Poverty,
Crime and Emigration', *Fraser's
Magazine for Town and Country*,
vol. 1, 1830, pp. 635–42.

... Since 1823, this unhappy country has been cursed by the visionary measures
of a set of men, than whom, greater fools or more mischievous empirics never
existed in any land. In 1823, the Liberals commenced their experiments, and
from that period we have been doomed to undergo all the alternations of increasing embarrassment and pauperism. The ministers then committed a fatal mistake.
They had not sufficient penetration to perceive that the reduction of wages,
prices, and profits, which they aimed at, and which they have unfortunately
accomplished, was a certain approach towards poverty. Cheapness in all countries, is only another word for indigence. Cheapness that affects the cultivator,
the manufacturer, and the labourer, without affecting the placeman, the
pensioner, the fundholder, the soldier, the sailor, or the mortgagee, is a term,
the proper definition of which, is—robbery. It is as much an offence against the
person and the property of the poor, as is the act of entering a man's house,
assaulting him in the presence of his servants, and carrying off his plate and
ready money. Had there been, since the death of Lord Londonderry, any man of
talent, of honour, or even of ordinary information combined with integrity in the
cabinet, the acts of spoliation which have been perpetrated, the loss of property
which has been incurred, the ruin of millions which has followed, could not have
taken place, and England would have been saved, even in defiance of its corrupt
and subservient parliaments. ...

   We trust that none of our readers belong to that class of sceptics, who would
here call upon us to produce satisfactory proof upon oath of the distress and
misery we have attempted to describe. Every man who has his eyes open—who
can read, or hear, or see—or is capable of comprehending what he reads, hears,

or sees, must assent to the accuracy of the picture. The common people are steeped in wretchedness to the very lips. England may have been, as Napoleon averred, a nation of shopkeepers; now it is a land of beggars. Nearly 10 millions of poor rates are levied annually to support, at the rate of from two shillings to five shillings per week, the infirm, the unemployed, and the destitute. And yet there is more real benevolence, more active philanthropy, and more charitable institutions in England, than in any three nations of Europe, if united. The great mass of the people are unable, by their utmost exertions, to earn wages sufficient to render them more comfortable, or more than one or two degrees more respectable or independent, than the actual pauper. Hence the prolific and increasing crop of criminals. …

… In short, if we were disposed to illustrate our hypothesis—that crime is caused by poverty—by examples we could fill the whole of this number of Regina, together with an appendix—twice the size of the *Quarterly Review*, advertisements included.

It is perhaps more desirable that we take a glance at the living authors of this demoralization, and these calamities. The representatives of the country are irresponsible agents. Those of them who buy seats, represent no interest but their own. They have nothing at stake, but the money paid to the seat-vendor; therefore *they* are independent! Those who have constituents cannot be called to account until that interesting period arrives, when they venture to solicit from their electors a renewal of their patronage. If they have jobbed with public money, trafficked with the minister for places and appointments, neglected the interests of the people and injured their country, their only punishment is the preference given to a new candidate, who, in all probability, may prove more venal than the former.

Be this as it may—however responsible these men are morally, they are not legally nor constitutionally responsible for the evils they inflict on the nation. But the ministers are responsible, even though they should plead the sanction of the houses of legislature. The ministers who have been in office since 1823, are responsible for all the pauperism and demoralization which have increased since that period. *Their* measures—not the measures of parliament—but the measures they have devised, recommended, and carried by majorities composed of their own retainers—have caused this increase in pauperism and crime. They are the guilty parties. Ignorance in a minister is as much a crime, as felony is in a mender of copper kettles. If he have done the state wrong, it is no defence to say he meant well. If by his policy he has reduced thousands of families to beggary, thence to poaching, thence to criminal acts generally, he is the author of both the suffering and the crime, and is more culpable than the sheep-stealer whom he transports, or the house-breaker whom he hangs.

For these reasons, we charge upon the ministers of the King, not only the distress that prevails, but the crime that degrades England in the eyes of the whole world—which places her lowest in the scale of morality, and paralyzes the example of her boasted benevolence, her apostolic missions, her public schools of instruction, her bible distributors, her cheap libraries, the purity of her reformed doctrines, and the excellence of her laws. We charge the increase of 23,841 criminals, since the year 1823, upon his Majesty's government. We affirm that they are answerable, at some bar of judgment, for the deep and incurable wounds they have inflicted upon the nation. ...

... If distress continue, crime, therefore, must increase. Its prevention, or its cure is not a matter of police. No gendarmerie can stay the 'superfecundity' of crime. They may detect, but they cannot restrain. They may fill the prisons, and load the hulks, and give an impetus to the increase of population in New South Wales; but they cannot eradicate the parent root of crime. Peel's soldiers, even though drilled on Sunday, are nothing more than clodpoles, armed with hangers, traversing a field of furze, and cutting down the green shoots and the withered stumps which they consider to be dead. With respect to this last indication they are mistaken. The roots are sound; the police may apparently clear the soil; but as they cannot, or rather dare not penetrate the surface, the shoots of next year will be more abundant than they were the year before.

To what then, it will probably be asked, must this state of things lead? The question may be pertinent, but we decline answering it. A candid compliance might involve us in the hazardous consequences of a legal tournament with Sir James Scarlett, and consign our sword and buckler, our shield and cuirass, and of course our unhappy person to the cells of Newgate. We would, therefore, advise the curious reader to propound his question to his Majesty's ministers. We stand upon our prerogative, satisfied that we do enough when we point out the evil. Others are paid to devise remedies—we are not. On them devolves the duty of relieving us; if they neglect this duty, it must be at the peril of a certain conspicuous adjunct of the human form, which is generally considered the guardian of the lower extremities. The head, says somebody, is to the feet, what a watch-box on a tower is to the sentinels who snore in the hall.

One word, however, before we conclude, with respect to the many-headed monster whose multifarious plans are offered as cures for the existing distress. The lesser quacks assume the character of legal reformers; the greater are trans-migrant philosophers. The latter propose to relieve us of our pauper dead-weight, by transporting the consumers of poor rates—by removing an English cottager, in order to make room for an itinerant corn-cutter from the Sister Island. These gentlemen monopolize but one idea, and this, they conceive, embraces the cause as well as the cure of penury. The cause is—a redundancy of population; the cure is—emigration. The present crisis, therefore, is quite a harvest for these persons. If by any chance or mistake the ministry were to adopt any salutary or corrective measure, their beautiful hobby would break down, and their system be blown up. If the Duke of Wellington should, by some happy blunder, commit violence on Peel's bill, and Huskisson's theories, these gentlemen would be unable to lay their hands upon a single beggar. The *materiel* of emigration would disappear; the 'young couples' would marry at home; and the philosophers would be deprived even of the consolation of a full workhouse. For these reasons they are, at the present moment, equally clamorous and industrious. And they are encouraged in their schemes by the government. They attract attention; and they entice the thoughts of the multitude from the real cause of their embarrassments. When the juggler wishes to deceive the sense, he diverts the eye. We are induced to look at the only thing we should not see; and as we gaze, the trick is accomplished, and we are imposed upon. Just so with the emigrationists. We find ourselves meandering in New South Wales, when we ought to be in England. We are discussing localities, sand-banks, and kangaroo soup with Mr. Thomas Peel, of the Swan river, when we ought to be spinning twist with his cousin, at Whitehall, in the City of London.

To show the folly of all this, on the part of the sincere encouragers of emigration, and the criminality of it on the part of the mere pretenders and the tools of the government, we have only to compare the condition of this country, at the present juncture, with that of France, antecedent to the revolution. Before that tremendous volcano burst forth, which poured its human lava upon France, the middle and lower classes in that country had long endured the most extreme privation. Famine had visited the poor. The queen had actually sold her plate to furnish food for the wretches who were dying in the streets of Paris. The finances of the nation were in a state of fearful derangement. Credit was paralyzed—confidence had fled. Had Neckar's currency plans been adopted, the nation might have been saved. But the philosophers of that day, like the philosophers of England in the present day, clung to a metallic medium, and poverty increased, wages fell, prices declined, profits diminished, just as the amount of available currency was hoarded from fear, or circumscribed by law. France, then was in a precisely similar state to that with which we are now contending. She had more labourers than she could employ—more artisans than she could support—more paupers than she could maintain. But did she then complain of a redundant population? Was there to be found a man so heartless or so depraved as to propose the deportation of her unemployed labourers? If such a philosopher had appeared, he would have been the *maiden* martyr of the guillotine. No man was so senseless or so wicked as to ascribe the suffering of France to providence, to improvident marriages, or to superfecundity. Events have proved that these were not the causes of either her calamities or her excesses. It was a long series of bad laws—of arbitrary measures—of oppressive monopolies—of despotic exactions—of insufferable favouritism—and of grinding taxes; which led to an event from which we fear the rulers of Europe have not learned those lessons which were intended for their instruction.

So much the worse for us under similar circumstances. Emigration is considered the sovereign and the only cure in England. Crime is to be diminished by banishing the virtuous. The arts are to be improved by expatriating the most useful and ingenious of our mechanics. The soil is to be rendered more productive by exiling the active farmer, and the industrious cultivator with his remnant of capital. The sinews of the country are to be strengthened by exporting its young blood and its 'young couples.' God forgive the heartless men who prescribe these remedies! The credulous only are their victims; and if the folly be chargeable on the nation, they alone are answerable for the guilt.

WILLIAM MAKEPEACE THACKERAY

William Thackeray (1811–63), novelist and journalist, was born in India, returning to England in 1817. His work for Fraser's Magazine *established his reputation in the early 1840s, and later he wrote for* Punch. *His most famous novel,* Vanity Fair *(1847–48), confirmed his status as a writer. He became editor of the* Cornhill *(1860–62). [DNB; LCVF]*

In his discussion on the 'earnest-minded writer' and his reports on 'our poor in London' in this piece, Thackeray is referring to Henry Mayhew's London Labour and the London Poor, *the first instalments of which were published in the* Morning Chronicle *in 1849 and subsequently issued independently in weekly parts.*

'**Waiting at the Station**', *Punch; or the London Charivari*, vol. 18, 1850, pp. 92–3.

We are amongst a number of people waiting for the Blackwall train at the Fenchurch Street Station. Some of us are going a little farther than Blackwall—as far as Gravesend; some of us are going even farther than Gravesend—to Port Philip, in South Australia, leaving behind the *patriæ fines* and the pleasant fields of old England. It is rather a queer sensation to be in the same boat and station with a party that is going upon so prodigious a journey. One speculates about them with more than an ordinary interest, thinking of the difference between your fate and theirs, and that we shall never behold these faces again.

Some eight-and-thirty women are sitting in the large Hall of the station, with bundles, baskets, and light baggage, waiting for the steamer, and the orders to embark. A few friends are taking leave of them, bonnets are laid together, and whispering going on. A little crying is taking place;—only a very little crying,—and among those who remain, as it seems to me, not those who are going away. They leave behind them little to weep for; they are going from bitter cold and hunger, constant want and unavailing labour. Why should they be sorry to quit a mother who has been so hard to them as our country has been? How many of these women will ever see the shore again, upon the brink of which they stand, and from which they will depart in a few minutes more? It makes one sad and ashamed too, that they should not be more sorry. But how are you to expect love where you have given such scanty kindness? If you saw your children glad at the thoughts of leaving you, and for ever: would you blame yourselves or them? It is not that the children are ungrateful, but the home was unhappy, and the parents indifferent or unkind. You are in the wrong under whose government they only had neglect and wretchedness; not they, who can't be called upon to love such an unlovely thing as misery, or to make any other return for neglect but indifference and aversion.

You and I, let us suppose again, are civilised persons. We have been decently educated: and live decently every day, and wear tolerable clothes, and practise cleanliness: and love the arts and graces of life. As we walk down this rank of eight-and-thirty female emigrants, let us fancy that we are at Melbourne, and not in London, and that we have come down from our sheep-walks, or clearings, having heard of the arrival of forty honest, well-recommended young women, and having a natural longing to take a wife home to the bush—which of these would you like? If you were an Australian Sultan, to which of these would you throw the handkerchief? I am afraid not one of them. I fear, in our present mood of mind, we should mount horse and return to the country, preferring a solitude, and to be a bachelor, rather than to put up with one of these for a companion. There is no girl here to tempt you by her looks; (and, world-wiseacre as you are, it is by these you are principally moved)—there is no pretty, modest, red-cheeked, rustic,—no neat, trim, little grisette, such as what we call a gentleman might cast his eyes upon without too much derogating, and might find favour in the eyes of a man about town. No; it is a homely bevy of women with scarcely any beauty amongst them—their clothes are decent, but not the least pictur-esque—their faces are pale and care-worn for the most part—how, indeed, should it be otherwise, seeing that they have known care and want all their days?—there they sit upon bare benches, with dingy bundles, and great cotton umbrellas—and the truth is, you are not a hardy colonist, a feeder of sheep, a feller of trees, a hunter of kangaroos—but a London man, and my lord the Sultan's cambric handkerchief is scented with Bond Street perfumery—you put it in your pocket, and couldn't give it to any one of these women.

They are not like you, indeed. They have not your tastes and feelings: your education and refinements. They would not understand a hundred things which seem perfectly simple to you. They would shock you a hundred times a day by as many deficiencies of politeness, or by outrages upon the Queen's English—by practices entirely harmless, and yet in your eyes actually worse than crimes— they have large hard hands and clumsy feet. The women you love must have pretty soft fingers that you may hold in yours: must speak her language properly, and at least when you offer her your heart, must return hers with its *h* in the right place, as she whispers that it is yours, or you will have none of it. If she says, 'O Hedward, I ham so unappy to think I shall never beold you agin,'—though her emotion on leaving you might be perfectly tender and genuine, you would be obliged to laugh. If she said, 'Hedward, my art is yours for hever and hever,' (and anybody heard her), she might as well stab you,—you couldn't accept the most faithful affection offered in such terms—you are a town-bred man, I say, and your handkerchief smells of Bond Street musk and millefleur. A sun-burnt settler out of the Bush won't feel any of these exquisite tortures, or understand this kind of laughter: or object to Molly because her hands are coarse and her ankles thick: but he will take her back to his farm, where she will nurse his children, bake his dough, milk his cows, and cook his kangaroo for him.

But between you, an educated Londoner, and that woman, is not the union absurd and impossible? Would it not be unbearable for either? Solitude would be incomparably pleasanter than such a companion.—You might take her with a handsome fortune perhaps were you starving; but then it is because you want a house and carriage, let us say, (*your* necessaries of life,) and must have them even if you purchase them with your precious person. You do as much, or your sister does as much, every-day. That however is not the point: I am not talking about the meanness to which your worship may be possibly obliged to stoop, in order, as you say, 'to keep up your rank in society'—only stating that this immense social difference does exist. You don't like to own it: or don't choose to talk about it, and such things had much better not be spoken about at all. I hear your worship say, there must be differences of rank and so forth! Well! out with it at once, you don't think MOLLY is your equal—nor indeed is she in the possession of many artificial acquirements. She can't make Latin verses, for example, as you used to do at school, she can't speak French and Italian as your wife very likely can, &c.—and in so far she is your inferior, and your amiable lady's.

But what I note, what I marvel at, what I acknowledge, what I am ashamed of, what is contrary to Christian morals, manly modesty and honesty, and to the national well-being, is that there should be that immense social distinction between the well-dressed classes (as, if you will permit me, we will call ourselves) and our brethren and sisters in the fustian jackets and pattens. If you deny it for your part, I say that you are mistaken, and deceive yourself woefully. I say that you have been educated to it through Gothic ages, and have had it handed down to you from your fathers (not that they were anybody in particular, but respectable, well-dressed progenitors, let us say for a generation or two) from your well-dressed fathers before you. How long ago is it, that our preachers were teaching the poor 'to know their station?' that it was the peculiar boast of Englishmen that any man, the humblest among us, could, by talent, industry and good luck, hope to take his place in the aristocracy of his country, and that we pointed with price to Lord This who was the grandson of a barber; and to Earl That, whose father was an Apothecary? what a multitude of most respectable folks pride themselves on these things still! The gulf is not impassable, because one man in a million swims over it, and we hail him for his strength and success. He has landed on the happy island. He is one of the aristocracy. Let us clap hands and applaud. There's no country like ours for rational freedom.

If you go up and speak to one of these women, as you do (and very good-naturedly, and you can't help that confounded condescension) she curtsies and holds down her head meekly, and replies with modesty, as becomes her station, to your honour with the clean shirt and the well-made coat. And so she should; what hundreds of thousands of us rich and poor say still. Both believe this to be bounded duty; and that a poor person should naturally bob her head to a rich one physically and morally.

Let us get her last curtsey from her as she stands here upon the English shore. When she gets into the Australian woods her back won't bend except to her labour; or, if it do, from old habit and the reminiscence of the old country, do you suppose her children will be like that timid creature before you? They will know nothing of that Gothic society, with its ranks and hierarchies, its cumbrous ceremonies, its glittering antique paraphernalia, in which we have been educated; in which rich and poor still acquiesce, and which multitudes of both still admire: far removed from these old world traditions, they will be bred up in the midst of plenty, freedom, manly brotherhood. Do you think if your worship's grandson goes into the Australian woods, or meets the grandchild of one of yonder women by the banks of the Warrawarra, the Australian will take a hat off or bob a curtsey to the new comer? He will hold out his hand, and say, 'Stranger, come into my house and take a shakedown and have a share of our supper. You come out of the old country, do you! There was some people were kind to my grandmother there, and sent her out to Melbourne. Times are changed since then—come in and welcome!'

What a confession it is that we have almost all of us been obliged to make! A clever and earnest-minded writer gets a commission from the *Morning Chronicle* newspaper, and reports upon the state of our poor in London; he goes amongst labouring people and poor of all kinds—and brings back what? A picture of human life so wonderful, so awful, so piteous and pathetic, so exciting and terrible, that readers of romances own they never read anything like to it; and that the griefs, struggles, strange adventures here depicted exceed anything that any of us could imagine. Yes; and these wonders and terrors have been lying by your door and mine ever since we had a door of our own. We had but to go a hundred yards off and see for ourselves, but we never did. Don't we pay poor-rates, and are they not heavy enough in the name of patience? Very true; and we have our own private pensioners, and give away some of our superfluity, very likely. You are not unkind; not ungenerous. But of such wondrous and complicated misery as this you confess you had no idea? No. How should you?—you and I—we are of the upper classes; we have had hitherto no community with the poor. We never speak a word to the servant who waits on us for twenty years; we condescend to employ a tradesman, keeping him at a proper distance, mind—of course, at a proper distance—we laugh at his young men, if they dance, jig, and amuse themselves like their betters, and call them counter-jumpers, snobs, and what not; of his workmen we know nothing, how pitilessly they are ground down, how they live and die, here close by us at the backs of our houses; until some poet like HOOD wakes and sings that dreadful '*Song of the Shirt*;' some prophet like CARLYLE rises up and denounces woe; some clear-sighted, energetic man like the writer of the *Chronicle* travels into the poor man's country for us, and comes back with his tale of terror and wonder.

Awful, awful poor man's country! The bell rings and these eight-and-thirty women bid adieu to it, rescued from it (as a few thousands more will be) by some kind people who are interested in their behalf. In two hours more, the steamer lies alongside the ship *Culloden*, which will bear them to their new home. Here are the berths aft for the unmarried women, the married couples are in the midships, the bachelors in the fore-part of the ship. Above and below decks it swarms and echoes with the bustle of departure. The Emigration Commissioner comes and calls over their names; there are old and young, large families, numbers of children already accustomed to the ship, and looking about with amused unconsciousness. One was born but just now on board; he will not know how to speak English till he is fifteen thousand miles away from home. Some of those kind people whose bounty and benevolence organised the Female Emigration Scheme, are here to give a last word and shake of the hand to their *protégées*. They hang sadly and gratefully round their patrons. One of them, a clergyman, who has devoted himself to this good work, says a few words to them at parting. It is a solemn minute indeed—for those who (with the few thousand who will follow them,) are leaving the country and escaping from the question between rich and poor; and what for those who remain? But, at least; those who go will remember that in their misery here they found gentle hearts to love and pity them, and generous hands to give them succour, and will plant in the new country this grateful tradition of the old.—May Heaven's good mercy speed them!

WILLIAM HENRY WILLS

William Wills (1810–80), British-born journalist and editor, was on the original staff of Punch. In Edinburgh, he was assistant editor of Chambers's Edinburgh Magazine (1842–45). From 1850 to 1869 he was sub-editor of and contributor to Dickens' Household Words and later, All The Year Round, of which he and Dickens were joint proprietors. [HW; LCVF]

'Safety for Female Emigrants',
Household Words, vol. 3, 1851, p. 228.

One of the greatest and most deplorable hindrances to the emigration of young women to distant colonies, is want of protection. That any class—but more especially women—should ever need protection in British ships manned by British seamen, is a little humiliating; but so many instances of brutality and immorality have been proved, that the treatment of emigrants during their voyage is now occupying the serious attention of the Legislature.

Meanwhile, Mrs. Chisholm's plan of emigration, which associates, in groups and families, the weak with the strong, has been found to work successfully in removing the wholesome dread which many well-disposed young women felt in venturing alone in emigration vessels. The pledge which was framed, and is regularly taken by the embarking emigrants of the Family Colonisation Loan Society, will show the excellence of, at least, their intentions: nor have we heard anything to show that these good intentions have not been zealously fulfilled. The resolutions forming the pledge were passed by a 'Group Committee,' composed of the elders of one of the groups.

'That we pledge ourselves, as Christian fathers and heads of families, to exercise a parental control and guardianship over all orphans and friendless females of good repute for virtue and morality, proceeding with the family groups; to protect them as our children, and allow them to share the same cabins with our daughters.

'We further resolve to discourage gambling, and not to take cards or dice with us, or to enter into any pernicious amusements during the voyage. We likewise resolve, by parental advice and good example, to encourage and promote some well-advised system of self-improvement during the passage.

'As the system of repayment proposed by this Society is one that, if honourably kept, will add to the credit of the working-classes as a body, and be the means of encouraging the generous and good to assist our struggling countrymen, we hereby solemnly pledge our honour as men, and our character as Christians, to repay the loan advanced to us, and to impress the sacredness of fulfilling this duty on each and all of the members constituting the groups. We also promise to aid the colonial agents in the recovery of such loans, and to make known, in whatever part of the colonies we may be, the means by which parties well to-do there may assist their relations in this county, through the medium of the Family Colonisation Loan Society.

'We further pledge ourselves not to introduce as candidates for membership of the Society any men but those we know to be of good character, or families but of good repute.

'We also determine not to accept of payment for any services we may render on board ship; but endeavour, individually and collectively, to preserve the order of a well-regulated family during our passage to Australia, and to organise and establish a system of protection that will enable our female relatives to enter an emigrant ship with the same confidence of meeting with protection, as respectable females can now enter our steamers, trains, and mail-coaches.

'That all members, constituting groups, be asked for their approval and fulfilment, as far as they may be individually concerned, of the above resolutions.'

ANON. _____

This is a reference to the series 'Australia'.

_____ 'Important Notice to Australian Emigrants', *Leisure Hour*, vol. 1, 1852, pp. 624.

It is in contemplation to issue before long another series of papers on AUSTRALIA, as a sequel to those, from the pen of a gentleman of high attainments in geographical science, which have already appeared in our journal. In preparing these papers, extreme care was taken to secure authentic and reliable information; … we reprint at large the regulations issued by the Government Emigration Office, 8, Park-street, Westminster.

QUALIFICATIONS OF EMIGRANTS.

1. The emigrants must be of those callings which, from time to time, are most in demand in the colony. They must be sober, industrious, and of general good moral character;—of all of which decisive certificates will be required. They must also be in good health, free from bodily or mental defects; and the Adults must,

in all respects, be capable of labour, and going out to work for wages. The candidates most acceptable are respectable young women trained to domestic or farm service, and young married couples without children.

2. The separation of husbands and wives, and of parents from children under 18, will in no case be allowed.

3. Single women, under 18, cannot be taken without their parents, unless they go under the immediate care of some near relatives. Single women with illegitimate children can in no case be taken.

4. Single men of the second class (described below) cannot be taken, unless they are sons in eligible families, nor can any single men of any class be taken without a corresponding number of young single women of good character to equalize the sexes.

5. Widowers and widows with young children;—persons who intend to buy land, or to invest capital, in trade;—or who are in the habitual receipt of parish relief;—or who have not been vaccinated, or not had the small-pox;—or whose families comprise more than four children under twelve years of age—cannot be accepted.

APPLICATION AND APPROVAL.

6. Applications must be made to the commissioners in the form supplied by them. The filling up of the form, however, confers no claim to a passage, and implies no pledge that the candidates, though apparently within the regulations, will be accepted.

7. If approved of, the applicants will receive a printed 'approval circular,' calling for the contribution required by Article 8, and pointing out how the money is to be paid. After it is paid, they will, as soon as the commissioners' arrangements will permit, receive an embarkation order (*which is not transferable*), naming the ship in which they are to embark, and the time and place of joining her. *They must not leave their homes before the receipt of this order.*

PAYMENTS TOWARDS PASSAGES.

8. The contributions above-mentioned (out of which the commissioners provide bedding and mess utensils, etc., for the voyage,) are as follows:—

CLASSES.	AGE.		
	Under 45.	45 and under 50.	50 and under 60.
I. Married agricultural labourers, shepherds, herdsmen, and their wives; also women of the working class—per head.	£ 1	£ 5	£ 11

II. Married journeymen mechanics and
artizans—such as blacksmiths, brick-layers,
carpenters, masons, sawyers,
wheelwrights, gardeners, etc., and their
wives, per head.   2   6   14

III. Single men, subject to the condition in
Article 4:-
    If accompanying their parents.   2
    If not accompanying their parents
       (when they can be taken).   3

IV. Children under 14—per head.   10s.

Passages from Dublin and Cork to Plymouth, from Glasgow to Liverpool, and from Granton Pier and places north of Hull to London, (according to the English port from which the vessel is to sail) are provided by the commissioners for emigrants. All other travelling expenses must be borne by the emigrants themselves.

CAUTIONS TO APPLICANTS.

9. *No preparations must on any account be made by the applicants, either by withdrawing from employment or otherwise, until they receive the 'approval circular.'* Applicants who fail to attend to this warning will do so at their own risk, and will have no claim whatever on the commissioners.

10. The selecting agents of the board have no authority to promise passages in any case, nor to receive money. *If, therefore, applicants wish to make their payments through the agents, instead of in the manner pointed out in the 'approval circular,' they must understand that they do so at their own risk, and that the commissioners will in no way be responsible.*

11. Should any signatures attached to an applicant's paper prove to be not genuine, or any personation be attempted, or any false representations be made in the papers, not only will the application be rejected, and the contribution forfeited, but the offenders will be liable, under the Passengers' Act, to a PENALTY NOT EXCEEDING £50.

12. Should any applicants be found on personal examination at the depôt, or on board, to have made any mis-statement in their papers, or to have any infectious disorder, or otherwise not to be in a fit state of health to embark, or to have any mental or bodily defect likely to impair their usefulness as labourers, or to have left any of their young children behind, or to have brought with them more children than are mentioned in their application form, or expressly sanctioned by the commissioners, or to have attempted any deception whatever, or evasion

of these rules, they will be refused admission on board the ship, or if embarked, will be relanded, without having any claim on the commissioners. If after embarkation emigrants are guilty of insubordination, or misconduct, they will be relanded, and forfeit their contributions.

13. If applicants fail to attend at the appointed time and place for embarkation, without having previously given to the commissioners timely notice, and a satisfactory reason—or if they fail to proceed in the ship—or are rejected for any of the reasons specified in the preceding article—they will forfeit their contributions, and will have no claim to a passage at any future time.

ANON. _____

While the author is unknown, the subject, Maria Rye, helped initiate the Female Middle Class Emigration Society (1862) as part of her work for the Society for Promoting the Employment of Women. Both groups were linked to the Langham Place collective.

_____ *from* 'Miss Rye's Emigrants', *Saturday*
Review, vol. 14, 1862, pp. 566–7.

A few weeks ago we ventured to make some remarks upon Miss Rye's project for the emigration of women of the middle class. It was a matter of painful surprise to us to find that our article upon 'The Export Wife-Trade' had excited very ungentle emotions in the bosoms of some of our fair readers. The article was intended to warn Miss Rye and her supporters against some dangers which seemed to us very imminent. We could not but express a fear that they were undertaking to supply a market with which they were imperfectly acquainted; and that, in attempting to dispose of our superfluity of educated women by furnishing colonial bachelors with wives, they might be involuntarily incurring dangers which they were very far indeed from contemplating. But Micaiah is in all ages a very unpopular character. Our suggestions drew down upon us a storm of invective, whose fury only those who are familiar with feminine controversy will be able to appreciate. It is a terrible thing to incur the wrath of philanthropists; and a controversy with the softer half of creation is notoriously a dangerous undertaking. But when benevolence of profession and gentleness of sex are combined in the same antagonist, a mere ordinary man of the world has no resource but to surrender at discretion. No purely secular nerves can be expected to withstand the vituperation which female benevolence pours out on those who meddle with its chimeras.

It is not, therefore, with any foolhardy intention of provoking another onset of female pens that we venture to recur to this dangerous subject. We are emboldened to do so only by the circumstance that we have been happy enough to make a convert, and that convert is no less a person than Miss Rye herself. Her original scheme was to provide an outlet for distressed governesses, by sending them to the colonies, in the hope that some at least of them would get employers, and that most of them would get husbands. They were to be sent out on speculation. It was argued, *à priori*, that Australian young ladies required education, and Australian young men required wives; and that, if educated young women who were in want of money could be persuaded to allow themselves to be consigned to the Australian ports, they would find a ready market for their talents in one capacity or the other. As a mere sum in political economy, an exercise in the rule of supply and demand, this calculation made a tolerable appearance upon paper. In fact, there were only two objections to it. One was, that the people who need education are not always the people who desire it; and the other was, that matrimony is not, even in the colonies, contracted upon principles so purely mercantile as Miss Rye and her estimable coadjutors appeared to imagine. Few settlers can afford, or think they can afford, the luxury of a governess, and therefore the majority of Australian young ladies must complete their education in some other way. The demand, accordingly, for governesses is limited and precarious; and women who go out on speculation, with no definite certainty of employment, will, in most cases, be disappointed. Their chances of marriage would be still more precarious. They would be too fastidious to be content to take a digger or a labourer for a husband; and the young men of their own class would be too fastidious to take them for wives. Englishmen of any education like to know something of the antecedents and connexions of the women they marry. It is rather an adventurous proceeding to bind yourself for better for worse to a lady of whom you know nothing whatever, except that she was No. 36 in Miss Rye's last emigrant ship. For the governess class of emigrants, therefore, marriage is an even more precarious reliance than employment. If Miss Rye had proceeded with her scheme as it was originally explained to the world, numbers of those whom she sent out must have been driven to depend for bare subsistence upon the liberality of others. We cannot regret that we have called the attention of the promoters of the scheme to these dangers in language which has compelled their attention. It is easy to compliment enthusiasts upon their good intentions, but nine-tenths of the harm that is done in the world is done by well-meaning people. Those who voluntarily assume to shape the destinies of others must bring something more than good intentions to the work. They are bound to make themselves certain, by adequate inquiry, that the promises by which they persuade others to risk their whole welfare are not mere figments of their own imaginations. If their sentimental ignorance is in reality deluding others to ruin, they must be exposed as unsparingly as if they were consciously wrong-doers.

Such censure, however, we are glad to say Miss Rye deserves no longer. The objections which both English and colonial writers have made to her first project have roused her to a sense of the dangers it involved. She acknowledges now, that 'if she were to adhere to the principle of sending out governesses only,' her whole scheme must fall to the ground.' So strongly has she now become impressed with the evils of 'sending out governesses by hundreds,' that she is going herself to the colonies to spend a year and a half there, to ascertain the real extent of the demand that exists for that class of labour, and to make arrangements, under which, in future years, it can be supplied without risk. For the present, the middle-class emigration scheme is practically abandoned. It has been superseded by the more sensible plan of exporting the class of women for whom both employers and husbands can be found without difficulty. Out of four hundred who have been sent out, only forty were governesses; and out of a hundred whom she is taking herself, only eight are governesses. The remaining nine-tenths belong to the classes who live by the labour, not of their minds, but of their hands, and for whose services there is a steady and abundant market. The Australian colonies form an admirable provision for the two extremes of the social scale, but (speaking generally) for none between. There is no better place for those who can take with them some capital to invest, or for those who can work with their hands. But for the intermediate class, who have received too high an education to be fit for manual labour, and yet have no capital to invest, the colonies offer but a doubtful and speculative subsistence. The rule holds good of either sex. Miss Rye thinks it necessary to apologize for her change of plan. She wishes it to be understood 'that she alone is responsible' for taking out the class that will succeed, and leaving the class that cannot possibly succeed behind. The patrons of the former scheme, who have a sentimental contempt for facts, and look upon them as the suggestions of a coarse mind, probably find it hard to stomach the change. ...

JOHN FRANCIS WALLER

John Waller (1810–94), Irish-born author and lawyer, contributed verse and prose to the Dublin University Magazine. *He later lived in London as a man of letters.* [DNB]

'The Emigrants', *Quiver*, vol. 11, 1876, pp. 620–1.

THROUGH the pathless waste of waters,
      With no land in sight,
Onward speeds the good ship ever
      In her lonely flight,
As a bird with pinion strong
O'er the desert speeds along.

All around the ocean stretches,
      All above—the skies,
Through the sails the breezes blowing
      Pipe wild melodies,
While along her strong-ribbed sides
Cleft waves murmur as she glides.

At the wheel, with eye on compass,
      Mute the helmsman stands;
On her course he holds her steady
      With his guiding hands,
As the skilful horseman guides
With the rein the steed he rides.

Weeks have passed since white-cliffed Albion
      Faded from the view,
Since the parting kiss was given,
      Sobbed the sad adieu;
Child from parent, man from wife
Doomed to live a severed life.

On she bears for Austral regions,
      With her precious freight—
Hearts that beat with high ambition,
      With strong hopes elate;
Souls cast down with doubts and fears
Strong men's moans and women's tears.

Two there are apart from others,
      Lonely on the deck,
With the noontide splendour o'er them
      And no cloud to fleck
With a shadow from the sky
Where the hot sun glows on high.

Ah! but there are shadows looming
    O'er their hearts to-day,
For their thoughts are with the dear ones
    Left far, far away;
Father, mother, friends are left,
Each of all but *one* bereft.

And the woman's lips are quivering
    With unuttered sighs,
And the un-shed tears are swelling
    In her heavy eyes,
As the tender, loving bride,
Leans against her husband's side.

Strong and true, and fond and holy,
    Love in woman proves,
When she gives herself confiding
    To the man she loves,
Cleaving to him as her life,
Leaving all to be his wife.

And the husband, with the passion
    Of his boundless love,
Sobered, saddened, looks down fondly
    On her from above,
Lays his hand with gentle touch
Upon that head he loves so much.

Oh, take courage, man and woman,
    Let your sorrows cease,
Love will make you brave to labour,
    Give you joy and peace;
God that bade you love will still
Keep you safe from woe and ill.

Let the sunshine that is round you
    Fill your hearts to-day.
Love, for which you've given up all things,
    Richly will repay.
Love the world itself can move;
All things yield to those that love.

WILLIAM JARDINE SMITH _____

William Smith (1834–84), London-born journalist, arrived in Melbourne in 1852. He became part-proprietor and editor of Melbourne Punch *(1866–69), was on the editorial staff of the* Argus, *and was an occasional writer for* Fraser's Magazine, Nineteenth Century *and other periodicals. [BR; NAP]*

This extract is from his response to William Feilding's 'Whither Shall I Send my Son?', Nineteenth Century, *vol. 14, 1883, pp. 65–77.*

_____ *from* 'Blue-blooded Boys.
An Australian Criticism', *Nineteenth Century*, vol. 14, 1883, pp. 840–53.

The paper by Major-General the Hon. W. Feilding which appeared in the April number of this Review, entitled 'What shall I do with my son?' has been read with interest by many people in Victoria, and doubtless by equal numbers in the other colonies of the Australasian group. The interest with which it has been studied is not attributable to any novelty in the views expressed, or to the insight of the writer. It springs, I think, from a feeling of mingled amusement and annoyance at finding that one more visitor has passed some time in our midst, and yet has failed to penetrate beneath the surface of things, or to carry away with him anything like a clear idea of the society in which he has moved. The mistakes made by many of the English writers who condescend to notice provincial affairs excite various feelings in the minds of colonists. In the thoughtless they produce laughter; but those who value the Imperial connection, who dream dreams of the part which the British race might play in the affairs of the world, if its power were to be consolidated by a federal pact, occasionally feel inclined to weep tears of vexation when they see caricatures and misrepresentations placed before their fellow-countrymen at home, which are calculated to prevent the growth of the complete understanding and close intimacy between the motherland and her numerous offshoots that must precede any thorough union of interests, and any course of hearty co-operation.

There is nothing in General Feilding's paper calculated to provoke bitter feeling. His feelings are principally of a negative character. He has been, and seen, but has evidently not conceived the faintest idea of what Australian colonists really are, or formed anything like just opinions about their habits of thoughts, their several conditions, and their ruling motives. It is difficult to imagine where the honourable and gallant gentleman picked up his notions concerning us and our affairs, so little do they correspond with existing facts. There is sufficient warrant, I think, for the use of the word 'us,' for, although the General treats of emigration in the abstract, his paper bears internal evidence of having been written with special reference to emigration to Australia. His recent visit to this country, in connection with the transcontinental railway which Queensland is about to construct, lends colour to this supposition. We need hardly say that this inability to understand the mind, temper, and circumstances of these colonies renders him a blind guide to those whom he wishes to assist. Speaking generally, the only really sound advice given in his paper is contained in the word 'emigrate;' all the rest is 'leather and prunella.'

... Immigrants, without family connections in the colonies, or that mysterious qualification known as 'colonial experience,' have now little chance of obtaining office employment, as they are confronted at every opening by swarms of the colonial-born furnished with these aids to merit. Unless young men who look to clerkships, &c., for the means of livelihood are of a robust nature, and capable of turning their hands to any employment that may present itself while waiting for appointments, they had better stay at home. There are too many of their kind here already, and soon their name will be legion.

But the fact that the supply of mercantile assistants in Australia is far in excess of the demand, and that for every vacancy which occurs there are usually about ten applicants, does not affect the young gentlemen whom General Feilding desires to benefit. The upper classes, he admits, have occasionally furnished recruits to the ranks of commerce. They have descended from their high estate, and served long apprenticeships as clerks; but he shudders when he thinks of what their refined natures must have had to endure while attempting to adapt themselves 'to uninteresting mercantile business routine, and to habits of thought and action foreign to' their 'former dreams, desires', and indeed to their 'very nature.' He would provide all young fellows of 'good family and high birth' who are reduced to the dreadful necessity of earning their own living with more suitable careers, would give them some desirable occupation, a lofty object of ambition, and aims worthy of men of their class and education. No one here would think of placing General Feilding's *protégés* at any disadvantage in the race of life simply because they happen to have been born in the purple, but at the same time very few would render them exceptional assistance as members of a privileged class. The prevailing disposition is to give all 'a fair field and no favour,' without any reference whatever to parentage or social rank.

Occupations in some way connected with land are, in General Feilding's opinion, the proper things for blue-blooded boys, although it is difficult to imagine why, in a new country, pastoral work so graphically described by Touchstone, or agricultural operations, should be considered more dignified than the business of the shop or the counting-house. Land in the colonies is not the sacred thing it is in older communities, nor are those connected with it regarded with special veneration. It must be remembered that the *rôle* of the practical settler is not that of supervisor. The General himself points out that 'in order to get the maximum of work out of a colonial labourer, the employer must not only know how things ought to be done, but able and willing to take off his coat and show how he wishes the work to be executed.' It may be more in keeping with high birth to have the hands befouled by the manipulation of sheep and cattle, or covered with the blood and dust of the branding yard, or coated with the soil of arable land, than stained by ink; but in countries where Jack considers himself as good as his master, people do not understand these nice distinctions. They are apt to think that such failures as General Feilding describes, young men of 'good family and high birth' but without sufficient industry, energy, or brains 'to win a commission in one of the professions of arms, to obtain practice at the bar, to enter into the Government service in any form, or *even into holy orders*,'* would be lucky, in the absence of pecuniary resources, to obtain any employment whereby they may keep body and soul together. However, I will not pursue this vein of thought further.

When a patrician parent decides the question 'What shall I do with my son?' by determining to send him across the seas to follow pastoral or agricultural pursuits, ordinary people would consider that nothing remains to be done but to buy him an outfit, take a passage, and despatch the emigrant. General Feilding, however, does not think that the valuable consignment should be treated in this rough and ready way. He would give him a prepatory training at home, through the instrumentality of an educational establishment about to be called into existence, 'in everything necessary to prepare' a youngster 'for direct entry into colonial life.' … One of the objects of the special settlement, we are told, is to people 'a large area of good land' with 'a fair sprinkling of young Englishmen of education and refinement, who will gradually act as an attraction to that portion of the country of a working population.' The idea is pretty and even idyllic, but it is 'such stuff as dreams are made of.' If the ordinary bush-hand, or agricultural labourer of Australia, were to hear that a number of young men had associated themselves together under the supposition that they were something superior to the general run of mankind, he would be far more likely to commend them to the infernal gods in a raging tornado of fancy swearing, than to be attracted by their 'sweetness and light.' If of a quiet disposition he might refrain from molesting them, but should he by any chance cross their path, he would soon show them that exclusiveness is not to his liking. All this may be very wrong, but it is true. The working man of Australia has little reverence for birth or rank. He will patronise both occasionally if he finds them ranged on his side in a political conflict. If any one whom he is compelled to respect as a *man* can boast of either, the horny-handed son of toil will not look down on him on account of his misfortune. People possessing more than a superficial knowledge of colonial life

---

*The italics in the above quotation are mine. I think the unconscious irony is exquisite.

are aware that even the very fairest 'sprinkling of young Englishmen of education and refinement,' given to the practice of thanking God that they are not as other men are, would beget no other feeling in the mind of the masses than one of wrath and repulsion. ...

'M.' [ANON.] _____

_____ *from* 'What Hinders Emigration to Australasia?', *Westminster Review*, vol. 139, 1893, pp. 402–13.

... The cardinal hindrance to Australasian immigration being efficiently promoted is the subserviency of the popular legislative chambers in the Colonies to the prejudices of the majority in the electorates who vote under manhood suffrage. The result is—class legislation, which often proves extremely oppressive to the large and intelligent electoral minorities. Under the Australasian Democracy there has sprung up widespread jealousy, amounting to positive aversion, to anything approaching organised emigration from Europe of able-bodied work-men of good character even though they may have been brought up to handle the plough. The bulk of men composing Australasian governments and legislative assemblies are in Parliament or in office, for a living. For the most part, they are professional politicians and apparently dead to the impulse of patriotic senti-ment. They are accustomed to pander to the whims of the working classes at whose mercy are their election and their salaries as the people's representatives. Speaking from years of careful observation on the spot I do not hesitate to say that the working men of Australasia are usually blinded to their true interests by the flattery of parliamentary agitators and proprietors of so-called 'Radical' newspapers. ... an absurd cry, 'Australia for the Australians,' has been invented by mob-orators to inflate the vanity of those of European descent born on the soil, who now largely outnumber comers from other countries. This watchword really means that the Colonists who have a footing in the country may stay, but that additions to the population from abroad (fellow subjects from the parent country not excepted), are not welcome unless they bring with them plenty of capital to give highly-paid employment to those already in possession, or to invest in land and thus raise the value of local holdings for the benefit of old colonists or their descendants. The colonial-born are trained by politicians to believe that they are in perpetual danger of being flooded with what in the cant of demagogues, is called 'the pauper labour of Europe'—a phrase indiscrimi-nately but purposely applied by them to all immigrant labour whatsoever. ...

Letters Home

ANON. _____

_____ 'Van Dieman's Land', *Mirror of Literature, Amusement and Instruction*, vol. 1, 1823, pp. 212–13.

In our last MIRROR we gave a description of Van Dieman's Land, and a view of its capital, Hobart's Town; and we now give an extract of a letter from a settler there, addressed to Mr. Owen, of New Lanark, of whose benevolent plan for ameliorating society it speaks very highly.

'*Hobart's Town, April 20, 1822.*

'Two hundred years hence, when the population shall have become more dense, and subsistence more difficult, I shall endeavour to obtain leave of absence from the dominions of Pluto, and the society of Proserpine, to re-visit this rapidly-increasing colony: and found, *after my decease*, an establishment, which it has been the grand aim of some small part of my early life to promote. Nothing has given me greater pleasure since I have been in this colony, than to see *that part* of your system practically proved, which has been so much and so dogmatically disputed and denied in England. I mean, the possibility of improving the habits and morals of that which we consider the *worst*, and most depraved part of the community, by a steady system of mild and kind treatment. I saw the hardest hearts softened by kindness, which no harshness of punishment has been able to touch. You know that the greater part of the servants of settlers and others, in this country, is composed of convicts, sent out for crimes committed. This it may be imagined would be the greatest evil the settler has to encounter. I have invariably found that where the master was wise, and kind, the servants have been good and faithful; and vice versa. The easiness of their condition—the removal of temptation—the certainty of subsistence; and, above all, the habit of honesty, causes a transformation as surprising as complete. The lot of the labourer in England is not to be compared with the condition of the labourer here. As a place of punishment this is the *last place* in the world to send a criminal. Crimes in this country are by no means so frequent as in England, and our population is the refuse of the mother country. What does this prove?—that the first incentives to crime among the lower orders are want, and the fretful uncertainty of procuring the common necessaries of life. These being removed, they return to the state whence they were artificially removed, and to the order of beings susceptible of kindness, and grateful for benefits.'

ANON. _____

_____ 'Letter From a Settler For Life in Van
Dieman's Land' (reprinted from *Hood's
Comic Annual*, 1833), *Chambers'
Edinburgh Journal*, vol. 2, 1833, p. 376.

To Mary at No. 45 Mount Street, Grosvenor Square.

DEAR MARY—Littel did I Think wen I advertisd in the Tims for annonther Plaice of taking wan in Vandemin's land. But so it his and hear I am amung Kangerooses and Savidges and other Forriners. But goverment offering to Yung Wimmin to Find them in Vittles and Drink and Close and Husbands was turms not to be sneazed at, so I rit to the Outlandish Seckertary and he was so Kind as Grant.

Wen this cums to Hand go to Number 22 Pimpernel Plaice And mind and go betwixt Six and sevin For your own Sake cos then the familys Having Diner give my kind love to betty Housmad and Say I am safe of my Jurney to Forrin parts And I hope master as never Mist the wine and brought Them into trubble on My accounts. But I did not Like to leave for Ever And Ever without treeting my Frends and feller servents and Drinking to all their fairwells. In my Flury wen the Bell rung I forgot to take My own Key out of missis Tekaddy but I hope sum wan had the thought And it is in Good hands but shall Be obleeged to no. Lickwise thro my Loness of Sperrits my Lox of Hares quite went out of My Hed as was prommist to Be give to Gorge and Willum and the too Futmen at the too next dores But I hop and Trust betty pacifid them with lox of Her hone as I begd to Be dun wen I rit Her from dover. O Mary wen I furst see the dover Wite clifts out of site wat with squemishnes and Felings I all most repentid givin Ingland warning And had douts if I was goin to better my self. But the stewerd was verry kind tho I could make Him no returns xcept by Dustin the ship for Him And helpin to wash up his dishes. Their was 50 moor Yung Wimmin of us and By way of passing tim We agreed to tell our Histris of our selves taken by Turns But they all turnd out Alick we had All left on account of Testacious masters and crustacious Missisis and becos the Wurks was to much For our Strenths but betwixt yew and Me the reel truths was beeing Flirted with and unprommist by Perfidus yung men. With sich exampils befour there Minds I wunder sum of them was unprudent enuff to Lissen to the Salers whom are coverd with Pitch but famus for Not stiking to there Wurds. has for Me the Mate chose to be verry Partickler wan nite Setting on a Skane of Rops but I giv Him is Anser and lucky I did for Am infourmd he as Got too more Marred Wives in a state of Biggamy thank Goodness wan can marry in new Wurlds without mates. Since I have bean in My pressent Sitiation I have had between too and three offers for My Hands and expex them Evry day to go to fistcufs about Me this is sum thing lick treeting Wimmin as Wimmin ought to be treetid Nun of your sarsy Buchers and Backers as brakes there Promissis the sam as Pi Crust wen its maid Lite and shivvry And then laffs in Your face and say they can hav anny Gal they lick round the Square. I dont menshun nams but Eddard as drives the Fancy bred will no Wat I mean. As soon as ever the Botes rode to Land I dont agrivate the Truth to say their was haf a duzzin Bows apeace to Hand us out to shoar and sum go so Far as say they was offered to thro Specking Trumpits afore they left the Shipside. Be that as it May or may Not I am tould We maid a Verry pritty site all Wauking too and too in our bridle wite Gownds with the Union Jacks afore Us to pay humbel Respex to kernel Arther who behaived verry Gentlemanny and Complementid us on our Hansom apearences …

CHARLES DICKENS & CAROLINE CHISHOLM

Charles Dickens (1812–70), famous English novelist, journalist and social reformer, established and edited Household Words *(1850–59). He supported Urania Cottage, a centre for prostitutes, who were encouraged to emigrate to Australia after rehabilitation. [HW; LCVF]*

Caroline Chisholm (1808–77), English social worker, visited Australia in 1838–46 and 1854–66. Disturbed by the plight of single immigrant women, she opened a Female Immigrants' Home in Sydney in 1841 and worked to provide employment opportunities for women. The Family Colonization Loan Society that she founded in London in 1849 was publicised in Dickens' Household Words. *[CDWB]*

from 'A Bundle of Emigrants' Letters',
Household Words, vol. 1, 1850,
pp. 19–24.

… These remarks have originated in the circumstance of our having on our desk certain letters from emigrants in Australia, written to relatives and friends here—to serve no purpose, to support no theory, but simply to relate how they are doing, and what they know about the country, and to express their desire to have their dearest relatives and friends about them. As the truth, whatever it may be, on such a subject, cannot be, we think, too plainly stated or too widely diffused in this country, we consider ourselves fortunate in the possession of these documents. We are responsible, of course, for their being genuine, and we write with the originals before us. The passages we shall give are accurately copied, with no correction, and with no omission, but that of names when they occur.

The first is from a man in Sydney, who writes to his brother. He 'would like to come to England for one day and no more to see the Railways and the baptist chappel.'

> If you can emigrate out i shall be able to provide for you Send me word in your next what progress you are making toward finding your way out here do not stop there to staarve for as bad as Sydney is no one that is willing to work need want i am beginning to think of expecting some or all of you out i have told you what i can do and look to God and he will do the rest for you dear brothere send answer to this as soon as Possoble that is if you can understand it but it is wrote so bad i think it will take some time to make it out.

The next is from a man at Melbourne writing to his wife:

> My dear and most beloved Wife this is the 7th letters I have written and sincerly hope this may find you and my dear children in good health likewise all my friends and acquaintances but I have not yet received one from you excepting the one Mr W brought I am realy very anxious about you particularly as I hear such bad accounts from home you are in my thoughts day and night Oh that I could see you here then you would spend the hapiest days you have ever yet spent there is not the care and trouble on your mind here as there is at home but God knows I have my share of it about you but I persevere for your benefit. My dear wife do keep up your spirits and come as soon as you can you will not have to study wich is the cheapest way to get a meal here you can judge for yourself when I tell you that the best flour is only 20 shillings the sack and such quality that you cannot buy in England the bread is the best bread I ever eat in my life and the meat very fine and no price at all for instance I saw a man on Saturday night last buy a very fine round of beef and a fine leg of mutton for 2 shillings and for all that Butchers is a very good trade here there are several Establishments called the boiling down houses where they boil down Bullocks and sheep for the fat only and one house alone will boil down 800 and sometimes a 1000 in one day this may seem almost incredible to you but it is a fact and the beast must be of the best quality sheeps heads and plucks you can have by wheel barrows full for fetching away for people never think of eating such stuff as they call it ox tails you can have for fetching away but you must skin them yourselfe so much for meat. Tea is 1s. 6d. lb but it can be bought for 1s by the chest Coffee is 9d lb wich can be bought for 5d but you must roast yourselfe or send it to the roasters but you can do it at home very well for every body has what is called a lamp oven here which costs about 7 or 8 shilling and you can

bake your bread or your dinners at your own fireplace […] I have taken a deal of notice in the people here they do not study economy as they ought if you where here we could save money first I am determined to buy a peice of ground shortly and I intend joining the building society but I don't know what to do untill I heare from you I am daily expecting a letter from you I know I could not have had one much sooner for I recon upon ten months to get an answer. I am still living in the little cottage and I have worked very hard lattely I dare say you will be surprised when I tell you that I have been at work as a joiner the last 3 months and I have made 3 Chests of drawers at home in my over time since for a Master Cabinet Maker I expect a winters work at the carpentering as there are a great many Buildings going on here I am happy to say that I enjoy most excellent health indeed it would be a sin to wish for a better state of health I never have had the slightest cough since I came here I have had a slight touch of my old Complant in the legs but I have got a presription which cures it directly the Chemist that made it up told me that my stomach must be like iron and my Constitution as strong as a horse to take it the doctor told me to wear flanell drawers so I got 2 pair and since then I never have it. Rents are rising rapidly here you cant get a cottage with 2 rooms under 7 or 8 shillings a week they have rose my rent to 5s I almost forgot to say that I shall have 10s monthly to pay in the Building Sosiety and 10s entrance it began in january so I shall have the back money to pay and it is expected that it will run out in six years and then you will get 120 pounds out if you let it lay the whole time there is two of them and they are going on flourishing. […] give my love to my dear children. Oh that the day may not be far distant when my happiness may be more Complete by seeing them and you on the happy shore in the *Province of Victoria* this is the new name given by the Queen for Port Phillip. My dear as soon as I get a letter from you letting me know that you are coming then I shall begin to make up things for my selfe but untill then I am unsettled which way to act for I have saved a few pounds wich will be very much wanted to lay out and I have bought myselfe several things since I have been here that I could not do without, I have been very carefull and am almost a Teetotaler I very seldom drink anything but I will live well and I feel the benefit of it in my strength for I have lately often worked from 4 in the morning till 11 at night and dont feel half so tired as I used with half a days work but sometimes I am almost compelled to go and get a pint of beer for the sake of company as I am at home by my selfe and no one to speak to. I get very dull there is no notice taken of Easter here. I worked all day on Good friday and Easter monday the Melbourn races are thought the most of it lasts 3 days but I worked all the time and did not go to see them I cant enjoy pleasure untill you come to share it with me.

This poor fellow seems to be possessed of an appetite which must have been very inconvenient to him at home. This is his account of a light supper he had one night:

I almost forgot to say that I wanted something for my supper saturday night so I went to the butchers to get some chops and I had a pound and half of the loin 2*d* fine sheep hearts and a sheep kidney and how much do you think they was why only 4*d* the lot a fine bullocks kidneys only 2 and a very fine shin of beef 4*d* or 6*d* what will the London butcher say to this. Poultry is rather dear but it is about the same price as at home. …

A gentleman who has been ordained as a clergyman of the Church of England, writes thus of Sydney at present:

Sydney is at present crowded with *respectable* young men,—Bankers and merchants' clerks, artists and such kind of people, are not wanted at all, so that many of them having but small means are quite in despair. They are almost useless to the settlers and people in the Bush and can find no occupation in town and are therefore liable to every temptation. I hope you will exert all your influence in preventing such people from coming out here, unless they come prepared to go into the Bush as shepherds, &c.

A vast number of the orphans who have come out here have turned out ill in consequence of the bad training at home. They fancy they are young ladies and that they ought to sit and knit or just take a walk on the race course or in the domain, with children. They have not the slightest idea of industry, nor do they understand what household work is. All this they should be practically taught in the old country, and it would save much disappointment and misery when they arrive here.

A poor woman at Sydney, re-united to her children, writes,—

Dear Friend,

Your kind note of Dec. 4th I have received informing me that you had obtained passage to this port for my children. They safely arrived by the Castle Eden all in good health. They however left their box of clothes behind at Plymouth and I have not as yet been able to get any account of it. It appears to be lost, but as *they* arrived safe I do not care to trouble any one to enquire for this. The oldest girl got married about five months since to a respectable young man a tradesman, a pretty good match—the next boy is apprenticed six months ago to the wheelwright business and the next boy is four months apprenticed to a boot and shoemaker—the other little one I have myself. My own health is pretty good, and although times are rather dull just now yet I hope that I shall find enough to do to keep along with. Many ships have arrived here with emigrants and this for a time causes rather more to be looking for situations than there are situations to be filled, but most of them go into the country.

An orphan girl at Bathurst, to whom the Emigration Company granted a free passage, writes thence to a lady in Ireland, 'If in case any emigrants were coming to Sydney, *to send me my little sisters which I left at home.*' Another sighs from 'Patrick's Plains, New South Wales,' for another sister. In these cases, and in that of the wife of the good fellow with the appetite, it seems to us that a society on the proposed plan would do great service, and run little risk. Also in such an instance as the following:

Melbourne, Port Phillip

My Dear Brother and Sister

I now take this opportunity of writing a more lengthened letter than my last which I wrote in haste in which I Enclosed a Draft for the sum of twenty five pounds £25 payable to you on the bank of Australasia in Austin Friars London thirty days after sight, which I hope you will get Safe. I also send by this ship's Mail another Draft for the same money only to Ensure the money safe in case one ship might get lost on the passage to London and one Draft I Keep myself. I hope as soon as you receive my letter that you will not make any Delay but write to me Immediately and I hope and trust you will send me a long letter for nothing will give me more pleasure than to hear a little about you all not Omitting one of you wrote to me for £30 but £25 is all I can spare for the present. I have been perfectly aware of the state of England Ever Since I left or I should have been among you many years since but now I have banished all thoughts from my mind of ever seeing England, the way to Say it is don't want, for ever since I have been here I *have not seen anybody in want* but at the present time wages is not quite so good as they were when I wrote to you first that is in Consequence of the late Influx of Emigration. ... I believe I told you I had separated from my wife some years since In Consequence of her taking to Drink but she followed me over to port phillip of late since you reed my letter. I gave her another trial and I expended about £20 but all to no purpose therefore I have left her about four months since she has kept me back considerably in pocket but still I Care not, so long as the almighty spares my health how happy I should be if you was with me, but please God in the meanwhile I will Endeavour to purchase about an Acre of Land on some of the Townships so that it will at all times be your Own and a home as long as you live but at the present time I hold a Ticket for which I gave five Guineas for landed property to be drawn in a Lottery in the port philip District at present belonging to the bank of Australasia when you take your Draft for the £25 which I remit to you ask any of the proprietors of the Bank and no Doubt they will Explain all to you about the Drawing for they are all prizes from 640 acres of land in a prize to 1/2 an acre as also Dwelling houses. should I be fortunate to get a grand Drawing it shall be all for the sole benefit of you and yours ... Everything will seem Quite strange if you come I must Initiate you in our colonial ways you will not be like many who arrives here strangers that know no one. I hope should you come you will bring as many newspapers as you can as also books should you have any for I am very fond of reading should you Engage with the Emigration agents to come Out you will Immediately post a letter in London to me stating the name of the Ship you will be likely to arrive in so that on her Arrival in port phillip I will come on board for you as also on your arrival here you will send a letter Directly from the Ship to me by the post as probably by that means I may get one Safe for where the Shipping Come to anchor is nine miles from Melbourne Just off williams Town. ...

The writer of the next, sent out as a labouring man, and then very poor, now holds an influential position at Sydney. The reader will smile at his description of 'mean and unmanly occupations:'

In Sydney times are rather dull at present—various causes have given rise to this; the disturbed state of Europe has sensibly affected commerce. The Gold hunting Mania of Chalaforina has put to flight many small capitalists, who will ultimately return if permitted by the daring freebooters of that Country. The steady stream of immigration pouring into Sydney has brought down to a fair standard the exorbitant wages given to female Servants. For this the Public are mainly indebted to you. It would be well if possible to advise all persons before leaving home, not upon any account to hang about the purlieus of Sydney, or the other Towns of the Interior for a dislike is generally acquired in those places for a bush life. It is deplorable to see the Number of able bodied men who eke out a miserable subsistence in Sydney in mean and unmanly occupations, such as hawking through the Public Street fish, fruit, vegitables, pies all hot—and various other things as equally disreputable, whilst they could if they possessed a spark of Manliness or common energy of mind obtain respectable employment in the interior, but their Weak and fantastic minds conjure up a thousand Hobgoblins in the Shape of Blacks, Snakes, flying foxes, Squirls, Mad Bulls, and other dreaded Animals, as equally ridiculous. A man coming to New South Wales 16000 miles in search of a living and remaining in Sydney after he lands, is like to an individual who digs all day long in search of some hidden treasure, who when he discovers it declines to take it up, because it would be too burthensome to take home.

The letter with which we shall conclude our extracts, is from a convict—the only one before us, from any member of that class.

New South Wales.
Dear Affectionate Wife and family
    I with pleasure embrace this first Oppertunity of addressing these few lines to you hoping by the blessing of God they will find you in the perfect enjoyment of Good Health as it leaves me at present thank God for it. I wrote you a letter to you while our stay at the Cape of Good Hope which I hoped you received. We abode there one week and we arrived at Port Jackson in Sydney on the 8th day of June after a fine and pleasing voyage for 4 Callender Months wanting two days only. Nothing worth Mentioning happened all the Voyage. Only 2 of our unhapy Number was taken away from us by death. While lying in Sydney Harbour I engaged for one twelve Month and am now for the present time situated up in the country, in not so quite a comfortable position as I should wish but I must bear it for a short time, and as conveniences will allow I shall be in Sydney to work. Dear Wife You can come out to Me as soon as it pleases you and also my Sister and I will provide for you a comfortable Situation and Home as a good one as ever lies in my power, And When you come or send You must come to My Masters House at Sydney. He is a rich a Gentleman known by every one in this colony, and you must come out as emigrants, and when you come ask for me as a emigrant and never use the word Convict or the ship Hashemy on your Voyage never let it be once named among you, let no one know your business but your own selves, and When you Land come to my Masters a enquire for me and thats quite sufficient. Dear Wife do not you cumber yourself with no more luggage than is necessary for they are of no use out here you can bring your bed and bedclothes and sufficient clothes for yourself and family. You can buy for yourself a tin hook pot to hang on before the fire in the Gally to boil tea at times when it is required. And a few Oranges and lemons for the Sea Sickness or any thing you please. Dear Wife this is a fine Country and a beautiful climate it is like a perpetual Sumer, and I think it will prove congenial for your health, No wild beast nor anything of the Sort out here, fine beautiful birds and every thing seems to smile with pleasure [...] I send my kind love and best of wishes to you all and every one related to you and me, to your father and Mother. Sisters and Brothers, acquaint-

ances and friends and to every one who may ask for me. I send my kind love to you all and especially to my wife and children.   Farewell.

These 'simple annals of the poor,' written for no eyes but those to which they were addressed, are surely very pleasant to read, and very affecting. We earnestly commend to all who may peruse them, the remembrance of these affectionate longings of the heart, and the consideration of the question whether money would not be well lent or even spent in re-uniting relatives and friends thus parted, and in sending a steady succession of people of all laborious classes (not of any one particular pursuit) from places where they are not wanted, and are miserable, to places where they are wanted, and can be happy and independent.

ANON. _____

_____ 'Another Voice From the "Diggings"', *Working Man's Friend, and Family Instructor*, vol. 2, 1852, p. 328.

Adelaide, South Australia
March 30, 1852.

DEAR COUSINS,— I take this opportunity of writing to you, hoping to find you all in good health, as it leaves me at present. This country affords a fine scope for industrious, healthy young men of any capacity. Here a man with £100 may, by frugality and industry, secure an independence for life. Say he buys 40 acres of land, £40; gets his crop in, with the fencing, will cost him £40 more; by the second year, he clears his £100, and has the land to the good to proceed on in after years, the profits of which will add to his 40 acres, or buy some stock such as cows, pigs, fowls &c.; or a good compositor will get good wages and permanent situations just now. A good boot or shoe maker will get his £2 per week without rations. The aspect of the country generally is very beautiful, more like our parks at home—such as Greenwich or Richmond—it abounds in copper, there is no end of it, and very likely gold, although it is not found yet; there has been a little found, but to no great extent; they are searching now for it, and I have no doubt by the time you get this we shall have a gold-field here. I will tell you the latest news from the gold diggings in the neighbouring colony:—The water is so scarce and bad, that the people are dying in hundreds with dysentery; little is doing except gambling and drunkenness; numbers get shot accidentally by means of others discharging their fire-arms when they come to the tent in the evening; the number of robberies is out of the question; in fact, it is all a lottery; some are fortunate, others are ruined. This colony is almost deserted, but numbers have returned for want of water to wash the quartz wherein the gold is contained. I shall not go till next December, if I go at all. At present I am shepherding. I have the charge of 1,000 breeding ewes; 3000 are to be added in a week's time from this. It is an easy, pleasant life, and through the scarcity of men just now, the wages are very high. I have been on the point of marriage twice, but broke off once on account of the fair one whistling, and would not stop when I told her I did not like to hear a female whistle; and the other, because she said she could drink as much as me without being drunk,—rather a bad sign, thought I, and dropt that speculation. When I find one that suits me, I intend to be spliced at once. I have one in my eye now. I read that one man, a tradesman of Adelaide, sold off his stock at half price, and took his wife and family with him to the diggings; he dug 14 holes, each of which you have to pay 30s. for licence; he had been at work for the last seven months, and found nothing, but himself ruined and starving, so made one more hole (in his head) with a pistol-ball, which made 15 holes. This is but one instance out of hundreds. I know the party well. Do not believe the papers; I have every opportunity of knowing the truth. The people pass (to and from the diggings) the station that I am at; besides, I have conversed with numbers of my acquaintance, who have been and come back, and persuade me not to go till next year, when there will be more order restored, better regulations, and plenty of water. They are making creeks— damming up other creeks; so that, by the time the winter is over, there will be plenty of water; and the gold digging is but in its infancy yet. I must have either a golden chain or a wooden-head.

(The other half of the letter is marked strictly private.)

ANON. ———————————————————————————

——————————————————————— *from* 'The Mails to the Antipodes',
Leisure Hour, **vol. 2**, 1853,
pp. 813–15.

… What a revelation of human life would be unfolded by an examination of the Australian mails! We have no wish to pry into the letter-bags. It is needless. Their contents may be inferred with general precision. In multitudes of instances the communications will have affecting and painful passages, sometimes tragic details along with cheering and hopeful representations. Besides mercantile advices, political intelligence, and family affairs, outward-bound letters will contain fond remembrances from parents, brothers, and sisters, with not a few anxious counsels, for many a thoughtless one to beware of the errors which blighted progress and sullied reputation in his native land. Homeward letters will have an equally checquered aspect, expressing impressions of hope and fear, with the experience of disappointment, dejection, suffering, success, and satisfaction.

There must be many odd addresses on the letters outward, for Australian nomenclature abounds with all kinds of oddities. Though the sites have in general been but newly named, the denominations are in many instances so whimsical as to baffle conjecture respecting their derivation; and names of English origin often make a strange medley with those that are native, by being placed in juxtaposition with them. A correspondent, for example, may have his whereabouts on Moonlight Flat, in Peg-leg Gully, Bendigo Diggings, Victoria; the squattage of another may be on Pig-face Plain, near Deniliguin, district of Murrumbidgee, New South Wales; a third may be located at Windy Corner; a fourth at Terry Hie Hie; and a fifth at Pudding-pan Hill. Letters have recently passed to and fro between Berlin and Buchsfeld in South Australia. …

Mishaps by thousands have attended letters outward to Victoria, after having accomplished the passage of the ocean. This has arisen from the peculiar condition of the province, the incessant shifting of the population, the vast increase of business at the post-offices, the want of effective organisation to conduct it, and the wilful carelessness of those employed. The negligence of the colonial post-masters and post-office clerks forms a prominent feature of complaint in all the Australian papers. The transmission of letters from one town and colony to another is slow and uncertain. Frequently they do not come to hand at all; more frequently their transmission and delivery are delayed for many days, and even weeks. In the capitals, the great banking-houses, commercial firms, and managers of public companies, may receive the correspondence addressed to them with something akin to regularity; probably because it would not be safe to exasperate those who have the means of enforcing redress. But persons of little importance and influence have to wait and petition before their correspondence is delivered; and if they write letters, they are never certain as to the time when they will be forwarded to their destination.

At the diggings this state of things is much worse. Owing to the badness of the roads, the mails come in and go out with disconcerting irregularity, and the post-offices of the capitals are slow to acknowledge the existence of new sites with fresh communities of gold-seekers. It requires many complaints in the local papers before the official dignitaries of Sydney or Melbourne can be induced to appoint a post-master for a newly-peopled district, and find for it a couple of messengers and bags. As for the transmission of correspondence to England, and the delivery of letters from the mother country, the complaints are still more frequent and acrimonious. 'Seldom,' says a document signed by fifty-two diggers

of Forest Creek, 'does a letter from friends—from wife, sister, or brother—ever reach the unfortunate immigrant. We travel about seventy miles to Melbourne for a letter. We live at great expense while there. It costs us at least 12s. per day. We spend hours, for days together, under a burning sun, before we can see an impertinent clerk, who, with perfect coolness, informs us there are no letters—ay, often without looking. If this answer does not dismiss the applicant, we frequently find a letter is at last given, and the post-mark and date prove that the letter has been lying at the office for weeks past.' Lamentable as are these circumstances, they are not surprising; for postal salaries, though raised to meet the exigencies of the time, are not prizes in a country where the price of ordinary labour is enormously high. Such situations are not, therefore, coveted by competent and energetic parties, but fall to the lot of these who are more or less incapable or indolent. The evil is thus to a great extent inevitable, and cannot be fully rectified while the position of affairs in the colonies continues so anomalous and extraordinary. …

Though grossly mismanaged, still some facts connected with the Melbourne post-office are highly interesting, as affording evidence of the progress of the colony. In 1851, as many as 229,670 letters and 206,674 newspapers went through the office of that city. In 1852, the number of letters amounted to 898,601, and of newspapers to 638,728. The mail brought by the 'Harbinger,' which arrived at Southampton from Port Phillip August 19th, was the largest that ever reached this country from the southern dependencies. It contained not less than 450,000 letters and newspapers; and, owing to the admirable management of the English post-office, the whole of this immense mass of correspondence was sorted and forwarded to its destination in twenty-four hours. The vessel belonging to the General Screw Steam Shipping Company is the first steamer that has made a successful passage between the mother country and the antipodes. To this company the honour belongs of having established the possibility of bringing the two distant regions into quicker intercourse, by the use of steam. Their ship, the 'Argo,' reached Southampton October 29th, having made the voyage *out* and *home* by Cape Horn in five months and nineteen days, spending upwards of six weeks in Australia. The actual time under steam and canvass was 121 days, and as the distance both ways is 27,900 miles, the average speed per day was nearly 230 miles, or slightly over 9½ miles per hour. Steam was only used as an auxiliary, the ship being fully rigged, and at times it was altogether dispensed with. The coals consumed out and in amounted to 2105 tons, of which 845 tons were consumed out, and 1260 home, an average of rather more than 17 tons per day. The 'Argo' run from Southampton to Port Phillip in 64 days; and a similar quick passage has been made from Gravesend to Adelaide by the 'Victoria,' belonging to another company, in 59 days, 22½ hours.

Colonial Life

ANON.

from 'Van Dieman's Land', *Mirror of Literature, Amusement and Instruction*, vol. 1, 1823, pp. 193–5.

As the British settlements in this part of the world are every year becoming of more importance, owing to the rapidity with which crime in this country is populating them, some account of them may not be deemed uninteresting. ...

Van Dieman's Land is an island nearly as large as Ireland, to the South of the colony of New South Wales, better known by the name of Botany Bay, from which it is separated by a strait of sixty miles in width, called Bass's Straits. This island has not so discouraging and repulsive an appearance from the coast as New Holland. Many fine tracts of land are found on the very borders of the sea, and the interior is almost invariably possessed of a soil admirably adapted to all the purposes of civilized man. This island is mountainous, and consequently abounds in streams. On the summit of many of the mountains there are large lakes, some of which are the sources of considerable rivers. Of these the Derwent, Huon, and Tamar, rank in the first class. There is, perhaps, no island in the world, of the same size, which can boast of so many fine harbours: the best of these are the Derwent, Port Davy, Macquarie Harbour, Port Dalrymple, and Oyster Bay. The first of these is on its Southern sides; the second and third on the Western, the fourth on the Northern, and the fifth on the Eastern side; so that it has harbours in every direction—a circumstance which must materially assist the future progress of civilization.

The climate of this island is healthy, and much more congenial to the European constitution than Port Jackson. The North-West winds, which are there productive of such violent variations of temperature, are here unknown, and neither the winters nor summers are subject to any great extremes of cold or heat.

The natives of Van Dieman's Land are few in number, considering the extent of country which they yet hold free from European invasion. It is probable that their extreme wretchedness forbids their increase. They have been always hostile, and by no means avail themselves of the freedom of our streets and houses, like the natives of Port Jackson. This feeling is ascribed to a fatal quarrel at the first settling, in which several of them were killed, and the memory of which has been kept alive by occasional encounters in the interior, between them and the solitary Europeans employed as stock-keepers. These are frequently assaulted by spears and stones, and are compelled to use fire-arms in their defence. The two parties live in mutual suspicion and dread; and time and conciliation towards such of the natives as afford opportunities of intercourse, can alone obliterate the present impression of long cherished animosity. Some intercourse has lately been effected with those of the western coast, and they appear free from all oppression of the colonists. Hence it would seem that, on the other side of the island, the native hostility arises from some ancient grudge, particularly since, from the difficult, if not wholly impracticable, nature of the western range of mountains, it is very doubtful whether the tribes have any communication, unless by the northern extremity of the island. The savages do not eat the cattle or sheep; but they often destroy them and burn the carcasses. They subsist chiefly on Kangaroos, opossum, and 'such small deer,' down to the kangaroo rat, migrating, in times of scarcity, to the coast for fish.

The great difference between the Indians of Van Dieman's Land and those of New Holland, though the countries are separated by a strait not a hundred miles wide, and studded with islands, by means of which canoes might safely pass, and though the rest of nature's productions are nearly the same in both lands, affords a subject of curious speculation. The islanders resemble the African Negro in physiognomy, much more than the natives of the continent; and the hair of the former is woolly, whereas that of the latter is coarse and straight. Both races are equally free from any tradition of origin, or acquaintance with each other—although their barbarism seems at the extreme pitch. Their languages are entirely different, and it is probable that they never had any connection with each other. ...

The British colonies in Van Dieman's Land have of late received a great accession of settlers from Great Britain. According to the last accounts they were gradually improving, and assuming more and more the appearance of a civilized community. From an account of a tour of inspection by Governor Macquarrie, it appears that, in July, 1821, the population of the island amounted to 6,372 persons, exclusive of the civil and military officers; and that it contained 28,838 head of horned cattle, 182,468 sheep, 421 horses, and 10,663 acres of land in cultivation.

Hobart's Town, the capital, was founded in 1804, and is situated about nine miles up the Derwent. As may be supposed, a capital of less than twenty years standing cannot be very large; it is, however, rapidly improving in size and comfort. And the settlement called Launceston has been founded about thirty miles from the mouth of Port Dalrymple, and 130 miles in a straight line from Hobart's Town.

We shall conclude this notice with a brief account of Michael Howe, the last and worst of the Bush Rangers, and who by his depredations became the terror of Van Dieman's Land. This account is abridged from the Life of Howe, printed at Hobart's Town in 1818, and was the first child of the press of a state not fifteen years old. ...

Howe was without a spark of even the honour of an outlaw; he betrayed his colleagues upon surrendering himself to government, and he fired upon a native girl, his companion, when she became an impediment to his flight. He was reduced at last to abandonment, even by his own gang; and one hundred guineas, and, (if a convict should take him) a free pardon and a passage to England, were set upon his head. He was now a wretched conscience-haunted solitary, hiding in dingles, and only tracked by the sagacity of the native girl, to whom he had behaved so ungratefully, and who was now employed by the police to revenge his cruelty to her. His arms, ammunition, dogs, and knapsack were first taken from him; and in the last was found a little memorandum-book of kangaroo skin, written by himself in kangaroo blood. It contained a sort of journal of his dreams, which shewed strongly the wretched state of his mind, and some tincture of superstition. It appears that he frequently dreamt of being murdered by natives, of seeing his old companions, of being nearly taken by a soldier; and in one instance only, humanity asserts itself even in the breast of Michael Howe, for we find him recording that he dreamt of his sister. It also appears from this little book that he had once an idea of settling in the woods, for it contained long lists of such seeds as he wished to have, vegetables, fruits, and even flowers.

These bush-rangers are now exterminated, and the colony on which they were a heavy drawback is consequently rapidly advancing in numbers and in civilization.

ALEXANDER ANDREWS

Alexander Andrews (c.1824–73), British writer, contributed miscellaneous articles chiefly to Bentley's Magazine, and wrote The History of British Journalism: from the Foundation of the Newspaper Press in England, to the Repeal of the Stamp Act in 1855 (1859). [WI]

'The Progress and Prospects of Western Australia', *Simmonds's Colonial Magazine and Foreign Miscellany*, vol. 1, 1844, pp. 321–3.

The last two years have been more important and eventful ones in the history of Western Australia than any which have revolved since her foundation. The population has received an accession of several hundreds—an increase not only of numbers, but attended to some extent by energy and capital; and the mischievous prejudice so actively kept alive against the colony has been dissipated by the wider dissemination of the truth. Two institutions, both calculated to be of great advantage to the colony, date their foundation in 1842,—the 'Vineyard,' and the 'Western Australian,' Societies. The former is established for the encouragement of vine cultivation, for which the soil and climate of the colony are found to be eminently adapted, and which has already been commenced on a rather extensive scale. Between fifty and sixty thousand varieties of the vine are already planted, besides Zante currants, melons and olives, and upwards of twenty acres are, we understand, systematically laid out in vineyards. It is not difficult to discern in the bright dawning of the future, the almost boundless benefit which will result to the colony from this addition to its products. The cultivation of currants and grapes, the manufacture of wine, and the distillation of brandy, must increase the wealth of the colony and give a vast impetus to its trade. Capital and labour are, of course, required before this enterprise can attain to any very great extent; but with the prospects which she has at present, it is not likely that Western Australia will long be depressed by the want of either, as the settlers have aroused themselves and resolved on no longer remaining silent and undefended. They have united themselves into a body to promulgate a correct knowledge of their state and prospects, and the resources and qualifications of their colony, and have commenced a systematic plan of operations for disabusing the mind of the British public, and righting themselves in the eyes of the world. These are the sole objects of the Western Australian Society, which abhors the idea of puffing or exaggeration as much as it is determined to make known the truth. This Society is located at Perth, and is designed to open a correspondence with England and other countries, and report from time to time the actual condition of the colony. The last reports, we are happy to find, are favourable; but yet much inconvenience appears to be felt from the want of labour, which has so long been the bane of the colony. We hope, however, to find this inconvenience speedily alleviated, by the accession of a fresh supply of emigrants, who will find ready means of employment in the extensive resources of the soil of the interior, and the seas which bound the coasts. We allude to agriculture and whaling, both of which have been hitherto contracted by the want of labour. But there is another product, indigenous to the colony, which will in time become a valuable article of export,—fine timber, adapted for ship-building and every description of work, rejecting barnacles and the white ant, and neither corroding with iron nor splitting in the working.

A colony with these manifold resources cannot long remain in the background when its settlers are determined on making known its real capabilities; but it possesses natural qualifications as great and as inviting to the emigrant as its resources are to the capitalist. The greatest of these is its climate, genial and invigorating, free from drought and fog, and beneficial in the highest degree to the invalid, especially in cases of pulmonary disease. Its situation, within a short voyage of the Indian Presidencies, is another important feature in its natural qualifications, and will ultimately tend to introduce capital into the colony. Invalids suffering from the ill effects of an Indian sun will anxiously fly for relief to the more wholesome atmosphere of Western Australia, and carry with them their families and wealth; and greater facilities for this transmigration must in a short time be afforded by the establishment of regular steam communication. It is impossible in the present rising condition of the Australasian Colonies that the advantage of steam should long be withheld from them, and the first ports with which such communication will be opened must be those of India. At present the Government schooner Champion, and other private vessels belonging to the colony, are employed in frequent transits to Calcutta and Singapore, and give opportunities both of correspondence by that route with England, and also for the return of invalid East Indians to recruit their health in the colony. With these prospects and resources, we think we are justified in predicting that Western Australia will speedily emerge from her obscurity—an obscurity caused by misrepresentation, and not by want of merit—and take her proper rank among the dependencies of Britain.

So much for the prospects of the colony: its progress seems to be sound and satisfactory. Several public works of importance and utility have lately been completed, and the appearance of the towns is now reported to be rapidly improving. Perth Church is approaching completion, and Fremantle Church has been lately opened; new roads have been laid out in the interior, superseding those which were before in use and which were hastily formed for expediency, but are now no longer in keeping with the progress of the colony, and affairs generally appear to be on a rapid advance, the letters lately received conveying pleasing assurances of prosperity. Not the least commendation of Western Australia is the respectability of its society, it having been the first Southern colony of free men, and convicts having from its foundation been jealously excluded. The state of crime has been consequently low, and the community, free from the contamination of criminals, and composed from honourable sources, has become confirmed in habits of morality and respectability. These several circumstances combine to render Western Australia most eminently qualified for colonisation; and it would be difficult to account for its former slow progress, did we not know that it has struggled on without advocate or vindicator, without an agent to protect its interests, and without a company to usher it into notice. As it is, however, its progress, slow and inadequate as it has been, is evidence of its eligibility; for assuredly, without many and obvious advantages, it could never have struggled through such difficulties or survived such shocks as it has sustained and triumphed over. We hope to hear frequently from this interesting colony, and shall have much pleasure in being enabled to report good progress, and give our readers frequent and favourable intelligence of our Western Australian friends.

The colony is at present on the advance, and decidedly progressing in the right way—slowly perhaps, but steadily, and without display or boast; and quietness of progress is not always indicative of absence of improvement, any more than a bright appearance of rapid growth and early maturity proves *true* solidity of foundation. For our own parts, although we would wish to see the colony rise into notice more rapidly, we look upon her tardiness of motion as the stronger evidence of her solvency, and are on that account the less disposed to regret it.

RICHARD HOWITT _____

Richard Howitt (1799–1870), British-born writer and poet, and brother of the writer and journalist William Howitt, arrived at Port Phillip (Victoria) in 1840. He farmed on the Heidelberg Road, returning to England in 1844. His Impressions of Australia Felix during Four Years Residence in that Colony *(1845) is a significant description of life in Australia at that time, and he also published volumes of poetry in 1830, 1840 and 1868. [ADB]*

_____ 'To a Small Australian Flower.
Written in New South Wales. (For
the Instructor.)', *Hogg's Weekly
Instructor*, vol. 6, 1847–48, pp. 8–9.

Meant to soften scenes austere,
    Or to speed the ling'ring hours,
Thou are blooming everywhere,
    Fairest of Australian flowers!

Star of Hope! with spring appearing,
    Prophet of bright coming days!
Wakener of benign emotions,
    Happy thoughts, and grateful praise.

Now the wattles forth profusely
    Hang their wreaths of paly gold,
Thee, e'en like a sportive fairy,
    In my pathway I behold.

Lonely, in these forests pond'ring
    On the distant and the dear,
With a smile of kindly welcome,
    Me, a stranger, thou didst cheer.

And, with each returning season,
    Round my footsteps thou dost rise,
To remind me that our Maker
    Is munificent as wise.

Goodness ever from Him growing,
    Solace 'midst the world's annoy:
Scatt'ring endlessly before us
    Life, and love, and living joy!

Native art thou in this region—
    Here alone hast birth and death,
Since God call'd thee in creation
    Into beauty with a breath.

Centuries was thy presence cheering,
    Whilst thy praise was yet unheard,
To thy woodland-wild companions,
    Wildest man, and beast, and bird.

Now the white man's eyes regard thee
    With a higher, holier aim—
Comprehends thy worth and graces,
    Though he names thee by no name.

Well he knows thy life is blameless,
    Spotless, or in blooms or buds;
Nor can be unknown or nameless
    To dusk wand'rers of these woods.

To the sun they may ally thee,
        Who art common as its light;
Or, for thy seraphic beauty,
        To some star that studs the night.

E'en the rudest human creature,
        With no kindliness to spare,
When his wand'ring eyes rest on thee,
        Must be conscious thou art fair.

And the sternest, thee beholding,
        Must relax his features hard,
Soften'd by thy gentle aspect,
        Ere thou fad'st from his regard.

Half the term of years, or longer,
        To which human life extends
We were strangers; now faith stronger
        Binds us than most common friends.

This I feel, thou lowly creature:
        Thou hast served me many ways—
In some things hast been my teacher,
        And therefore I sing thy praise.

Whatsoe'er is pure and graceful,
        Unto joy allied, though lowly,
Serves the cause of highest natures,
        Is God's servant, and is holy.

Therefore though thou of the many
        Held be as a noteless thing,
I will prize thee in thy station,
        And thy worth will boldly sing.

Long thy light was from me hidden—
        Soon, will be no longer seen,
By the solid globe divided
        As we heretofore have been.

Still for thy pure look benignant,
   And for hours which thou dost cheer,
I, in that far land of beauty,
   Fain would see thee, and revere.

Yet to see thee chill'd and drooping—
   Hard return for solace given—
Were unmeet, and more so stooping,
   Where the skylark sing to heaven.
                    August 1843.

ANON.

The measures noted in the following verse included the establishment of responsible government. A new government Bill for the colonies was debated in the British Parliament in 1849–50. The Australian colonies were to be granted the right to draw up constitutions, but there was still to be a division between imperial and colonial legislation. (See Paul Knaplund, The British Empire, 1815– 1939, *New York, Howard Fertig, 1969 [1941], pp. 206–7.)*

'Good Measures for the Colonies. J. Russell and Co., *Downing Street, Home and Colonial Tailors,* **Invite attention to their New System of Colonial Measurement',** *Punch, or the London Charivari,* **vol. 18, 1850, pp. 75, 77.**

With joy and pride a parent sees
His children climb about his knees;
Pleased we regard the tiny elves,
The little dittoes of ourselves;
It is a gratifying sight
To witness their increasing height,
And mark, as every father knows,
How quickly they outgrow their clothes.
A change of garb, too, must be had,
Soon as the child becomes a lad;

Richard Doyle, 'Lord John Taking the Measure of the Colonies', *Punch, or the London Charivari*, vol. 18, 1850, p. 75.

Doyle, Richard (1824–83), London-born artist and illustrator, became associated with *Punch* in 1843. A virulent anti-Catholic campaign run in 1850 by the editor, Mark Lemon, offended Doyle, a practising Catholic. He left that year, and later worked for the *Cornhill*. [LCVF]

We then select a manlier style
Of clothing for the juvenile.
With little Bulls JOHN BULL is blest,
'Tis time that they were rightly drest;
RUSSELL AND CO. will undertake
The requisite costume to make.
With needful measures duly squared,
To meet all wants they're quite prepared.
Suits they provide for every age,
Of growth according to the stage,
Adapted to each size and shape,
Yes; from Australia to the Cape,
Jamaica, Canada, Ceylon,

RUSSELL invites to try them on;
Easy they're warranted to sit,
Full freedom to combine with fit,
And elegance with what must be
Resistless—strict economy,
In which all other firms compete
In vain with RUSSELL's, Downing Street.

*Measures to order, and a New (Blue) Book will shortly
be published.*

ANON. _____

_____ *from* 'Stray Notes on Australia and
the Diggings', *Leisure Hour*, vol. 1,
1852, p. 640.

AUSTRALIAN COTTON.—A lively interest has been excited in Manchester by the
report of the Chamber of Commerce of that great manufacturing capital on some
samples of Australian cotton submitted for examination by the Rev. Dr. Lang.
There were nine samples of various qualities. Altogether, they are considered by
the highly competent President of the Chamber as 'indisputably proving the
capability of Australia to produce most useful and beautiful cotton, adapted to
the English markets, in a range of value from 6*d.* to 2*s.* 6*d.* per pound.'

ORIGIN OF THE WORD 'NUGGET.'—This word, now so common amongst our population, is a strange sounding word, and destitute of any apparent etymological
meaning. It originated at the Ophir diggings in New South Wales, and is probably
a corruption of 'ingot,' which is itself a corruption of 'lingot,' a little tongue. The
wedge of gold which Achan purloined is called, in the original Hebrew, a 'tongue'
of gold, as a reference to a Bible with marginal readings will show. In California
the word 'lump' is generally used, and sometimes the Spanish word *pepite*. ...

ESTIMATED PRODUCE OF THE AUSTRALIAN MINES.—By papers from Sydney, up to the
8th of May, we learn that the gold said to be now produced throughout Australia
amounts to 60,000 ounces weekly, being at the rate of 3,120,000 ounces per
annum. This, at the European price of gold, would amount to £12,000,000
per annum. The quantity sent into Melbourne from Mount Alexander alone is said
to be 50,000 ounces weekly. This, with fewer hands, would at once place the
Australian gold fields in advance of California. The New South Wales yield is
stated at 10,000 ounces weekly, the comparatively limited production of the latter

'An English Gold Field', *Punch, or the London Charivari*, vol. 23, 1852, p.58.

colony being owing to the superior attractions of the Port Philip mines. What the yield will be when a much larger population has found its way to the Australian colonies it will be impossible to prognosticate. Enough is now apparent to render it certain that it will be without a parallel in the world's history. ...

FIREWOOD is selling in Melbourne at £3 the cart load.

PURCHASE OF LAND BY GOLD DIGGERS.—A cheering fact amongst the New South Wales gold diggers is that, in most cases, as soon as they have procured sufficient means, their first step is to purchase a piece of land, and settle down upon it. It is delightful to see this, as it proves that the men are not, as might have been supposed, absorbed in the vice of avarice; and it proves that which is of more consequence, that Australia will rapidly be peopled with a race of sturdy yeomen, who but the other day were labourers. ...

DISPROPORTION OF THE SEXES.—The men who are traversing the route to Australia are reckoned to be in the proportion of 15 or 20 to one woman. We do not hear, however, that adequate means are being taken to rectify this frightful and growing evil.

REMITTANCES FOR RELATIVES.—There has recently been published a second remittance roll for the reunion of families in Australia. The gross sum remitted was nearly £3,000, and the several contributions, 136 in number, varied in amount

'A Gold Field in the "Diggins"', *Punch, or the London Charivari*, vol. 23, 1852, p.59.

from 12s. to £150. We observe that a shepherd has sent £100 for the emigration of his relatives; a labourer sends £80; a blacksmith £60; a bricklayer, £50; and a builder, £50 for the like purpose. Labourers, servants, and mechanics contribute the most to the kindly office of rescuing parents, children, relations, and friends from poverty, and of making them share in the prosperity now enjoyed by the emigrant donors. It is a pleasing subject to contemplate, and does honour to the industry and self-denial necessary to the accumulation of such a sum, and in so short a time. No class gives so largely as the labourer. There is no other than he that had the fortune or the virtue to save £130 and £80, except a shoemaker, who sent his brother-in-law £150. Hopeful and good as all this is, it must be in candour confessed that the Irish stand conspicuous for similar and greater generosity; they having remitted, in little more than a year, £900,000 for the emigration of their relatives. A new country, new hopes, and good employment seem in both nations to rouse the qualities that 'the thorny point of bare distress' had suppressed at home.

IMPORTANT TO EMIGRANTS.—Mr. Mansfield, the magistrate of Liverpool, lately gave his decision in an important case. The point involved was, whether the charterer of an emigrant ship, in case of the detention of that ship beyond its appointed day of sailing, is liable to the passengers for the return of the passage-money, and compensation for loss of time. The complainant was a person named M'Turk, who, with others, had taken passages in the 'City of Lincoln' for Australia; and the defendant was Mr. J. Johnson, the charterer of the vessel. Johnson had failed to pay the whole of the contract-money to the owner, who detained the vessel in the river fifteen days beyond the specified day of sailing. It was contended, for the defendant, that he was not the cause of the detention of the passengers in the sense of the 32nd section of the Act, recently passed for the protection of emigrants. There were two ways in which the payment of the first £5 by the plaintiff might be regarded, namely, either as a deposit, or part payment of the contract; but so far from the day of sailing not having been specified, that was one consideration for the payment of the money. Then, as to Mr. Johnson not being the owner of the vessel, he had certainly acted as such, and could not now be allowed to repudiate the ownership. The wording of the Act at one time led him to think that the case did not come within its meaning, but further consideration had changed that opinion. The plaintiff was therefore entitled to his £15 passage-money, and £3 compensation.

ANON.

'Hot Weather in Adelaide', *Eliza Cook's Journal*, vol. 8, 1853, p. 416.

FRYING and dying, and boiling and roasting,
Perspiring and tiring, and broiling and toasting,
Smothered and bothered, and covered with dust,
And grimy and slimy, and baked to a crust;
Full of bile all the while, but attempting to smile,
Dead beat with the heat, merely walking a mile,
Your hair in a flare, or a sop like a mop,
Red-hot every spot, if you stop you must drop;
In a fire hot as bricks, and as cross as two sticks,
The glass up, alas! at a hundred and six,
Every day in this way, every night in a fright,
With the bugs in your rugs, though the light be in sight,
And the fleas on your knees, which you scratch to get ease,
While they bite left and right, and just tease as they please;
I know no condition can well be called rummer,
But such is our state in an Adelaide summer.

GERALDINE ENDSOR JEWSBURY _____

Geraldine Jewsbury (1812–80), English-born novelist, essayist and long-time reviewer for the weekly
Athenaeum, was also an influential publisher's reader for Richard Bentley. She produced six novels
in the years 1845–59 which directly engage with the 'Woman Question', but today her career as
publisher's reader and reviewer attracts most critical interest. [BWW; LCVF]

_____ '"Our Library Table", *Lights and*
Shadows of Australian Life. By
Mrs. Charles [Ellen] Clacy'. Review,
Athenaeum, 11 November 1854,
p. 1333.

—After travels, come tales. The modern fashion of turning every scrap of knowledge and grain of experience into immediate print for profit's sake, is as tiresome
to the public as it is tempting to authors who care little for the art of authorship,
and who regard only the sale of the greatest number of pages. Mrs. Clacy's narrative was an addition, of its slight kind, to our books concerning the New Land of
Promise [*vide*, Athen. No. 1358]; but her tales are commonplace, romantic, and
mawkish,—sometimes where she means them to be terrible. We already knew
concerning Australian life, that Hood's exaggeration has become of late almost a
reality; and that young Ladies are almost asked in marriage through speaking-
trumpets ere they step ashore from the ship. We had already heard how belated
wanderers are glad of a Kangaroo chop for supper, if they can shoot down one of
those jumping denizens of the wilderness; and that when they are 'out' for a day
or two, they may be compelled to bring themselves down to that dainty—dear to
the aborigines—a fine nutty maggot from beneath the bark of the gum-tree. Mr.
Rowcroft had already in his 'Bushranger' displayed to us what manner of *Corsair*
or *Bethlem Gabor*—otherwise reckless and shocking criminal—the settler may
chance to meet in out-of-the-way places. One or two more facts and traits
like these—marking locality—are all that distinguish Mrs. Clacy's tales from the
commonest Annual ware. The period of vicissitude which they illustrate is too
universally violent in its contrasts to be very tractable for purposes of Art,—but
were it the reverse, our authoress is no artist in fiction, and seems to have spun
out this second book (as we said at the beginning) merely because the first
pleased its readers.

MRS CHARLES [ELLEN] CLACY _____

Ellen Clacy (1830–?), British-born writer of fiction, autobiography, children's stories and social commentary, visited Australia briefly in 1852 and produced an excellent account of life on the Victorian goldfields, A Lady's Visit to the Gold-Diggings of Australia in 1852–53 (1853). Her fictional work includes novellas and short sketches dealing with bushranging, Aboriginals, gold-digging, and bush and city life. [AWW; BALP]

This extract is from Lights and Shadows of Australian Life, *vol. 1, 1854, pp. 61–4. See the preceding review by Geraldine Jewsbury.*

_____ 'An Australian Home', *Bow Bells*,
vol. 1, 1863, p. 768.

As it was almost dark when he had arrived, it was not until the next morning that he obtained a view of his new abode; but when he did so, his delight at the beauty of all around him was at first unalloyed by any other feeling. The house itself was built of stone, and was large and commodious, with a shady verandah, which was nearly hidden beneath clusters of wild creepers and ferns. Some distance beyond the station rose a barrier of rocks, which sheltered the spot from the cold south winds; groves of the palm and Indian fig-trees were scattered here and there; the elegant leaves of the tea-fern were reflected in the waters of a small lake; and to complete the picture, were some cattle luxuriating on the fresh green herbage, and the gay prattle of childish voices, as they sat upon the ground outside the verandah, caressing a large kangaroo-dog which lay at their feet. It was a scene of calm loveliness; and, as I have said, George experienced no feeling but delight as he first gazed upon it; but as his eye fell upon the stock-keeper's merry children, and caught sight of a graceful womanly figure bending over them, other recollections passed over his mind, and a deep sigh burst from him. In the danger and excitement of the last few days—in the gaiety and dissipation of Sydney, he had lost sight of many bitter remembrances, and given himself up to the passing moment, without recurring to the memory of bygone days. But here, secluded almost from the world, in a place where peace and happiness seemed to pervade every living thing, he looked back upon the past—upon the principal events of his own thoughtless and undisciplined existence, and then turned to the hopeless future—to the life-long penalty his past follies would entail upon him. And thus he sorrowfully mused, till a return of the old reckless-ness came over him and he shook off, as it were, the temporary depression of spirit, and with lighter steps walked slowly towards the house. He had been hidden from sight by a group of trees intermingled with fern; and as he advanced, still concealed from the little party before the verandah, he obtained, without being himself seen, a closer view of them. The children were sitting, as before, upon the ground, twining some wild flowers round the neck of their canine companion: beside them stood a young girl of about seventeen: and George had little doubt that she was Janet Mortimer, the only child of his host. Janet had been born in the colony, and was therefore a 'currency lass,' as they are termed. Her figure was slight and very tall; her hair and complexion dark as a brunette; her eyes were of a deep blue, yet when they were cast upon the ground, so long and black were the fringes that overhung them, that a casual observer would have declared them of the same colour as her hair. She was simply attired, and stood in an easy, graceful attitude beside the children: now caressingly curling their long fair locks round her fingers; now gently stroking the smooth skin of the kangaroo-dog.—*Australian Life.*

MRS H. W. [EMMA] COBHAM BREWER _____

Emma Cobham Brewer (dates unknown), British-born editor, translator and writer, published books including Gold: or, Legal Regulations (1877), The Condition of Nations (1880) and a translation of G. F. Kolb, as well as Mrs. Brewer's Statistical Chart of London (1882). She wrote regularly for the Girl's Own Paper on such topics as 'The Colonies and Dependencies of Great Britain' (1882); 'The Girls of the World' (1885–86), using what she termed the 'wonderful science' of statistics; 'The Romance of the Bank of England, or, The Old Lady of Threadneedle Street' (1886–87); and 'The Flower Girls of London' (1891), a social document indicting the conditions under which these children worked. [GGW]

This extract is from a four-part series which includes: South Australia, pp. 728-31; Western Australia; Queensland, pp. 755–8; New South Wales, pp. 804–7.

_____ *from* 'Our Australian Colonies and New Zealand' (First Part), *Girl's Own Paper*, vol. 4, 1882, pp. 676–80.

These colonies are, perhaps, the most interesting of all our possessions. A little of the past history is necessary to enable us to appreciate their present condition, and on our way thither we shall have ample time to consider their origin, their wonderful progress, and their vast contributions to the necessities of the mother country.

We, passengers in the 'Girl's Own,' have a special interest in this visit beyond the enjoyment we anticipate in seeing the beautiful works of Nature and Art. We desire to see personally some of the girls who have already made their homes in these colonies, and to inquire what chances of remunerative labour and independence exist for girl immigrants in the future.

The voyage will be a long one, and before starting some few arrangements must be made. Our time must be fully and usefully occupied, according to the special knowledge which each may possess. Some of us will take charge of the kitchen, and if any very good dish should be sent to table, we will dot it down for the use of those who by-and-by may have homes of their own. All will take part in keeping our beautiful ship—the 'Girl's Own'—clean and pure. …

Our farewells are spoken and our ship is off, but not until England is lost sight of can we settle down to our daily tasks. As we look back we talk of those girls who have been compelled to leave the dear old country, and take upon themselves the responsibilities of life alone and in an unknown land, and we honour them for being courageous enough to break away from the old life, in order to lessen the burdens of those they love. We think it just possible that the information we may glean on this tour may make separation less painful to those left behind as well as to those who go, for knowledge always clears away doubts and difficulties.

… Most of us have friends in one or other of these colonies, and according to our tastes we have picked up and remembered certain facts concerning them. [a description of early history follows].

Such is the little history we have collected among us of the Mother Colony of New South Wales. The time came, however, when her household became too large for her to manage, and she did what many another mother has done before and since, settled her children in homes of their own and started them in life with a new name. The first to leave the mother's care was 'Tasmania,' the most beautiful of all her children. She has done well, and gradually obtained the confidence of all who were attracted to her home. In 1834 the most exemplary of the family took her place in the world under the name of South Australia; she gave no trouble as a child, and her course has been one of steady industry and integrity, and none have had cause to repent becoming her subjects. The rebellious, ambitious child was Victoria, who wanted to assume the reins of government before the mother thought her capable, and, therefore, without the mother's leave, she asserted her independence in 1850, and took her place in the world as Victoria. The youngest child, who was launched under the auspicious name of Queensland in 1859, is making progress in wealth and position, and offering a home to the children of other lands who desire to work under her banner. We have left West Australia to the last, because from her starting in life in 1829 she has had many and overwhelming difficulties to contend with; she has been depressed and well-nigh crushed, but by her intelligence and perseverance she is coming out a conqueror and able to stand side by side with her prosperous sisters without shame.

One law is common to all these homes, viz., that they will not extend their protection to the idle; all who seek them must be willing and able to work, and accept as their motto, '*Labour is honourable.*'…

'J.C.' [ANON.]

'Kangaroos at a Cricket Match. A True Story', *Boy's Own Paper*, vol. 13, 1890–91, p. 634.

Allan and Robert Hart prided themselves upon the fact that they had lived all their lives in the Bush. They were Bush boys, and desired no better fate. Their father owned what is called a station or run, in a thinly-populated part of New South Wales. People who lived fifteen miles away were called neighbours, and a distance of eight or ten miles was spoken of as next door.

Under these circumstances you would suppose a cricket match impossible; but our Bush boys are not fond of that word, and, except during the busy shearing or lambing seasons, they contrived to meet pretty often for a game.

One afternoon so large a party of young men and boys had assembled, that Mr. Hart's home was nearly surrounded by horses; some tied to rings in the wall, others to branches of trees. Cricket was the order of the day, and no one had eyes or thoughts for anything else. All at once a cry was heard, 'Look at the kangaroos!' and there, sure enough, were two large kangaroos, sitting up side by side in a corner of the field, watching the game with grave interest.

In one moment the scene was changed as if by magic. The field was deserted, and each man and boy made a rush for his horse.

The sporting instinct is keen in young Australia. He is fond of cricket, but fonder still of a hunt. He will tell you that, as a kangaroo eats as much grass as a cow, it is the duty of every farmer's son to kill one when he can.

Our cricketers were only too eager to perform this duty. They sprang upon their horses, whistled up their dogs, and gave chase to the kangaroos. One was speedily overtaken and killed; the other bolted straight towards the house. The door stood open, and, to Mrs. Hart's dismay, it seemed disposed to seek refuge within; but, fortunately, it bounded past the door, round the corner, and over the hedge into the fields beyond.

Helter-skelter went the pursuing crowd of men, boys, and dogs, and the air was filled with shouts of laughter. At a little distance flowed a stream, called in the bush a creek. The kangaroo wisely decided to put this creek between himself and his pursuers. He reached the bank, and prepared for the vigorous bound needed to carry him to the further side. At this moment Allan rushed down the bank, and, as the animal rose, he caught hold of his tail and held on firmly with both hands.

A trial of strength between an 'old man' kangaroo and a boy of fourteen could have but one end. Away went the kangaroo, boy and all, amidst the laughter of the spectators on the bank. But after all Allan had the best of it, for the 'old man' in calculating his spring had not reckoned upon a stout boy hanging on to his tail; so, instead of landing, as he would have done, on the opposite bank, his jump ended in the middle of the creek, when he plunged his unwelcome follower into ten feet of cold water. Here the dogs soon put an end to the conflict, and Allan emerged from the creek, dripping from head to foot, but looking very jolly in spite of his ducking. His companions greeted him with peals of laughter and clapping of hands.

'Let those laugh who win,' cried Allan, as he marched off homewards. 'I caught the kangaroo.'

And so he maintains to this day.

Women

CHRISTIAN ISOBEL JOHNSTONE _____

Christian Isobel Johnstone (1781–1857), Scottish pioneering editor and co-proprietor of Tait's Edinburgh Magazine (1834–46), contributed over four hundred articles to the magazine. She actively encouraged women writers, and reviewed the work of almost every new woman writer of the 1830s and 1840s. [BWW; WI]

This article was published in February 1835, possibly as a companion to 'What Shall we do with Our Young Fellows?', published the previous September.

_____ 'A Page For the Lasses', *Tait's Edinburgh Magazine*, vol. 2, 1835, pp. 128–9.

Our literary and poetical, our scientific and our political friends, will surely forgive us for devoting a single page, once in three years, to the service of the lasses. We are not aware how many, or indeed if any of our own country maidens have hitherto volunteered for the Australian Colonies, candidates for places in the first instance, and not without some remote idea of matrimony:—the most natural idea in the world, by the way; and that which, by every ship, carries out two or more accomplished young ladies to India, with but one string to their bow, while the lasses have two, as they are required to work, as well as to charm. It is as respectable workers they are wanted; the other advantages to the colony are but prospective: and we need not intimate that it is not altogether for the mere pleasure of their company, that the young women are invited out by the Committee for Promoting the Emigration of Females. The gentlemen of the Committee say they will urge no one, however highly they may think of the advantages of emigration to females of good character and industrious habits. Neither shall we. On the contrary, all our affections and sympathies are with the lasses, and we do not care one fig for the Committee; nor should we be greatly concerned, though the colonists were considerably put about for female servants; but we are well aware, that, though young females of the description wanted are far from being the worst situated persons in our crowded society, there are thousands and tens of thousands of destitute, friendless, and distressed maidens, who would gladly embrace the offer of being safely conveyed to a better market for their industry, and for their domestic qualities, if they were acquainted with its advantages, and the mode of proceeding. Having said that we would advise no young woman to emigrate who has connections, or who can do even tolerably well at home, and warned every one, we shall now briefly tell what all may expect, and how they should proceed.

The class most wanted are girls bred in farm-houses, or house-maids, and maids-of-all-work. The Government defrays the expense of their passage out, upon the advance of £5; or a girl that is approved by the Committee, though without money, is taken out, on giving her note of hand for £6, to be paid out of her earnings in the colony, within a reasonable time. The emigrant ships generally sail from London. A surgeon, with a superintendent and his wife, accompany the females, to watch over their health, and maintain order. They are furnished with bedding, and are taken care of on their landing at Hobart Town or Sydney; they are then shown a list of situations, with the wages offered, and left, we are assured by the Committee in London, consisting of many respectable individuals, *perfectly free* to act and decide *for themselves*. There are marriages very suddenly struck up at such times, we understand, but we would have our prudent Scotch damsels think of nothing but service till they have time to look about them.

A girl who has made up her mind to emigrate, either from the desire to better herself by her own industry, or because she has friends before her in the colony, or friends about to go out, must apply, by letter, to Mr. Marshall, agent to the Committee, 26, Birchin Lane, Cornhill, London, under cover to the 'Under Secretary of State, Colonial Department, London;' and in her letter she must enclose a certificate of her character from a resident clergyman in her parish, or some other respectable person to whom she is known. The possession of the £5 will be, of course, a considerable recommendation. The voyage lasts from four to five months; and in order to accomplish it with health and comfort, the Committee require each female to be provided with a bonnet, two dark caps, two dark gowns, one pair of stays, two flannel petticoats, six pair dark hose, one pair of good shoes, eighteen shifts, six coarse towels, one cloak, six pocket handkerchiefs, four dark aprons, six night-gowns, twelve night-caps, one strong bag, two combs; soap; one small knife and fork; one table and one tea spoon; one pewter or tin plate; one pint tin pot; one half-pint tin panakin; one work bag, with appurtenances. We would add, a New Testament. Of these articles as many must be put into a small bag as will serve for four weeks use, as the boxes containing their clothes will, at intervals of four weeks, be brought on deck during the voyage, when each female *must* exchange the clothes she has used for clean ones.

For this necessary outfit credit will also be given to the woman to the extent of thirty shillings, to be afterwards paid back from her wages; and the more clothes of a useful kind the emigrant female can take with her the better it is when she reaches the colony—but the above are indispensable. However large her stock of clothing, it will be taken free of cost. We must observe that the emigrant vessels are, from economy, sufficiently crowded—but the voyages have hitherto been short and fortunate.

WILLIAM RATHBONE GREG ⎯⎯⎯⎯⎯⎯⎯⎯

W. R. Greg (1809–81), essayist and economist, industrialist and social critic, made prolific contributions to the major journals of his day, including the Contemporary, Edinburgh, Fortnight-ly, National, North British *and* Westminster Reviews. *[WI]*

This extract is from what was ostensibly a review of L'Ouvrière *by Jules Simon and* My Life, and what shall I do with it? *By an Old Maid. Greg based his statistics for the most part on the population census of 1851.*

⎯⎯⎯⎯⎯⎯⎯⎯⎯⎯⎯⎯⎯⎯⎯ *from* 'Why are Women Redundant?', **National Review**, vol. 14, 1862, pp. 434–60.

… The problem, … appears to resolve itself into this: that there is an enormous and increasing number of single women in the nation, a number quite dispropor-tionate and quite abnormal; a number which, positively and relatively, is indica-tive of an unwholesome social state, …

… We must redress the balance. We must restore by an emigration of women that natural proportion between the sexes in the old country and in the new ones, which was disturbed by an emigration of men, and the disturbance of which has wrought so much mischief in both lands. … of the 440,000 women who should emigrate, the larger number are wanted for the longer voyage to Australia. …

FRANCES POWER COBBE _____

Frances Cobbe (1822–1904) was born in England, rejected evangelical religion and left home after her father's death. She travelled to Europe and the East. Philanthropic work in England led to an interest in women's rights and suffrage, and she worked as an advocate for married women's property rights. She published Criminals, Idiots, Women and Minors *in 1868, and earned a living through journalism, writing for the* Contemporary, Fortnightly, Modern *and* Theological *reviews among others. [BWW; WI]*

This extract is from a response to W. R. Greg's 'Why are Women Redundant?'.

_____ *from* 'What Shall we do with our Old Maids?', *Fraser's Magazine*, vol. 66, 1862, pp. 594–610.

… It appears that there is a natural excess of four or five per cent. of females over the males in our population. This, then, might be assumed to be the limits within which female celibacy was normal and inevitable.

There is, however, an actual ratio of thirty per cent. of women now in England who never marry, leaving one-fourth of both sexes in a state of celibacy.

… we cannot but add a few words to express our amused surprise at the way in which the writers on this subject constantly concern themselves with the question of *female* celibacy, deplore it, abuse it, propose amazing remedies for it, but take little or no notice of the twenty-five per cent. Old bachelors (or thereabouts) who needs must exist to match the thirty per cent. … All the alarm, compassion, reprobation, and scoldings are reserved for the poor old maids. …

… Whatever other offences our young ladies may be guilty of, or other weaknesses our young gentlemen, obduracy on the one hand, and dying for love on the other, are rarities, at all events. Yet one would suppose that Zoroaster was needed over here, to judge of the manner in which old maids are lectured on their very improper position. 'The Repression of Crime,' as the benevolent Recorder of Birmingham would phrase it, seems on the point of being exercised against them, since it has been found out that their offence is on the increase, like poaching in country districts and landlord shooting in Ireland. The mildest punishment, we are told, is to be transportation, to which half a million have just been condemned, and for the terror of future evil doers, it is decreed that no single woman's work ought to be fairly remunerated, nor her position allowed to be entirely respectable, lest she exercise 'a cold philosophic choice' about matrimony. No false charity to criminals! Transportation or starvation to all old maids!

… The woman who arrives in a colony where her labour, of head or hands, can command an ample maintenance, stands in the precise condition we have desired to make marriage—a matter of free choice. She has left 'Hobson's choice' behind her with the poverty of England, and has come out to find competence and freedom, and if she choose (but *only* if she choose), marriage also.

It is needless to say that this scheme has our entire sympathy and good wishes, though we do not expect to live to see the time when our reviewer's plans will be fulfilled by the deportation of women at the rate of thirty or forty thousand a year. …

An important point, however, must not be overlooked. However far the emigration of women of the working classes may be carried, that of educated women must at all times remain very limited, inasmuch as the demand for them in the colonies is comparatively trifling. … The reviewer to whom we have so often alluded, does indeed dispose of the matter by observing that the transportation he fondly hopes to see effected, of 440,000 women to the colonies, will at least *relieve the market* for those who remain. We cannot but fear, however, that the governesses and other ladies so accommodated will not much profit by the large selection thus afforded them among the blacksmiths and ploughmen, deprived of their proper companions. …

ANON.

Alfred Ernest Albert, Duke of Saxe-Coburg and Gotha and Duke of Edinburgh (1844–1900), entered the navy in 1856 and was made Captain in 1866. He commanded the Galatea *on a voyage around the world, landing at Glenelg, South Australia, on 31 October 1867. The first English prince to visit Australia, he spent five months visiting Adelaide, Melbourne, Sydney, Brisbane and Van Diemen's Land. In Sydney he was shot in the back by an Irishman, O'Farrell, recovered within a month, and was back in England in June 1868.*

'Britannia To Australia', *Punch*, vol. 54, 1868, p. 44.

[Accompanies 'Our Australian Cousin' by John Tenniel.]

My dear daughter,

You have come out. You have been presented to my sailor Prince. You have pleased your old mother vastly by your splendid celebration of this one of the greatest events in your life, and she is eager to offer you her thanks and congratulations.

I hear you are a fine, handsome lass, with a bush of golden hair, blooming and buxom, who have not yet done growing—figure rather fuller than mine, but features much the same. I hope the family likeness will be preserved through

OUR AUSTRALIAN COUSIN.

PRINCE ALFRED. ' WELL, MISS AUSTRALIA, I KNEW YOU WERE A *GREAT* GIRL,
BUT I'D NO IDEA YOU WERE SO BEAUTIFUL.'

John Tenniel, *Punch, or the London Charivari*, vol. 54, 1868, p. 39.

John Tenniel (1820–1914), London-born illustrator and cartoonist, replaced Richard
Doyle at *Punch* in 1851. He became principal cartoonist on the departure of John Leech
in 1861, and produced over two thousand drawings for the magazine. He was also the
noted illustrator of Lewis Carroll's *Alice's Adventures in Wonderland* (1865) and *Through
the Looking Glass* (1871). [LCVF]

many centuries and cycles to come, and that when you are as old as I am you may
look as well as I do, and have as few wrinkles and furrows, as after all my years
and trials, my time-beaten visage shows.

So young, too! only four-score! for Sydney will keep her eightieth birthday this
very year. I am conscious that when I was your age I was not able to give balls
and banquets, or dazzle with transparencies and illuminations (piping times

for your gas-fitters), or breed Mayors and Corporations, or erect Exhibition buildings as big as your old friend Westminster Hall. I am afraid I was subsisting on acorns and berries, and painting myself a warm blue, and going and coming nude as your own aborigines. So spread, so developed at 80, what will you not be at 800? You are the superb young beauty, the rose on your cheek, the brilliant in your eye, full of life and expectation, with many squires to hold up your train of cloth of gold, and a long and triumphant career before you. I am the mature matron, with a silver thread here and there in my glossy hair, and a line or two on my ample brow, but handsome and stately still, proud of my bonny daughter, proud to be told that she resembles her mother, wondering whether she will make the great conquests I have made, or stand amidst the affluence of possessions that I can command, and wishing her with heart and voice all the happiness that I have known, without a tithe of my suffering, or a tenth of my sorrow.

My Daughter, do not listen to those who will tell you that I have seen my best days, and that there is no prospect for me but decrepitude and decay. I mean to be the Methuselah of nations, the evergreen of kingdoms. I have no intention, at present, of dismantling London Bridge, or converting St. Paul's into a picturesque ruin. I mean to live to see your future prosperity as far exceed your present, as your present does that forlorn time of COOK and BANKS from which our own is separated by such a scanty handful of years. You, in your turn, will have to colonise and emigrate, and you will bless me with lusty and vigorous grandchildren. Your stride will lengthen, your pace will quicken; but don't make the running too soon, don't go too fast.

You resemble your mother in many things. Like her you have your Ministers, your Parliaments, your Speakers; your Rechabites, your Druids, your Odd Fellows. You would not be a woman if you had not your Opposition; you would not be my child if you were without your jobs and blunders. I doubt not that you have your Usher of the Black Rod, your Beadles and your Waits. I am sorry that you have no Lord Mayor, but I hope, as some compensation, that you are not Vestry-ridden. I notice that you have what I cannot afford, your 'Free Gardeners,' and 'Free Banquet.' Send me the Gardeners' address, and some dinner tickets, will you? and a case or two of your beef (without bone) would not come amiss. Are your Metropolitan streets as dirty as mine? In the bustling thoroughfares of Melbourne, or Sydney, or any other of your several capitals, do you take a human life nearly every other day in the year, as indifference and stupidity do in London? Are you old enough to have vested interests and a National Debt?

In some points I cannot compete with you. I possess no marsupial creatures for an active young Duke to stalk down (partridges at Sandringham, and pheasants at Osborne, will be tame sport after elephants at the Cape, and kangaroos in the Bush); I cannot emulate your emus, except, perhaps, in the enclosures of the Zoological Gardens; the Ornithorhyncus is not one of my domestic animals;

there are no auriferous diggings in Regent Street, and at present I have not heard of nuggets being picked up in the Strand by zealous agents of the Goldsmiths' Company; my sheep-walks and cattle-drives are mere toys and playthings compared with yours; you enjoyed a Session of Parliament lasting exactly three-quarters of an hour; 'and not a single person was put into the lock-up that night for misbehaviour.' Bravo, Melbourne! and not a teetotal population either. Hull, and Newcastle, and Nottingham, and other towns of mine of about the same size as Melbourne, mark, learn, and copy. But, my Daughter, we have one necessary of life in common; there is one great banner of which we both hold a pole, and the blazon that sparkles upon it is *Punch!*

I wish your geography was rather simpler. My young men, whose education has been carefully neglected—wealthy foundation schools, wealthy Universities, and so forth—complain that they are perplexed by Victoria, and New South Wales, and Queensland (is not *all* Australia Queensland?), and South Australia, and Western Australia, and Van Diemen's Land, *alias* (convict-like—I congratulate you on being free from that settlement on you) Tasmania, and New Guinea, always staunch to the Old Sovereign; and they would be relieved if you could fix on some one city as your capital, and cease to divide your favour between Melbourne, and Sydney, and Adelaide, and Ballarat, and Brisbane, and Perth, and Hobart Town, whose respective geographical positions they find great difficulty in accurately discriminating.

Send me home my young Salt of a Duke, my 'Queen piccaninny,' when he has had enough of boomerangs and waddies, whoops and coroborees, unless you determine to place him on a throne of your own virgin gold, as Australia's first king, to be, perhaps, the second ALFRED THE GREAT. I don't advise him to exchange his epaulets for a crown.

I must not keep the mail longer waiting. Only a word about those rumours from time to time blown to us over the sea, that when you are a little older you mean to leave me, and set up for yourself in life. I have no wish to part company, I should like to keep you and all the rest of my children by my side all my days. But if there should come to you that aspiration for freedom which dignifies all noble youth, though there may, though there must be sorrow at my heart, there will be no feeling of displeasure at your independence, no thought of resistance to your wishes. *Floreat Australia!*

Your affectionate Mother-Country,

BRITANNIA

P.S. (Woman-like.) I have addressed you by your usual name, but properly, you know, you ought to be styled Australasia. So let it be *Floreat Australasia!* Have you any pet name? What say you to Kangarooia?

LOUISA LAWSON

Louisa Lawson (1848–1920), Australian-born journalist, started a journal, the Dawn *(1888–1905),
to campaign for women's rights. As editor, she wrote most of each issue for its seventeen-year run. The*
Dawn *offered household advice, fashion, poetry, a short story, and reported women's activities both
local and overseas. In 1889 Lawson began a campaign for female suffrage, and the* Dawn *helped to
mobilise support.* [ADB]

This article was first published in the Woman's Journal, *Boston, in July 1889.*

'The Australian Bush-woman', *The
Englishwoman's Review of Social and
Industrial Questions*, **15 August,
15 October 1889, pp. 383–4, 469–74.**

The Government statistician estimated that at the end of 1887 there were in the
colony of New South Wales about 471,000 women and girls, so that I suppose
there were at that time, in various stages of growth, about 471,000 different
kinds of woman. This is rather too large an assortment to be separately described
in the *Woman's Journal*, unless you will place me on the staff as a life contributor.
This suggestion can be considered at leisure. Meanwhile, for hasty purposes, my
colonial sisters may be roughly sorted into three heaps—city women, country
women, and bush-women, and it is of the last I will write; for it is of their grim,
lonely, patient lives I know, their honest, hard-worked, silent, almost masculine
lives. My experience lies chiefly among the women of New South Wales, but I
think in the main, and as far as generalisations can describe a large number of
units, my description will apply to the bush-women of all Australia.

The city women in Australia are for the most part like all other English-speaking women. Their civilisation is pretty nearly up to date, and the tragi-comedy of
their lives is of a type common to all the cities of the world. The country women
have also no features which are unique. As everywhere, they drag behind the
town in fashions, they imitate the town in a leisurely, bucolic way; they are a little
healthier, a little less clever, and a little less artificial. But the bush-women are a
race apart. No 'foreigner' can seem so strange to them as a city woman does. A
bush-woman in town is as lonely, as helpless, as homesick, as an Esquimaux
landed at Honolulu. What does she know of domestic comforts? She desires
none. There is nothing for her to do. She cannot keep house: she who comes
perhaps from rounding up lost cattle or ring-barking trees. She is independent,
taciturn, and the regularities and measured methods of town life appal her. If the
cattle were lost, she would be all day long in the saddle, working as well as any
of the men, and she would do what little had to be done in the house on her
return—whenever that might chance to be. It would not anyhow be much more

than the making of a 'damper' in a tin dish and putting it in the ashes. She is not one to be easily moulded to the hours and times of city customs. For by bush-women I mean not the wives of settlers in accessible country, near a railroad or town, but the wives of boundary-riders, shepherds, 'cockatoo' settlers in the far 'back country;' women who share almost on equal terms with men the rough life and the isolation which belong to civilisation's utmost fringe.

Progress begins at the seaports, and it is a long while before the ripples reach the bush-woman. It is less than five years since I saw one start out to tend sheep, taking among her few necessaries a flint and steel. Half a century of advance lies between her and her daughters, educated at the public schools; but the bush-woman herself, Australian-born, and the daughter or granddaughter of a pioneer, retains her characteristics in spite of the march of the times.

The bush-woman is thin, wiry, flat-chested and sunburned. She could be nothing else, living as she does. She lives on meat; sometimes she does not even eat bread with it. She rarely sees vegetables, and no costly bouquet of orchids could so surprise and delight a city dame as a cabbage would gratify and amaze a bush-woman. She is healthy and full of vigour, but it is a leathery, withered, sun-dried health. You would call her a poor starveling in appearance, if you contrasted her with one of the fair, fresh-looking, plump city women whom two miles' walking would utterly exhaust. If the energy of the bush-women could only be put to some profitable use, they might be millionaires; but they live in perpetual feud with the sun. They try to keep bees, but the heat starves them out. If they have cattle, the drought or the pleuro kills them. When they do get a wet season, the flood rots all they have in the ground. Two-thirds of their labour is wasted. They are lank, yet wiry, sun-cured while alive, but able to do, and almost always doing, the work of a strong man. In the city, a wet day is accursed; it makes people melancholy; every one abhors dulness and damp; but the bush-woman's ideal home is a place where it is dark and wet, some damp, lush, grassy hollow. Let her be ever so miserable, ever so ill-fed and hard-worked, her life becomes full of bliss when she hears the rain pattering on the roof. There is no sorrow that a good shower will not wash away.

Though she is not egotistical, she has no patience with the ways of city folk. She is disgusted at their fastidiousness. They want soft, comfortable beds; but she can sleep anyhow. Often, in the self-abnegation which is natural to her, the supreme recognition of the claims of hospitality, which is only with her a habit and ingrained custom, she relinquishes her bed to a stranger and sleeps on the floor. As to food, the heel of a 'damper' and the fag-end of a piece of beef will do for her. She is utterly self-neglectful. The white plump women of the city seem soft to her. They cannot walk a mile without fatigue, while she will tramp five miles with a heavy child on her hip, do a day's washing, and tramp back again at night. She works harder than a man. You may see her with her sons putting up a fence, or with the shearers, whistling and working as well as any. She has a fine, hard patient character; she is not emotional, nor very susceptive, but she has no conception of the little jealousies, the spite and petty meannesses of city women. Her generosity to any sort of stranger is natural, for society of any kind is at a premium. The monotony of the ever-green (or rather ever-brown) Australian bush, and its years of unbroken drought, tend to make time seem as if it had no changes and no periods. To hear of a life she does not know, to get news and speech of outside things from even the most worthless stranger, is payment enough for all the shelter, food, and assistance that she offers. It is such an incursion of novelty into her dreary domain of changeless months, that it is a pleasure and a relief no town-bred woman can understand.

Of her own life she never speaks. To her oldest friends she does not talk of her hardships, though her life may be nothing but a record of ill-usage. She may be an isolated woman prey, alone in the wilds with a brutal husband, yet she does not complain; she suffers silently. She thinks her lot peculiar to herself. Resource she has none, nor escape, nor redress. She is tough and patient, and works till she dies without murmuring. Reform can never come through her, for should one speak to her of anything touching her own life or fate nearly, she would look at her askance, and shrink from her. People who think must be 'cranks,' for he who lives in the bush and thinks, goes mad. She may have ideas, but she never exchanges them. She is a slave, bound hand and foot to her daily life. If an educated man—and there are such, with strange histories behind them—goes into the bush and becomes shepherd, hut-keeper, or the like solitary exile, his mind recoils on him. In the solitude he becomes at the least a 'crank,' and there is no more respect for him. So with a bush-woman; she does not speak of what she has discovered or thought out, she does not go beyond her daily life, because they would say 'She hasn't got all her buttons,' she is a 'crank.' Nevertheless she is not mindless; she loves poetry and pictures, and what newspapers come in her way she reads carefully. She often knows more of letters than her sisters of the city, for what she reads she reads earnestly and remembers. She cuts out the articles which she values and preserves them. You would not suspect they lay among her treasures, for she says nothing. Her thoughts and actions are all alike uncommunicated and self-contained.

She has no pleasure nor comforts. When she is sick, she leaves it to nature, or treats it with one of the three remedies she recognises as a complete and sufficient pharmacopœia—salts and senna, castor-oil and Holloway's pills. She would laugh at a medicine-chest; she could not be bothered with it. Many of these women even endure a confinement almost without aid. Some will mount a horse and ride for the nurse themselves. In one case the husband, with the customary indifferent, indolent, non-interfering habit, left his wife to ride alone to the midwife. She became ill on the way, and was never seen alive again. The native dogs watched her agonies and ended them.

There is one thing the bush-woman hates—it is discipline. The word sounds to her like 'jail.' System, regularity, method, her life has nothing to do with. The domestic affairs of town women, which are ordered with the precision of an almanac, are an abhorred mystery to her. You could not put her to worse torture than by setting her to dust the drawing-room every morning at a fixed hour. Her home among the eucalyptus bush or on the 'ironbark' ridge is guiltless of drapes and mantel boards and ornaments; her domestic duties are merely the simplest of cooking; her life is out-of-doors in the broiling sun and the dry wind. She can handle a stock-whip better than a duster, she can swear mildly when the cattle are very refractory and the dogs utterly unmanageable, and she would far rather break in a horse than flutter around pictures with a feather broom.

There is also one thing in which she becomes particularly expert, the weather signs. The one hope of her life is for rain. She is always on the watch to wrest from nature the earliest news, and she can tell you whether the showers will come or the drought continue. She hates the cry of the 'hard times bird' who shrieks in the dry, dewless nights and parching days of drought seasons; she watches the colour of the sky, the clouds, the sun as he rises and sets; she hearkens to the frogs, and can tell from the colour which the atmosphere gives to distant objects whether the drought will break and the cattle live.

The bush-woman's husband, if he be also Australian born, is like herself, spare and wiry. He is inured to wind and weather, cold and heat, and what is better, he can *fast* well. He is not, as a rule, dissipated, nor is he brutal to her. He has a tendency to leave her to manage the business, and he is rather indolent and neglectful. He will sit with others talking, while she, a thin rag of a woman, drags two big buckets of water from the creek, for instance, and if he stands by while she chops the wood, he sees no unfitness in the arrangement. They are a comparatively cold and impassive pair, inured to weather and hardships and rough living. They are never jealous of one another, and rarely unfaithful, so that the bush-woman, if married to an Australian, has generally a smooth life enough. She is fortunate in such a marriage, for the native is innately mild and not ill-natured, even in a life which seems to intensify in other men all the brutality they possess. To generalise roughly, one must say that the bush-woman's life is, however, on the average, a sad one. The Englishmen, Germans, Scandinavians, and, indeed, all the men of whatever nationality who took to bush life, were generally of rough, coarse character, or, if they were not of such nature originally, the solitude and the strange, primitive life must have made them so. In those remote and isolated spots, man is king and force is ruler. There is no law, no public opinion to interfere. The wife is at the man's mercy. She must bear what ills he chooses to put upon her, and her helplessness in his hands only seems to educe the beast in him. There is a vast deal of the vilest treatment. Some are worked to death and some are bullied to death; but the women are so scattered and so reticent that the world hears nothing of it all. In town, the fear of the law operates insensibly; we know that a woman can, if she needs, reach a police-station in five minutes, and charge her husband with an assault; but out in that loneliness of mountain and plain, where is the redress, where the protection? She cannot ride a hundred miles in search of a magistrate; she cannot leave the hut and the sheep and the cattle to look after themselves in her absence; the law is not accessible, even if she would use it; if she writes a letter, it may lie a fortnight before the chance comes of sending it on. Besides, she is not the kind of woman to run to the law. She keeps her sorrows to herself, and endures everything. I have known a woman to be up in a tree for three days, while her husband was hunting for her to 'hammer' her. It is horrible to think such things are possible, yet worse things happen daily. Time and our efforts may help to mend the world.

A bright and promising story follows the saddest part of this narrative of the bushwoman's life. The best qualities of her live in her girls, and they will make their mark on a fairer page of Australian history. I have heard it urged against them that they are very shy. It is a true bill. They are as shy as the kangaroos and emus, their wild fellow-lodgers in the bush. You may catch sight of two girls astride a horse. They see you and are gone in a flash. They have no curiosity about strangers. I remember a man telling me that he had often caught a brief glimpse of a girl about a certain district, and that some day he meant to get a horse and run her down. In the old days the children used to get a little schooling in the evenings from some shepherd who could boast of education; but now wherever a dozen children can be got together, there is a school. Many of them walk or ride very long distances, but they get there; for the bush-woman is anxious for her children to get on, and is proud of their successes. Anything is good enough for her, she thinks, and if any comfort or advantage comes with growing civilisation, it falls to the children's share. The girls are of very quick intelligence; they learn everything rapidly, and surpass the boys. Where they have a chance they make clever women, and a great number become school-teachers, but in those who get no schooling this astuteness turns to slyness and cunning. Take them all round, they are fine girls, always ready in an emergency, and capable of anything. Tough, healthy, and alert, they can cook or sew, do fancy-work or farm-work, dance, ride, tend cattle, keep a garden, break in a colt. They are the stuff that a fine race is made of—these daughters of bushwomen. The men are more idle, and besides they have always the drink washing away their prospects; therefore we look to the girls for the future.

So as the bush-women, one by one, end their sad, lonely, hard-worked lives, these girls, quick, capable and active, will be ready to step into their places, and the iron strength of character, the patience, endurance and self-repression which the bush-women practised and developed, passing to a generation more enlightened and progressive, will give us a race of splendid women, fit to obtain what their mothers never dreamed of—women's rights.

MARY SPENCER

No biographical information has been found.
This extract is from the first in a two-part series. Part II, pp. 225–8.

from 'Woman's Life in Australia. I',
Young Woman, vol. 5, 1897,
pp. 174–7.

Not long since a well-known woman's journal gave in answer to a correspondent some extraordinary statements concerning Australian life. The inquirer was evidently coming out to begin housekeeping in Victoria, and was seeking information as to her new home. She was told that she must be prepared to perform all household duties herself, as in the interior of the colony only black servants were to be obtained. Also that the best material to make her dresses of would be grey woollen or something that would not show the dirt, for the dust in Victoria was very trying to either dark or light clothing. The unfortunate lady was also told that she must do her weekly washing by night, as the heat was too great to work hard during the day, and besides, the night air in the Southern Hemisphere had a wonderfully purifying effect.

These statements were evidently written in all good faith, and no doubt were implicitly believed. One can imagine the unfortunate English girl arriving in Melbourne on a scorching summer day with only a collection of dingy grey woollens—a sort of natural wool trousseau. How she would vow vengeance on the well-meaning deceiver in the English newspaper office, as she panted down Collins Street, noting with envy the cool and pretty linen dresses of the Melbourne girls! No doubt before she reached Australia she would find that the other statements were only the wanderings of an inventive imagination.

Perhaps it would interest English readers to put before them some idea of the life led by their Australian sisters. Home-life has by many critics been reckoned as playing a small part in the existence of the Australian. The climate, the opportunities for sport, the national character, have all in turn been blamed as the cause. No doubt this accusation must be in some degree true, but I think it applies chiefly to the lives of men and not of women, so that we need not discuss the point here. Women in Australia as elsewhere are proud of their homes, and do not as yet show any signs of abdicating the house for the election booth or the football field. The life of the home in the Colonies is very varied in its demands and opportunities, that of the station or the farm differing essentially from that of the city or township. Housekeeping in any Australian town would present no great difficulties to any woman newly arrived from the old country. Houses are comfortably built, and are supplied with gas and water. We may safely say that wherever there is a population of over a thousand there are no great discomforts to be dreaded, except in the exceptional cases of mushroom mining towns, which spring up in a few months, and where life must necessarily be of the roughest description. …

All the Colonies have plenty of good openings for reliable servants. Well-trained girls from the old country may be certain of obtaining good situations if they have the courage to emigrate. Lady helps are also in demand, but they must not expect wages. The only difference between a lady help and a servant is that the former has her meals with the family, and has rather less time to herself than the well-paid servant. It seems to me that any self-respecting girl would rather be independent as a servant in a good house than the nondescript article known as a lady help or mother's help—equivalent to a nursemaid, only without the nurse-maid's pay. In the Colonies servants are treated well, and trusted more than in English homes. A Colonial girl would feel insulted if the ordinary household stores were kept under lock and key, and certainly the result of this trust seems to be that one seldom hears of dishonest servants.

One consequence of the scarcity of domestic servants is that Australian girls accustom themselves to all sorts of household duties. Even in houses where several servants are kept, the girls take a pleasure in arranging the rooms and flowers, and in trying their hands at cookery of the more elaborate sort. In the country it is essential that a woman should know how to cook, not in theory, but in practice. Many women attend advanced cookery classes, and possess books full of recipes for purées and galantines, but if they were called upon to step into the kitchen and cook a plain dinner of meat and vegetables, how few would come through the ordeal successfully. …

In Australia we need to learn lessons in the art of house decoration. The furnishing of most drawing-rooms is truly hideous. Plush and tapestry and bright Brussels carpets are considered the height of grandeur, and walls are still strewn with cheap fans, gilt horseshoes on plush mounts, and glaring oleographs. The most remarkable room I ever came across was in a farmhouse on the Murray. The only wall decorations were three oleographs of the Queen, all exactly alike. …

But Australians are gradually learning more wisdom in the matter of furnishing, and are adapting their household arrangements to the hot climate. The Brussels carpet, the plush-covered suite, the heavy moreen curtains, are becoming things of the past, and in their place we have Indian mattings, light cane furniture, and dainty muslin curtains. ... Bathrooms are to be found even in the humblest cottages. In towns they are comfortably appointed, but in the bush some queer contrivances are met with. A favourite place for the bathroom on stations is at the foot of a tree near a tank, perhaps a hundred yards or so from the house. The shower-bath is hung to the branch of a tree, and round the shower is a covering of canvas reaching to the ground. For a woman, a visit to such a bath is fraught with many small excitements. First of all, to get there you must run the gauntlet of curious eyes, then when inside you must undress, place your clothes outside, and take your bath, all the time holding together the canvas which flaps wildly in the wind. One becomes inured in time to all such things, and as long as there is a bath one does not care where or how it is placed. ...

Men

ANON.

from 'Young Women in the Colonies',
Eliza Cook's Journal, vol. 6, 1851–52,
pp. 241–3.

Emigration heretofore has been too one-sided. It has been held up as a means by which young *men* might better themselves in the world, and lay the foundations of good fortune. And, generally speaking, emigration has greatly improved their circumstances, and made life comparatively easy, comfortable, and prosperous, for them. In a good colony, a young man gets out of the sphere of intense competition, and enters upon a new and untilled field, where ability and industry have full and free play. There the steadiest worker invariably succeeds the best. The young man labours in constant hope, for he knows that his reward is sure. He not only lives well, but accumulates property for his children, whom he leaves behind him without any fear or anxiety as to their future, so far as worldly means are concerned.

It is indeed a subject of complaint with many prosperous emigrants, that they have no wives or families to whom to leave their worldly goods. After all, life without woman is 'stale, barren, and unprofitable.' Do as he will, man's happiness is, to a very large extent, dependent upon woman's presence,—in the Australian bush, as in the crowded cities of the old world. That most cherished part of a man's life,—which centres in *home*,—can scarcely have an existence but for her. The poet, addressing woman, says—'We had been brutes without you;' and 'tis true. Where she is not, a gross low life of the senses is apt to set itself up. Woman softens man's nature and sweetens the breath of his home. He is thus humanized and civilized. And then comes responsibility, with fatherly joys and cares, attendant upon the introduction of first one, and then another, little being into the family circle. ...

... In New South Wales, at the last census, there were 118,927 men, and only 77,777 women. It is obvious that serious evils must arise out of such a disparity in the numbers of the sexes, which need not be specified here. We have somewhere seen it stated, that in some districts, the number of women was so small, that when it became known that a new woman was coming into the district, men would come from distant stations to see her pass along the road! Whether this be a joke or not, certain it is that in the more remote districts the want of female help is greatly felt. Men act as hutkeepers, dairymen, and household servants; thus, homes in the bush are often no homes; they want the cheering voice and the tidy help of women to make them cozy, clean, and comfortable, as homes should be. But where women are so scarce a commodity, they often cannot be had either as servants, or, what is still more wanted, as wives; and thus the colonial well-being seriously suffers.

Fancy a colony of men only! What a pandemonium it would be! It must not only live miserably, but die without issue. It could not exist but for a generation, and then expire, unless kept up by new draughts of men from the old country. ...

CHARLES KINGSLEY

Charles Kingsley (1819–75), Devonshire-born clergyman and author, demonstrated his Christian socialism in early novels like Alton Locke (1850). He probably coined the term 'muscular Christianity' often invoked by writers encouraging lower middle-class and working-class people to emigrate. He also published historical works, and developed an active interest in marine biology in the early 1850s. [LCVF]

This extract is from a review of six books on seaside studies.

from 'The Wonders of the Shore',
North British Review, vol. 22, 1854,
pp. 1–56.

... A frightful majority of our middle class young men are growing up effeminate, empty of all knowledge but what tends directly to the making of a fortune; or rather, to speak correctly, to the keeping up the fortunes which their fathers made for them; while of the minority, who are indeed thinking and reading men, how many women as well as men have we seen wearying their souls with study undirected, often misdirected study; craving to learn, yet not knowing how or what to learn; cultivating, with unwholesome energy, the head at the expense of body and of heart, catching up with the most capricious self-will one mania after another, and tossing it away again for some new phantom; gorging the memory with facts which no one has taught them to arrange, and the reason with problems which they have no method for solving, till they fret themselves into a chronic fever of the brain, which too often urges them on to plunge, as it were to cool the inward fire, into the ever restless sea of doubt and disbelief. It is a sad picture. There are many who may read these pages whose hearts will tell them that it is a true one. What is wanted in these cases is a methodic and scientific habit of mind; and a class of objects on which to exercise that habit, which will fever neither the speculative intellect nor the moral sense; and that physical science will give, as nothing else can give it.

Moreover, to revert to another point which we touched just now, man has a body as well as a mind, and with the vast majority there will be no *mens sana* unless there be a *corpus sanum* for it to inhabit. And what outdoor training to give our youths, is, as we have already said, more than ever puzzling. This difficulty is felt, perhaps, less in Scotland than in England. The Scotch climate compels hardiness; the Scotch bodily strength makes it easy; and Scotland, with her mountain-tours in summer, and her frozen lochs in winter, her labyrinth of seashore, and, above all, that priceless boon which Providence has bestowed on her, in the contiguity of her great cities to the loveliest scenery, and hills where every breeze is health, affords facilities for healthy physical life unknown to the Englishman, who has no Arthur's Seat towering above his London, no Western Islands spotting the ocean firths beside his Manchester. ...

... athletic exercises are now, in England at least, so artificialized, so expensive, so mixed up with drinking, gambling, and other evils of which we need say nothing here, that one cannot wonder at any parents' shrinking from allowing their sons to meddle much with them. And yet the young man who has had no substitute for such amusements, will cut but a sorry figure in Australia, Canada, or India, and if he stays at home, spend many a pound in doctors' bills, which could have been better employed elsewhere.

WILLIAM JARDINE SMITH

See biographical note on p. 107.

from "'Wanted—A Career!"
A Colonist's Advice to Certain British Fathers', *St. Pauls Magazine*, vol. 11, 1872, pp. 738–48.

... Let the British father of the middle-middle class, who sees a family of stalwart sons growing up around him, take heart of grace. Every year the avenues to advancement in the old country become more and more crowded, until a dead-lock appears inevitable; but if in imagination he will ascend a sort of domestic

Pisgah, he may look out across the waste of waters and see the lands afar off, which flow with milk and honey. There lies a career for his children, and thousands more,—a field of operations where their energies may find free scope, and where certain success is the reward of virtue and industry. When I think of the numberless young men who plod on from year's end to year's end in over-populated England, with but little hope to buoy them up, I can but think how much happier had been their lot if the advantages the colonies held out had been better appreciated. At home a man walks in swaddling clothes; he is hedged round on every side by the rules of social etiquette: for the class I am speaking of, to work with its hands, is to lose caste. Indeed, it might almost as well commit crime as descend to manual labour.

In Australia, however, it is otherwise. Away from the large towns a man may do what he pleases in connection with any pursuit which is likely to attract those who have been brought up as gentlemen. Those who take to farming or grazing may go through a lot of hard manual toil of a description undreamt of in Mayfair, or many other less pretentious localities. But they are not the less welcome in the drawing-room in consequence, nor less fitted to shine there. Any educational advantages they may possess are not eclipsed by the roughness of their surround-ings, but rather shine forth with greater brilliancy. Those who lead a bush life, as it is called, enjoy a sense of freedom, and exhilarating feeling of independence which is unknown to those who are chained to a desk and drilled into machines. They can 'rejoice in their youth.' Perhaps they have to push out into the wilder-ness, as others have done before them; but the dangers and difficulties they may meet with, will surely have the effect of developing the better parts of their natures, and of 'making men of them.' With gradual but ever-advancing flow, the great wave of civilisation will roll on and surround them, while villages will spring up and homesteads arise, where lately stood the black fellow's 'mia-mia.' The few hundreds, which was all that the parental purse could afford, and which would have gone no way in England, have probably developed into an independ-ence by the time middle life is reached. Although, perhaps, it is in connection with land that the great advantages offered by the colonies are most conspicuous, we may safely affirm that in every way a living is much more easily and surely made than in England, and the chances of arriving at an independence are fifty times as great. If a parent is satisfied of the moral and physical soundness of his sons, if he knows them to be as sensible, brave, persevering, industrious, sober, upright and honest as a good example and careful training can make them; if he feels assured that he has furnished them with that sort of education which is calculated to fit them to meet emergencies and make the best of whatever circumstances they may be placed in, then I say that he could not do them a greater kindness than to send them to some country where such qualities meet with their highest earthly reward. It may be said that 'young men so furnished would make their way anywhere,' which is true, but not only would they progress more quickly in the colonies, but their absence would afford a better chance to those who are forced to remain at home. Thus emigration blesses those who leave and those who stay. But the frivolous and the idle, the empty-headed fop and the premature *roué*, the shiftless, purposeless, hesitating noodle, and the feeble creature that cannot say 'No,' had better stop at home. Transplanted to an uncongenial soil they run to seed and perish with marvellous rapidity, under circumstances more or less disgraceful both to themselves and those who get rid of them, without a care for their ultimate fate. I have known young men in Victoria hurried along by the devil which possessed them to an early grave, whose death must lie heavy on the souls of those who first neglected and then abandoned them. Emigration is not a good thing for such as these; but so surely as they fail, so surely do their opposites succeed.

ISABELLA LUCY BIRD [MRS BISHOP] _____

See biographical note on p. 61.

This short piece on larrikinism is all the more interesting for Bird's misconceptions about the term. She told her sister: 'At first when people said of a man that he was a larrikin I thought it meant a member of some lodge or society so called. I don't think the Australians are behind the Americans in inventing words.' See Isabella Bird, Letters to Henrietta, *edited by Kay Chubbuck, London, John Murray, 2002, p. 48.*

_____ 'Australia Felix: Impressions of Victoria. I', *Leisure Hour*, vol. 26, 1877, pp. 39–44.

Melbourne on the whole is an orderly city, but at dark a state of things sets in in certain quarters, not always the lowest, by no means creditable. In the list of crimes and offences which daily disfigures the columns of the 'Argus,' there is frequently a paragraph headed 'Larrikinism.' 'Larrikinism' is not the name of a new virtue, though it may be said to designate a new colonial product, and a product specially manufactured in Melbourne. The 'larrikin' is as much a growth of Melbourne as the 'hoodlum' is of San Francisco, and there is little to choose between them. The 'larrikin' is an embryo ruffian, a boy in years, but a man in vices. He gambles, cheats, drinks, chews, smokes, sets outhouses on fire, rifles drunken citizens' pockets, insults respectable women, is proud of his familiarity

with the non-virtuous, rings bells, wrenches off knockers, and has a fatal precision in the use of obnoxious missiles. He is only in his element after dark, when
he terrifies quiet people, and parades the streets singing atrocious songs. The
bands of 'larrikins' infest particular localities, and, like pariah dogs, refrain from
poaching on each other's preserves. The existence of this numerous and well-
defined class of juvenile 'rowdies' may be traced partly to the number of parents
of both sexes who are drunkards, partly to the increasing relaxation of parental
control, and partly to the homeless mode of living of many families, sleeping in
crowded lodgings, feeding in restaurants, and spending the evenings in saloons,
or among the lowest amusements of a city. Bad example is infectious; the lawless
life of the 'larrikin' has great fascinations, and even well-to-do and well-meaning
parents often lose all control over their boys. They run wild, and won't go to bed,
and from the time that 'stopping out nights' begins, to howling about the streets
in the glory of full-blown 'larrikinism,' is one of the shortest roads to ruin that is
anywhere traversed.

W. A. G. BRUNTON

*W. A. G. Brunton (1867–1938), Australian-born businessman and politician, served his apprentice-
ship as a carpenter and joiner, and rose to hold directorships in several firms, including Australasian
Advertising. He was knighted in 1926 and elected alderman in 1929. [ADB].*

*This piece is from an eight-part series that includes: I. 'Pharmaceutical Chemist', pp. 269–70;
II. 'Supreme Court Solicitor', pp. 366–7; III. 'Barrister-at-Law', p. 383; V. 'Tea-planter', pp. 590–1;
VI. 'Ranching', pp. 638–9; VII. 'Land Agency and Auctioneer', pp. 797–8; VIII. 'Inspector of Weights
& Measures', p. 815.*

'What Shall I Be? IV.—Jackeroo Life',
Boy's Own Paper, vol. 20, 1897–98,
pp. 574–5.

Almost every boy manifests a keen interest in tales of life and adventure in
far-away countries, and nothing excites his imagination more. The thought of
going abroad has romance for all, but at no time stronger than in boyhood. As
the youth merges into manhood his desire to go to foreign parts is, however,
generally subjected to what his parents or guardians deem best for him. In the
majority of cases it is decided that he shall remain at home and enter some
profession or business. But it may be decided, or be necessary, that he should
go abroad.

The question then arises—Where should he go and what should he do? To one
of our colonies the youth is most likely shipped off, with many blessings, and a

well-furnished and, for the most part, useless kit, to enter upon a life which he knows next to nothing about. In nine cases out of ten the boy fails to succeed, really through no fault of his own, but because of not knowing before arriving in the country what he should have to undertake. I hope in this article, by faithfully portraying the life led and what work had to be done in the bush of the Australasian colonies, to be of assistance to some boy who intends or desires to go to these parts as a wool grower.

It is interesting to note that the present year is the centenary of Australia's greatest industry—wool. In 1798 there were in the land of the kangaroo only two thousand sheep; now there must be over one hundred and twenty millions. The first shipment of wool amounted to 245 lb. The latest returns show that the wool clip is above 750,000,000 lb., the value of which may be put down as £20,000,000.

Australia has lately, as everyone knows, passed through a serious crisis. Although matters are now assuming a much brighter appearance, still things are not as they were some years ago. Employment is much more difficult to obtain, and wages are on a lower scale. That the present depression is only temporary cannot be denied, for a country with such a beautiful climate, and endowed with a wealth of mineral and other resources, must ultimately take a foremost place in the world. Considering the difficulty of getting employment, it may sound paradoxical to say that the chief drawback to the development of Australia is its lack of population. Nevertheless, such is the case, coupled with the want of capital.

On the life in the cities of Australia I shall not enter in detail, as it is almost in every way similar to that led in the large cities of our own country. There is as keen competition for a vacant post in colonial cities as there is at home. Many people here think that a young man has only to go to the colonies to at once jump into some lucrative situation. They do not seem to understand that it is just as difficult, if not more so, for an English youth to obtain a billet in, say, Melbourne, as it is for an Australian to do so in London; unless, of course, strong personal influence is brought to bear. It is extremely improbable that the new arrival in the colonies, who is armed merely with a few letters of introduction, will obtain an entrance to any office. Before the crash five years ago, the banks paid their clerks well; since then salaries have been very much lowered, and a colonial bank clerk is now little better off than his *confrère* at home.

I shall now endeavour to briefly state what bush life is, and what prospects it affords. 'Bush' was at first applied to the vast forests of gum-trees which cover so great an area in the Australian continent, but is nowadays used simply to denote 'country.' Although all country is designated 'bush,' there are different degrees of it, as the word is applied to the country district around a township, as well as to the huge tracts of land in the 'Never-never' country remote from any centre of activity. Sheep and cattle raising are the chief pastoral pursuits of the country. Stations, as the properties are called on which the stock is kept, vary in size from a few thousand to considerably over a hundred thousand acres. Some are purely devoted to sheep, others to cattle, and, again, others raise both. To these stations many youths from this country go, with, I may safely say, an extremely hazy idea of what work will have to be done. They think life on a station consists in riding a horse all day, and if fond of horses they unhesitatingly choose a bush life. Once in the colonies and on a station, they find out their mistake, and, either disliking or unable to do the work, they leave and go to a town in the hope of obtaining employment there. Failing to do so, if they do not return home these lads begin to aimlessly drift about the colonies, many lapsing into evil ways. To those who understand what is expected of them, and are willing to work, the healthy out-of-door life is enjoyable enough. In fact, after living in the bush for some years it is hard to leave it.

A boy goes on a station as a cadet, or, as more commonly termed, a 'jackeroo.' Before going further, let me say—beware of the premium-seeking squatter. It is quite as unnecessary to pay a premium in Australia as in Canada, where the fleecing, by this system, of young fellows going on to ranches, has lately been exposed. If a lad cannot at least earn his board, he is not worth his place on, nor is suitable for, a station, even if he be willing to pay a premium. On some stations there are several cadets who live in barracks—cottages or huts set apart for their use. If there be only one or two, they generally live in the station-house as members of the squatter's family.

One of the first questions put to the 'new chum' is, 'Can you ride?' Riding to the bushman does not mean hacking along a road, but being able to sit a buck-jumper and to gallop through rough country after cattle. The newcomer, in ignorance of the true purport of the above question, will probably reply that he can. His horsemanship will soon be tested by his having to mount a buck-jumper, by which he will speedily be thrown amid the laughter of the onlookers. Unless really a good horseman, it is safer to say that he is only learning. In that case, quiet animals will be given him for some months until he is capable of managing spirited ones. On a station I know, the rule is to give the jackeroo for the first six months easily ridden horses; after that he has to mount any horse he is ordered to. It is said that the Australian bushman is unsurpassed by any horseman in the world. Considering he commences riding at the early age of five, and is thereafter constantly in the saddle, it is not much credit to him.

After being shown the various paddocks on the estate, the jackeroo will be given two or three of them to superintend. These paddocks may embrace many hundreds of acres. Twice or thrice a week he will have to ride round the boundary fences, observing if these are in order; if not, he must do the necessary repairing. He must see that the sheep are all right. If he finds one of them dead, he has to skin it, burn the carcass, and bring home the pelt. A watchful eye must be kept on the state of the grass and the amount of water in the creek or dam. On mustering days—stock in a paddock brought together and probably yarded—he has, along with the other station hands, to take part. It is necessary in this work to know how to handle a stock-whip, which is not learnt without some trouble and practice. Carrying rations to the boundary riders who may reside on the outskirts of the estate is another of his duties. These, if somewhat monotonous, form the most pleasant portion of his work. Now comes the part which the young Englishman does not understand nor care to do. He is made to groom horses, milk cows, clean out pigsties and stables, grub tree-roots, chop firewood, and other such duties. He has to learn to use an axe and saw; to cut down trees, saw and split them into proper lengths for posts and rails for fences, sink holes in the ground for these posts; and, in general, do exactly what a labourer does in this country. Let it be clearly understood that the above form a very considerable part of what is called 'colonial experience'; and, unless the youth determines to do such work without cavilling, it is needless for him to go on a station.

Practical jokes are always played on the new chum, in fact he is considered the fitting butt for them. If he keeps his temper and shows that he can give as good as he gets, these will soon be dropped. If he does not—woe betide him!

In short droving trips the jackeroo is taken to light the fire, boil the billy, and get the food ready. He has to look after the blankets and cooking utensils and place them on the pack-horse, which is under his charge. Long droving trips from Queensland to the other colonies, extending over some months, I will not discuss, as they do not come under the duties of a cadet. The most busy season of the year is shearing time. For several weeks—according to the number of sheep to be clipped—the work is very hard, and from dawn to dusk the cadets are kept busy mustering, dipping, etc.

The principal reason for going on a station is to learn about the raising and management of stock. The instruction in this should be given by the squatter or his overseer, but more often the boy is left to pick up information the best way he can. Much valuable knowledge of stock and of bush matters can be had from the elder stockmen, who have spent all their lives in the bush. These are the men of whom it is said that once having seen a horse they will always recognise it again.

After having spent the necessary number of years learning squatting, the youth must determine what he is going to do. Posts as managers are very scarce, and the salary is not large nor is it progressive, so it means either buying a station or taking up land from the Government. In both cases capital is required, and in the latter much hard work will be necessary—the estate having to be fenced, a homestead built, yards put up, ground cleared for cultivation, etc.

I shall not enter into the method of taking land on leasehold from the Government; it is sufficient to say, if the quondam cadet does so, he will require to go to the back blocks, as all land in desirable places is already taken.

Parents and guardians cannot pay too much attention to the fact that if a boy is to be successful in squatting he must have capital. It is unfair to send a boy to the colonies to learn sheep farming if he cannot thereafter command capital, because otherwise there is really little prospect of bettering his position. In the colonies to-day there are many Britishers with a perfect knowledge of bush life unable to obtain better situations than those of a boundary rider or stockman.

I do not wish to discourage boys from entering on the life of a squatter; I merely desire to tell them exactly what to expect. If a boy has made up his mind to go on a station, then forewarned is forearmed. If he is not physically fit, it will be much better to try some less arduous work.

For those who are strong, willing to work, to endure hardships, and who, above all, have capital, squatting may be successful. The charm of life and work in the bush is well expressed in the following lines by the Australian poet, Adam Lindsay Gordon:

> Twas merry in the glowing morn, among
>   the gleaming grass,
> To wander as we've wandered many a mile,
> And blow the cool tobacco cloud, and watch the
>   white wreaths pass,
> Sitting loosely in the saddle all the while.
> 'Twas merry 'mid the blackwoods, when we spied
>   the station roofs,
> To wheel the wild scrub cattle at the yard,
> With a running fire of stock-whips and a fiery run
>   of hoofs;
> Oh! the hardest day was never then too hard!

ANON. _____

_____ *from* 'Young Men in the Colonies.
A Chat on Australia with the
Reverend W. H. Fitchett', *Young Man*,
vol. 13, 1899, pp. 397–9.

… Mr. Fitchett, who, by the way, is a Wesleyan minister, is thoroughly imbued with the imperial spirit; and, living as he has done in the Colonies practically the whole of his life, he has formed a conception of the Empire which does not come so easily to the man whose life is spent only in the British Isles. He has high hopes of the future of the Colonies, especially of Australasia, and his advice to all clever young men of good character who want a change of sky is to make their way to the other side of the world. A representative of THE YOUNG MAN has had a chat with Mr. Fitchett on this subject.

'There are some things Australia does not offer,' Mr. Fitchett said. 'It does not offer, for example, opportunities of sudden and easily won wealth, and it is scarcely the field to which young fellows who fail here ought to be sent, in the hope that they will succeed there. Australia is sometimes treated as a sort of moral sanatorium, and all sorts of moral wrecks are sent there in the hope that a change of geography will bring a change of character. But "they change their skies but not their souls" who cross the sea. There are some things, however, which Australia does offer. It offers a perfect climate, easier social conditions than England has, and open doors to every vocation in life. England is gridironed with almost impossible social barriers. A young fellow born in one class does not find it easy to climb to another. Now with us social differences are faint, labour is light, all classes are pretty much on a level, no one Church has any social or legal preference over another; and so Australia does offer conditions of life which make the maximum of comfort and the maximum of freedom possible. I know of no other country in the world where men earn their livelihood more easily, and flavour labour with holidays and enjoyment more abundantly, than in Australia.'

'Do you want a special kind of young men?'

'The young men who have the best opportunity in Australia are those with a business training and a little capital. A young fellow with character, intelligence, and business knowledge, without capital, may get on admirably, but he has some risks; he may have to wait for a while. If he has a little capital he can almost certainly find a business opening, which won't prove a short and easy cut to a great fortune, but will give him an assured position and all the comforts of life. But if possible he ought to have some little resources of money, as the area of employment in commerce is, I imagine, about as preoccupied in the Colonies as in England. Yet any Englishman or Scotchman, with the excellent commercial training which England and Scotland give, and with the severer standard of application to which they are trained,—severer than is known in the Colonies,—will, as a rule, go ahead of the colonial youth himself.

'Another class to which Australia offers a career is young fellows trained to some handicraft or to agriculture, or gardening, or dairy-work. If such a young fellow, again, has a little capital, he has an additional chance of success. He will find in all the Colonies land abundant, cheap, often at an absolutely nominal rent, with railways near; and while the climate has its uncertainties, I don't know that the Australian climate is more capricious than any other. And the market for Australian produce has been of late years steadied, and amazingly enlarged, by the better trade relations established with the United Kingdom. Dairy produce and fruit are flowing into British markets from Australia, with the result that Australian dairy farms and orchards become highly profitable forms of industry. If a young fellow knows a handicraft and has no money, he will find resources enough in his hands to make him sure of a comfortable livelihood; and if he has character, is sober, diligent, and honest, he will quickly make a happy home for himself.'

'But how is it, if Australia offers so many attractions, that its population grows so slowly?'

'Australia has really a more spacious geography and, taken as a whole, a more genial climate than even the United States, but its distance from Europe makes its growth in population somewhat slow. In one sense that is a drawback; in another and larger sense it is a very great advantage. It is the law of nature that slow growths are enduring, and in Australia we shall undoubtedly build up a community of a less mixed type, and of a better moral fibre, than in the United States. So that the young man who comes to Australia knows that he is linking himself to a nation with a future, and his children will have a fortunate place in the world. Already, for example, every child in Australia has a school within reach, with a trained teacher, a good educational system, and absolutely no fees. Education is as all-embracing, and about as costless, as the atmosphere, and a clever Australian lad may climb, almost without expense to his parents, from the kindergarten class to the University degree; and, like the late Premier of Queensland, find every vocation and every position in the State open to him. So that if a young fellow takes into his calculation not only what Australia offers to himself, but what it will offer to his children, he may find it a very tempting field to live in.

'There are, of course, differences in the Colonies. Queensland, perhaps, offers the widest diversity of climate and industry; Victoria the most settled and ordinary form of society; New Zealand the most advanced socialistic type of government. But all the Australian Colonies at last are melting into political unity. They are rich in mineral wealth and in agricultural possibilities; and, taking them altogether, I think the Queen's flag flies over no other realm so wide, so happy, so free from evil elements, and so rich in possibilities as the seven colonies of Australasia.'

'But Australia has its dangers for young men?'

'Human society always includes many evil elements. Where can a young fellow go where he will not find temptation? God never planned this world to be a garden of ease without temptations. But I think, as a whole, a young man has less of evil environment in Australia than perhaps anywhere else in the world, save perhaps in an English or Scottish village, where everybody knows him and he knows everybody, and where a wholesome supervision increases the difficulty of going astray. In Australia the liquor traffic is more sternly restrained than in England, and the tone of public feeling on the drink question is much more wholesome. We have no public-houses open on Sunday. No Australian woman, unless she was of known bad character, would think of going to an open bar to drink.'

'But is not gambling, on the other hand, very rife?'

'We are supposed to be much given to gambling. So we are. There are facts in our history which predispose us to gambling. Victoria was built on the discovery of gold. That, in its very nature, was a sort of huge industrial lottery. A stroke of the pick might make a man rich, and that predisposes us to be greedy of sudden and easily won wealth, which is the passion at the root of all gambling. But I do not know, after all, that we are more given to gambling than you in England. Our anti-gambling laws are better than yours. All the Colonies but one shut the mail bags against sweep circulars, and the sweeps have taken refuge in one corner of Australia. In Tasmania they still reap a rich harvest. But the fact that five out of six Colonies have prohibited sweep advertisements, and shut the post-office against them, is a wholesome sign. Bishop Moorhouse, the Bishop of Manchester, said the present peril of Australia was not drink, not gambling, but lust; and there are elements in our climate and in our habits of food—an Australian table has meat three times a day—which do stimulate unduly the physical side of human nature. But Australian life is cleaner certainly than life on the Continent, and the illegitimacy rate is lower than in Scotland. No,' said Mr. Fitchett, slowly and with emphasis, 'the young fellow who wants to live a clean life and serve God may do that in Australia as easily, and find as many helps in the doing of it, as under any other sky.'

'What is the chief characteristic of the Australian young man?'

'The young Australian ripens soon, and is on that account, I think, less likely to have enduring physical fibre than the sturdy British stock from which he sprang. But he is quick-brained, active, intensely given to field sports, enthusiastic in his hates and loves. The typical Australian is an Englishman with a dash of sunshine in him. He takes an intelligent interest in public affairs, too. About the strongest political force in Victoria is the Australian Natives Association—nearly all young men, intensely loyal, intensely imperialistic. Our politics are, from the humanitarian and social points of view, much in advance of yours. Our Conservative would be an advanced Liberal here. And we have greatly enlarged the function of the State. The State owns all the railways and telephones, as well as the post-offices, and is expected to assist all struggling industries and to kill all social evils to a degree which would seem alarming to the sober English folk. It lends money to farmers, buys up big estates and subdivides them for men of small capital, limits the hours of labour, and more than one Colony has undertaken old-age pensions. In a word, the State is generally expected to be—sometimes in a quite absurd degree—a sort of human Providence.'

Then we talked of the bond between the Mother and the Child. Nobody who has read either *Fights for the Flag* or *Deeds that Won the Empire* will need to be told that Mr. Fitchett has a great conception of the Empire and a keen sense of its responsibilities and possibilities. 'How little they know of England who only England know' is a quotation often on his lips. I suggested that perhaps some day the Colonies would break away from England. Mr. Fitchett took up the point earnestly.

'I will tell you what would break up the Empire,' he said, 'what would cost England the faith and affection of her children across the seas—that is, if England loses her sense of her place in the world. England is as much a nation called to a special providential task as the Jews were, and that task is to carry out Christian ideals of freedom and civilisation in non-Christian lands. Why has God given to England nearly all the waste places of the earth, unless she is to fill them? And we in the Colonies think that England would be abandoning her providential mission if she surrendered the imperial side of her politics. Nothing could be more fatal to the hold England has on her Colonies than the prevalence of a "Little England" doctrine. We have no Little Englanders in Australia. So long as England has faith and pride in herself, her children across the seas will have faith and pride in her.

The Chinese

JENNER PLOMLEY

Jenner Plomley (c.1815–69), doctor, first practised in Northiam, Sussex. He probably lived in New South Wales after 1837, and married a widow, Frances Howson Ayrane, at Rio de Janeiro in January 1849, having met her on board the Tasmania, *which sailed from Sydney in 1848. He practised medicine in Sydney from 1862 to 1868. [SG]*

from 'Chinese Emigration',
Simmonds's Colonial Magazine and Foreign Miscellany, vol. 3, 1844, pp. 41–2.

SIR—The opinion is daily gaining ground that slavery and the slave-trade can only be terminated by the promotion of systematic emigration from India, Africa, and China, to our various tropical possessions, so as to enable planters to raise tropical produce cheaper by free than it can by slave labour; and that the measures which have been adopted by this country for putting a stop to the slave-trade, entailing an enormous expenditure and loss of life, have only tended to aggravate its horrors without materially diminishing its extent.

... As colonists, the Chinese are undoubtedly superior to the natives of India. They are a hardier and more industrious race, endowed with a more robust constitution—better able to endure fatigue, and to withstand vicissitudes of climate, and superior to the Indian labourer as agriculturists. Moreover, they are more likely to become permanent residents on the soil, and the hope of their conversion to Christianity under more favourable auspices than obtain in their own country, is anything but chimerical. Next to the English, perhaps the Chinese, of all the nations of the earth, are most disposed to emigrate; and the extent to which emigration has reached of late years among them is truly surprising, when we consider that it is left to individual enterprise. It has been computed that upwards of fifty thousand adults, chiefly males, annually emigrate from the shores of China to seek a home and livelihood in a foreign land. These emigrants have found their way in great numbers, and at their own expense, to Siam, Borneo, the Philippine Islands, Moluccas, Java, Singapore, Malacca, Pinang, Madras, Calcutta, Bombay, Mauritius, and to the Islands of Bally and Lombock, situated only a short distance from the Australian continent. In

Singapore they form the bulk of the labouring population, and are, with few exceptions, the only clearers and cultivators of the soil. In Borneo, in the very teeth of its hostile inhabitants, they have formed flourishing settlements. At Batavia, they form a large and industrious portion of the population; the same at Manilla. Thousands exist under British rule at Hong Kong, where all the public and private works are carried on by them. In his own country the pay of a Chinese labourer averages from fourpence to sixpence a day; on this stipend he contrives to maintain himself, together with his wife and family. His food is principally rice and fish, with occasionally a little meat.

From the inquiries I made when in China, of persons long resident there, I am satisfied that with the prospect of bettering their condition, any number of Chinese labourers and mechanics of every description might be easily induced to emigrate, and form settlements on the northern coasts of New Holland, and when the country should become known to them, multitudes, at their own expense, would speedily find their way thither.

The fisheries in Torres Straits might be rendered productive in the hands of the Chinese; and the colonisation of New Guinea, one of the largest and most fertile islands on the globe, would not be far distant.

I am further confident that the country which shall direct and promote the emigration of the Chinese cannot fail of reaping a rich harvest therefrom, and of giving a death-blow to slavery and the slave-trade.

The experiment might be easily tried at or near Port Essington, and that at an inconsiderable expense.

I am, Sir, your most obedient servant, Jenner Plomley.

ANON. _____

_____ 'Chinese at the Diggings', *Leisure Hour*, vol. 4, 1854, pp. 639–40.

The discovery of gold in Australia has proved a great stimulant to Chinese enterprise. Ship after ship, heavily freighted with Chinese, anchors in Hobson's Bay. For the last eighteen months they have been arriving in quick succession, and yet still they come. During one week we saw no less than eleven hundred Chinese land on the wharf at Melbourne, and the latest news from Victoria tell us that the inhabitants were expecting, with some misgivings, if not alarm, the arrival of eight thousand Chinamen, who had left Hong Kong in twenty vessels all bound for Melbourne.

The first advent of this singular race was regarded by the colonists with complacency. Years before the discovery of gold, occasional importations of Chinese to Sydney had occurred, but they were usually received into the families of wealthy settlers in the capacity of servants, and often assumed a position little superior to that of a slave. They were found to be economical as shepherds, and their patient, contented habits rendered them suitable for that very monotonous occupation. During the dearth of labour, therefore, their arrival in Victoria was looked upon as a fortunate circumstance for the colony, and it was said that the luxury of domestic servants would now be within the reach of all—for who so easily contented and so unambitious as John Chinaman! He could do all the scrubbing and grubbing and shepherding for easy wage, whilst others looked after more profitable matters.

It soon became apparent, however, that these strange adventurers had more independent ideas in seeking the Australian shores. Their destination was invariably the diggings. On landing at Sandridge, or on the wharf, each man shouldered his bamboo cane, with his baggage slung on the ends; in this way it is surprising what ponderous chests and huge baskets they will carry with comparative ease. In long procession of single file they stagger through the town, loaded like a swarm of ants in harvest time, and thus tacitly proclaiming to the colonists that they come among them willing to work and help themselves. The majority appear of the most impoverished class. Here and there a mandarin or one of superior wealth and influence may be seen among them. They usually pitch their tents on an eminence lying to the left of the St. Kilda road on the south bank of the Yarra. Arriving at this spot, they soon unpack their baggage, and in an incredibly short space of time the rising ground is covered with small fragile calico tents. John Chinaman is not the sluggard we took him to be. He is evidently endowed with a goodly share of that practical Robinson Crusoism which is an element so valuable in a new colony, and so essential for 'roughing it' at the diggings. Whilst some are rigging the tents, others dig out little hollows in the earth and kindle fragments of wood into a blaze. Their pots and kettles are in active requisition, a mat is laid on the ground, and by the time the tents are up, many a curious mess of cunning cookery, many a mystery in hodge-podge and stew is steaming in bowls and platters, amidst circles of large, grinning, moon-like faces. Chopsticks are set to work, and the bowls are cleaned out with marvellous rapidity and relish. Thus regaled after their fatigue, they have now an eye to business, and spread out on a piece of matting before their tent, what little articles they may possess likely to attract the attention of visitors.

Their location near Melbourne is quite a temporary one; they merely want a little time to look about them, to exchange their nick-nacks for cash enough to purchase necessary tools, a pair of American boots, of which they are especially proud, a little stock of salt fish and rice, and then they as suddenly strike their tents and are off to the diggings. They leave the city as they came, loaded with baggage and cooking utensils, carrying their boots in their hands and walking barefooted in the middle of the road. Spades and washing dishes are strapped to their 'swags,' and indicate that they are bent on a search for gold. They are good pedestrians, in spite of bare feet and rough roads, and reach the diggings in a few days. They generally resort to surfacing in preference to the more laborious process of digging for gold; for although in emergencies they will manifest considerable energy and physical endurance, their naturally lymphatic temperament tends perhaps to encourage habits of indolence. It appears to be a maxim with them never to dig if they can obtain the desired treasure by any other means; and being satisfied with very moderate gains, they prefer obtaining a few pennyweights by washing the surfacing left by the diggers, to the chance of gaining ounces by the more laborious process of the pick and spade. They rarely sink a hole of any depth; if they commence one, they do so to 'shepherd' it; that is, to secure the claim by making a show of working it, for the purpose of selling it to others. Thus it is that they crowd at Castlemaine and swarm at Bendigo, because there particles of gold are found near the surface; but the riches of Ballarat are to be reached only by descending hundreds of feet into the bowels of the earth. Chinese creeks, Chinese gullies, and China towns, are familiar words in the gold regions.

There are at present residing at Bendigo, 5000 Chinese, the great majority of whom have arrived in the colony during the last eighteen months. So important are their numbers in a commercial point of view, that stores have been opened by Chinese to supply their countrymen, and a keen competition is kept up between them and the European traders to obtain the custom of the celestials. Rice, herrings, and mess pork, provisions of which they are particularly fond, and upon which they almost entirely subsist, are seen marked in Chinese figures. Hebrew gold-brokers proclaim in Chinese characters their determination to give the highest price and the most exact weight for the produce of the mines. As a body, the diggers regard the Chinese with prejudice and animosity. They accuse them of many vices. They are strongly addicted to gambling, and some will not rise from their mats until the whole of their earnings have been lost. They are also uncleanly in their habits; and by puddling in the creeks, and throwing into them filth of every description, they render the water at times unfit for domestic purposes. This, where good water is so scarce as at the diggings, is a grievous public offence, and at Bendigo on more than one occasion it has led to serious outbreaks.

In trade, the Chinese drive hard bargains. They will not sell a pennyweight of gold without a most rigid examination of weights and scales, and many suspicious shakes of the head; nor will they buy a herring without haggling about the price. Great is the invention of their cunning, and rarely is a bargain arranged but, when the settling comes, John Chinaman finds he is a shilling or a sixpence short of the stipulated sum. They are remarkably shrewd in prospecting, but prefer using the discoveries of others to spending time in searching for new spots. They shuffle quietly among the claims, keep a sharp eye on those who work them, and generally manage to worm out the secrets of the digger. John has picked up a few words of English, and he ventures to inquire—'Much gold here?'

'Oh, plenty of gold here,' perhaps the digger will pettishly reply; 'five ounces to the tub; there's gold all along this gully.'

John Chinaman walks on; a knowing grin dilates his broad features, and a cunning twinkle dances in his small, black eyes. He is quite certain the fellow is finding no gold, or he would not own it. He stops again; he watches keenly a man who is digging away with a steady purpose, evidently a man who has not time to be lazy. Again John uses his scrap of English.

'Gold much here—eh?'

'Gold,' replies the digger; 'not a speck; a regular *schicer*; not a spangle in the whole claim.'

A lie will never bear looking in the face. John sees through it in a minute. Several ah! ah! ahs! and as many nods of the head, is all the reply he gives; but the cautious digger is surprised on reaching his claim next morning to find the hitherto quiet scene of his labours surrounded by Chinese, who have already mapped out their claims as close as possible to his own.

In some respects the Chinese have set an example to the diggers. At Bendigo their attention to religious matters has been strongly manifested in their desire for the establishment of a place of worship—not after the manner of Confucius, but after the manner of the Christian church. The Testament in the Chinese tongue is read in many a tent on the diggings. Not content with this, they have, through Mr. Emmett, applied to the colonial government for a site for the erection of a Protestant church. The reply of the surveyor-general to the application was as follows:—

> Sir—Having received an application from the Chinese who are now residing at Sandhurst (Bendigo) for a site suitable for the erection of a church in that township, I should feel obliged if you would obtain for me the following information, which it is necessary I should be possessed of, before submitting their application to the consideration of the lieutenant-governor:—
>
> 1st. What ecclesiastical authority, if any, is exercised by any of them?
> 2nd. What religion do they profess?
> 3rd. Under what trust would the church be placed?
>   I have the honour, &c.,
>
> A. CLARKE.

The following is Mr. Emmett's reply.

Sir—With reference to your letter, I have the honour to state that I have had several interviews with the most intelligent Chinese here, and find that they are estimated at over 5000 on this field. I have had several communications with a Chinese missionary, who professes the protestant religion, and who purposes conducting worship by interpreting to his countrymen the bible and service of the church of England. He has been partly educated in England, and appears to have great influence over his countrymen. He also undertakes to find several of the principal Chinese who will become trustees.

I have the honour, &c.

E. N. EMMETT.

To the Hon. the Surveyor-General.

As a manifestation of the working of the Spirit of God, as a sign of the passing away of old idolatry, and as showing the appreciation of christian truth by a strange people, amidst circumstances unfavourable to the fostering of religious habits, this movement will be regarded by the christian church with lively satisfaction.

JOHN POPE-HENNESSY _____

John Pope-Hennessy (1834–91), Irish-born colonial governor, entered the British Parliament in 1859, the first Roman Catholic to do so. An advocate of prison and mine reform, he worked actively to amend the Irish poor laws. He contributed articles to various periodicals. [DNB]

_____ 'The Chinese in Australia',
Nineteenth Century, vol. 23, 1888,
pp. 617–19.

The Government of the United States and the various Australian Governments object to the immigration of Chinese. In each case the popular vote has guided the Government. Those who admit that the objection to the influx of Chinese into an Anglo-Saxon community is well founded will probably acknowledge that the objection is really stronger in Australia than in the United States. Nevertheless the United States have succeeded, where the Australian Governments have failed. It was announced in New York on the 14th of March that a treaty between the United States and China prohibiting the entry of Chinese labourers into the United States for a period of twenty years has been signed. Whilst this effectual remedy has been secured for the United States, the Australian colonies are still fighting the question with their hands tied.

At the very moment when American diplomacy had succeeded, the Premier of Queensland issued an address to the North Brisbane electors in which he declares his belief that all Queensland can be cultivated by whites, and that the Chinese should be excluded; but the exclusion is to be partial only, an exclusion dependent on the operation of an increased poll tax, the prohibition of naturalisation, and a tax on residence.

In Sydney, Victoria, and New Zealand leading statesmen are propounding remedies somewhat similar to Sir Samuel Griffiths'. But all their speeches are in a half-hearted and despairing vein. For ten years past the Chinese have paid a poll tax, and have continued arriving in Australian ports in larger numbers. Every one knows that they will pay the increased tax, but that their numbers will not diminish. No foreign nationality is so indifferent to the advantages of naturalisation in our colonies generally as the Chinese, and the threat of stopping the naturalisation of Chinese will have no real effect on their immigration.

The partial remedies discussed more warmly than ever in Australia have all been tried and have all failed in the United States. Why should not our self-governing colonies adopt the radical cure that the statesmen of America are now applying? The answer is, they are not allowed to do so. Downing Street rightly interprets the sentiment of the House of Commons in objecting to the prohibition of Chinese. Our Foreign Office, directly under the same influence and moved indirectly by some Indo-Chinese questions, objects to prohibition. Therefore we say to our self-governing colonies, 'In this matter, of such general interest to you and so vital to your future, you are not to be self-governing.' There is a twofold danger in this: there is the direct injury to Australia; there is the risk of embittering the relations between Australia and England.

I believe the parliamentary sentiment on this subject in England is founded on a misapprehension, and that the traditional policy of the Foreign Office is mistaken.

The common opinion in Parliament is that the governing classes in China as well as the people of China would be offended if we prohibited Chinese immigration into a British colony. During the five years that her Majesty entrusted to my care the government of British China, that is the island of Hong Kong and the territory of Kowloon on the mainland of China, I had some opportunity of ascertaining how far this common opinion was well founded. When I assumed the administration of Hong Kong in 1877 I entertained a similar opinion. But direct communication with intelligent Chinese, and especially with the *literati* of China (from whom the governing classes are drawn), soon taught me that I was mistaken. My interviews at Tientsin with Li Hung Chang and at Peking with Prince Kung and other members of the Tsung-li-Yamen convinced me that the experience I had gained in Hong Kong and Canton was well founded, and that, so far from there being in China any general objection to the policy of prohibition, such a policy would be viewed at least with indifference and probably with satisfaction.

The argument on the subject was briefly stated by an interesting guest that I had the honour of entertaining. When the Chinese envoy to the German emperor was returning from Berlin to Peking, in speaking of Prince Bismark he gave two reasons for doubting the infallible statesmanship of the Prince, one connected with the overgrown armies that he traced to him; the other he thus referred to: 'The Prince said that China and Germany were natural allies, because, unlike Russia, England, or France, no territorial jealousies could arise, and because there were plenty of German steamships now ready to convey away the surplus population of China to San Francisco, to Australia, to Peru, and other places suited to Chinese emigrants.' 'Fancy,' said the envoy, 'a European statesman addressing the latter argument to me—to me, a Chinaman!' And then he went on to explain how hateful to a true Chinaman was the idea of Chinese emigration to foreign countries—how objectionable it was on political and religious grounds. He described vast regions of the Chinese Empire where a migration of the agricultural population was taking place followed by an increase of food sent in to the great cities. 'We have no desire,' he said, 'to see the enormous resources of our own country undeveloped by our own industrious people. He is a bad Chinaman,' he said emphatically, 'who, except on the Emperor's business, leaves his country, for every Chinaman has duties to his family, to the village community in which he lives, and to the Emperor, which cannot be discharged when he emigrates.' He explained how essential it was for every Chinaman to visit at stated periods the graves of his ancestors. Again he repeated, 'The Chinaman who voluntarily puts thousands of miles of sea between himself and the graves of his ancestors—between himself and the ancestral tablet—is a bad Chinaman, always excepting a servant of the Emperor proceeding abroad on official duty.'

But even without meeting leading Chinamen in Hong Kong, Canton, or Peking, a careful observer of the sources of Chinese emigration will have some reason to suspect the true feeling of the Chinese Government and people on this subject. Chinese emigration is practically conducted through the British colony of Hong Kong. That colony is the conduit pipe of Chinese emigration to Australia. When I discovered that it had been the practice to export Chinese convicts from Hong Kong to Australia, I issued a proclamation denouncing the system, and with reference to the general employment of coolie ships I gave instructions to the harbour officials which tended to check Chinese emigration to Australia. What happened? No complaints came from the Australian Governments or from the Government of China. On the contrary, the Premier of New

South Wales, Sir Henry Parkes, wrote to thank me warmly, and the Viceroy of Canton also cordially supported me. But complaints, loud and persistent, were made by British, American, and German shipowners in Hong Kong. Even one of my harbour officials wrote to Downing Street complaining that my action threatened injury to a flourishing branch of Hong Kong trade—the Chinese coolie trade to Australia. It is easy to guess the result. A trade from which a few influential shipowners in Hong Kong make a profit has been kept up, though it has been alike distasteful to the governing classes of China and to the people of Australia.

And is there no remedy for all this? Evidently there is if Lord Knutsford can do that which has enabled him to solve with success some older and more difficult problems—if he can get at the real facts and can induce the Foreign Office to act upon them.

No doubt the unsettled question of treaty revision with China indirectly complicates the question. For temporary purposes it may suit Chinese officials abroad to make a grievance of a prohibitory act in Australia if such an act were passed. But if we learn to treat China frankly and with more justice, or if we would probe the whole of this question to the bottom, our Government would soon secure for Australia a treaty similar to that which President Cleveland's Cabinet has obtained for the United States.

JOHN WILLIAM FORTESCUE _____

John Fortescue (1859–1933), military historian, wrote mainly for Macmillan's Magazine. *His books include* A History of the British Army *in twenty volumes (1910–30);* Wellington *(1925) and* Marlborough *(1932). [WI]*

This article provoked a response from Howard Willoughby, 'The Seamy Side of Australia. A Reply from the Colonies', to which Fortescue replied with 'Guileless Australia. A Rejoinder', Nineteenth Century, *vol. 30, 1891, pp. 292–302, 430–43.*

from 'The Seamy Side of Australia',
Nineteenth Century, vol. 29, 1891,
pp. 523–37.

… Now, there can be very little doubt but that the very best people that can be obtained to develop tropical Australia are the Chinese. Polynesian labour is unsatisfactory; African negroes are not to be had; Indian coolies would not be supplied by the Indian Government on the terms desired by the Colonial Governments; Chinese alone remain, and are from every point of view the most desirable. They are admittedly orderly, thrifty, and industrious, and safer than Indian coolies as citizens because less subject to religious fanaticism.

In the face of these facts how do we find the Colonial Governments behaving? First we discover a series of enactments to discourage Chinese immigration dating in Victoria from 1855; in New South Wales from 1861; in South Australia from 1857, and in Queensland from 1877; and a bitter hatred of the Chinese, constantly taken advantage of by politicians when a political cry is wanted, the whole culminating in the violent anti-Chinese agitation of 1888.

The first symptom of that agitation appears in a letter written in November 1887 by Sir Henry Parkes, Premier of New South Wales, to his brother premier, Mr. Gillies of Victoria. In it he speaks—*à propos* of nothing in particular—of the advantage of getting all the Australian colonies to agree in a measure of restriction, 'or, more properly speaking, practical prohibition of the influx of Chinese into Australia.' The subject, he added, was difficult, owing to questions of climate, but ought, in his opinion, to be settled in view rather of the better qualities of the Chinese—their thrift, industry, &c.—than of their worst characteristics. Altogether a very quiet and peaceful letter was this, and admirably timed, as it turned out. In April 1888, ships with Chinese immigrants on board began to arrive in the Australian ports, which immigrants were promptly refused admission. Such refusal was, of course, absolutely illegal, and was pronounced to be so by the Supreme Courts of Victoria and New South Wales; but the Governments having set the example of lawlessness, the people promptly followed. On the 4th of May a mob of 5,000 people invaded the Parliament House at Sydney, and extorted from Sir Henry Parkes a promise that no Chinese should be allowed to land. On the same day a Chinese camp was destroyed by fire under suspicious circumstances, and two days later a gang of 200 'larrikins' invaded the Chinese quarter of Brisbane, completely wrecked many of the shops, and stoned the inhabitants.

Some weeks before, the Imperial Government had been requested to settle the whole difficulty for the colonies by negotiation; but that was a mere matter of form. A stringent Bill against the Chinese was hurried through the Sydney Parliament, which, in combination with the other previous violent measures that could not be considered likely to further negotiations, showed that Sir Henry Parkes was not going to wait, but meant to take the law into his own hands. When confronted with his illegal action in the Assembly, he replied that he cared nothing for technical law: that he was obeying a superior law, 'the law of the preservation of society in New South Wales.' He also declared that neither for Her Majesty's representative on the spot, nor for Her Majesty's ships of war, nor for the Secretary of State, did his Government intend to turn aside from its purpose, which was to terminate the landing of Chinese for ever, except under the provisions of a Bill which practically amounted to prohibition. Needless to say that this violence was heartily to the taste of the working man of New South

Wales, for whose appetite indeed it was designed. The other colonies, of course, joined in the cry; but Sir Henry Parkes very cunningly outbid all the other Premiers, and thus secured for himself what he chiefly wanted—the leadership of the movement. Of course, not the least attention was paid to the treaty obligations, which give the Chinese right of access to all British dominions, in return for the opening of the Chinese ports which we wrested from China at the bayonet's point.

The next step was to hold a Colonial Conference at Sydney. The delegates met on the 12th of June, and by the 14th had settled matters to their satisfaction. Three days sufficed to thrash out infinitely the most difficult and complicated question that has yet arisen in the colonies. Lord Knutsford suggested to the Conference that all foreign immigration should be restricted alike, in order that no invidious distinction might be made. The proposal was quietly put aside by the Conference, which, after resolving that the restriction of Chinese immigration could best be secured by diplomatic action on the part of the Imperial Government, proceeded, after the manner of Australian politicians, to at once secure it for itself by violent legislation. Why the solemn farce of summoning a Conference, and calling upon the Imperial Government to intervene, should have been performed at all is incomprehensible; for the Australian politicians had really no intention of letting the Imperial Government have any say in the matter. This is clear enough, because Lord Knutsford had warned the colonies that the premature action of New South Wales was an obstacle to successful negotiation. Still, it was thought necessary by the Conference that some excuse should be made for its precipitation, and that excuse was thus put forward in an official minute:—

> As the length of time to be occupied in negotiations between the Imperial Government and the Government of China is uncertain, and as the colonies in the meanwhile have reason to dread a large influx from China, the several Governments have felt impelled to legislate immediately to protect their citizens from an invasion which is dreaded because of its results, not only upon the labour market, but upon the social and moral condition of the people.

To understand rightly the absurdity of this pretext, I must inform my readers that there were at that time in all Australasia but 52,000 Chinamen against three-and-a-quarter million Europeans. If, therefore, the number of Chinese had been increased by one-half during the progress of the negotiations, there would still have been but one Chinaman to fifty Europeans. The moral condition of Australia must be highly sensitive if it can be so easily corrupted, particularly as the Chinese in Victoria (for which colony alone we have access to statistics) have a lower criminal rate than any other nationality.

The minute continues thus:—

In conclusion, the Conference would call attention to the fact that the treatment of the Chinese in the Australasian colonies has been invariably humane and considerate; and that in spite of the intensity of popular feeling during the recent influx, good order has been everywhere maintained. In so serious a crisis the Colonial Governments have felt called upon to take strong and decisive action to protect their peoples, but in so doing they have been studious of Imperial interests, of international obligations, and of their reputation as law-abiding communities.

These statements were too much even for Australians. A member of the Legislative Council of South Australia said in his place that the allegation as to 'humane and considerate treatment' was absolutely untrue. 'The Chinese,' he said, 'have complained, in a memorial to the Conference, that the laws had been strained to torture and oppress them, and even broken to inflict harsh treatment and injustice; and that, by the hasty and violent conduct of various Colonial Governments, the more ignorant of the population had been incited and encouraged to outrage the feelings and show contempt and hatred to their countrymen.'

I affirm, unhesitatingly, that the Chinese have told the truth and that the Conference has not. It is hardly necessary for me to prove it, for every hon. member must know that hardly a month passes that news does not come from one or other of the colonies of harsh and inhuman treatment of the Chinese, of assaults upon them, or even of their murder. Not long ago a case occurred in the northern territory, in which some Chinese who attempted to start in business were disgracefully treated by some Christian Europeans. These men hamstrung the Chinaman's horses, and did it on several occasions. This is only one of a dozen illustrations which might be given to show that the statement of the Conference is not borne out by fact.

But the last paragraph of the minute of the Conference is the sublimest in the matter of effrontery. The Colonial Governments have shown themselves 'studious of Imperial interests' by persecuting Chinese subjects and irritating China, whose alliance they knew to be of importance to England; 'studious of international obligations' by flying in the face of well-known treaties; 'studious of their reputation as law-abiding communities' by a course of violence (quite irrespective of mob outrages) which their own courts of justice pronounced to be illegal.

I have told this story at some length because it gives such an excellent sample of the procedure of Australian politicians, and makes it easier for readers to understand that their behaviour in other affairs by no means raises them above suspicion in matters of finance. Here we see all the old traits repeated: blind subservience to the mob; complete recklessness in the pursuit of their own ephemeral ends, total blindness to the future, and unblushing misstatement in presenting their account to the British public. This anti-Chinese agitation was in reality wholly factitious, and was recognised and denounced as such by not a few prominent Australians.

The main lesson to be drawn from it is this: that the Australians are prepared, not to say determined, to leave a vast extent of their territory untouched and unprofitable sooner than admit another race that can turn it to account; in other words, to cancel a considerable portion of the assets on the security of which they have borrowed and are borrowing millions of money.

This is the end for which the Australian working man, represented by a few unscrupulous politicians, employs British protection. ...

Federation

ANON.

'Australasian Federation',
Westminster Review, n.s. vol. 64,
1883, pp. 431–7.

Whenever the question of Federation is referred to by the leading politicians or public journals in Australia and New Zealand, it rarely happens that a single argument is advanced against the proposal to create a United Australasia. Colonists, who hold opposite opinions on many political questions, generally agree on the desirability of Federation as a broad principle. They assert, 'it is merely a matter of time,' and there the subject is now allowed to rest.

Going further afield we find English statesmen, irrespective of party, apparently unanimous in urging these colonies to federate; and, not perceiving how the object they have in view is to be gained, generously conceding that the colonists should be left to make the necessary arrangements without Imperial interference.

The arguments in favour of Federation are usually based on the following considerations. Federation, we are told, will enable us—

1. To provide a more powerful defence against the enemies of the British Empire.
2. To secure a better and more economical form of Government.
3. To obtain a quicker and healthier advancement of the various industries; and
4. As a check to the tendency to further subdivision, as well as for the creating of more friendly feelings than at present exist between the residents of different localities, Federation, we are assured, offers the best, if not the only means.

With one army and navy we should naturally expect and provide a defence force far superior in power to what we can now boast of. The expense of maintaining this united force might not be less than the present annual outlay on colonial defences, but it requires no elaborate argument to prove that any extra cost would be fully compensated for by increased efficiency.

In other directions a greater economy in administration, and especially in the construction of public works of an intercolonial character, would more easily be secured, both by the amalgamation of Government offices, and by the higher ability we could afford to jointly pay for. Eleven hundred and fifty pounds per annum is considered to be a high salary for an Engineer in Chief in South Australia. It is more than any Minister of the Crown in that colony receives; but it certainly will not arouse envious feelings in the minds of first-class professional men in England.

That the industrial enterprise of these colonies would be ultimately greatly benefited by the removal of vexatious tariffs on each other's products freetraders and protectionists must alike admit. It is here, however, that we touch on one of the chief obstacles in the path of Federation, for it is held by many that intercolonial freetrade would give Victoria, whose industries have been established under protection, an undue advantage in manufacturing over the other colonies. Leaving this and other objections for the moment, we may certainly claim that Federation would put a stop to any further subdivision of these colonies.

Victoria and Queensland have split away from New South Wales, and it is within the realms of the possible that the residents of the northern territory may some day seek to legislate for themselves, and that the large area known as Western Australia may be divided under two or more independent Governments. There is also a feeling of what some describe as jealousy, but which certainly cannot be called excessive friendliness, existing between the inhabitants of, let us instance, New South Wales and Victoria. It may be due to 'a spirit of healthy rivalry,' but among people of the same race and language all animosity, in however mild a form it may show itself, ought to give place to honest goodwill. There is always a danger while the colonies are disunited of those little differences arising which tend to create antagonistic feelings. Sweep away all chance of such matters cropping up, and there will be no longer any cause for squabbling.

Having mentioned the principal benefits to be derived from Federation, let us consider what are the chief difficulties which stand in the way.

At present each colony has its own debt and system of taxation, and no two have the same method of dealing with waste or Crown lands. Are the debts to be consolidated? Will the taxpayers in New South Wales or Victoria quietly consent to assist in paying the interest on borrowed money squandered in New Zealand, or *vice versâ*? Would New South Wales adopt the South Australia plan of dealing with unalienated land? Unless we answer Yes to these questions, we are forced to admit each colony must be permitted to provide the interest on its debt in such manner as the contributors, or taxpayers, may deem most expedient. If we do not object to the consolidation of our loans, to uniformity in our customs tariffs, land systems, railway charges, and in obtaining other sources of revenue, then

Federation might be easily achieved. But the merest tyro in colonial politics will acknowledge that so great a change is bound, under the most favourable conditions, to be the work of many years. The Government of each colony has, in undertaking the execution of important works of development, stifled individual enterprise; and it would certainly act prejudicially to the interests of the poorer colonies if the present system were abandoned, and the future construction of public works, such as railways, jetties, &c., were left to private individuals to carry out. Nor could we, with any advantage to ourselves, trust to the tender mercies of a central Parliament to sanction the necessary expenditure for the construction of such public works as we require.

If an intercolonial Parliament attempted to decide where railways, &c., should be constructed out of borrowed monies, it is pretty certain the less influential countries would fare badly, even if the difficulty did not result in a deadlock caused by the pressure of work, and the obstruction raised by powerful minorities. There is already too much jealousy between the northern and southern districts in several of these colonies. In an intercolonial Parliament this feeling would be intensified when the question of expenditure on the construction of proposed public works was brought forward.

While, therefore, it is evident that the initiation and execution of public works of a local character must necessarily be remitted to local Parliaments, it is also clear that any proposed consolidation of the several public debts must be abandoned as impracticable, and each colony left to provide for the payment of its own indebtedness—left, in short, to manage its financial affairs and public works as the cities are allowed to do.

Compelled to meet the liabilities it incurred, each colony would naturally desire to raise a revenue as it deemed most expedient. Nor is there any reason why such powers should not be granted, with this restriction—viz., that no taxes should be raised which were opposed to commercial intercourse. 'There's the rub.' Each colony might retain its revenues derived from Crown lands, waterworks, wharves, railways, and by any tax on the property or income of private persons, and even from its jointly authorized customs duties; but the majority of the advocates of Federation would certainly insist on intercolonial freetrade. There must be no vexatious imposts on each other's produce, either at the borders or at the ports.

It is very difficult to discuss questions affecting the policy of Freetrade or Protection without arousing an extraordinary amount of bitterness. In Australia, where Protectionists are, comparatively speaking, numerically stronger than in England, the subject is apt to arouse the passions of the disputants more quickly than a theological argument. In England the majority often calmly dismiss all discussion by briefly telling the minority that no one in his proper senses can be a Protectionist. It is, therefore, more difficult to persuade persons in England that many of the men known as Protectionists in Australia are looked upon as leaders by the people, and that an allowance must be made in discussing the question of Federation for the prejudices of Protectionists as well as for the fancies of the freetrader.

It has been already stated it is frequently asserted that intercolonial freetrade would give Victoria, whose industries have been established under protection, an undue advantage over the other colonies in manufacturing.

'Why,' it is occasionally asked by our Protectionists, 'should Victoria manufacture for South Australia? What natural advantages does she possess as a manufacturing country which we do not? And, further, what should we gain if our struggling manufactories were to be closed from exposure to Victorian competition? To meet our financial engagements with the English bondholder, to maintain the price of property, to ensure further progress, we require population. Close our manufactories and we not only restrict the increase of population, but we induce our factory hands to emigrate to Victoria.'

The freetrader naturally regards these statements as exaggerated, and laughs at the fears of the manufacturers who advance them. He also claims that 'the great impetus intercolonial freetrade would give to business would fully compensate for any loss we might sustain by the change.'

We have assumed, and not without reason, that Victorians would not object to intercolonial freetrade, and we might safely go to the length of taking it for granted that if the whole of the electors in the Australasian colonies were polled, there would be a majority in its favour. But whether we are justified in assuming this or not, we must admit that directly we couple with intercolonial freetrade a uniform customs tariff on all foreign goods, the matter assumes another aspect. Although it is not essential to Federation, it is at least desirable that these colonies should adopt a uniform tariff, and the question arises whether the opposition of the Protectionist party in Victoria and elsewhere should be courted by insisting on low duties. Prudence dictates that in the early stages of the introduction of a new system of government it is well not to insist on too much. Give the Central Parliament or Federal Council power to arrange a tariff, and it will not be long before the customs duties are fixed to suit the wishes of the majority of colonists.

It may be found advisable in the interests of Federation not to insist even on the amount of customs charges to be levied on foreign products being relegated to the decision of any central authority, but to wait until after that central authority has been created, and then to agitate for this addition to its powers.

Having shown that Federation is desirable, and dealt with the alleged disadvantages or objections raised against it, we may proceed to discuss the following questions:—

1.   How is Federation to be secured?
2.   What powers should be entrusted to the Federal Government?
   Federation cannot be forced on the people of these colonies. It is necessarily a
matter of slow growth, and those who are in favour of it will the more quickly
attain the object they have in view, if prepared to be thankful for small mercies.
As the colonies have separate Parliaments, the first step is to induce some of the
leading members of Parliament to adopt Federation as a plank in their political
platforms. Australian politicians are in need of a subject of this sort, and a word
from Government House would be sufficient to persuade the leaders to promise
on the hustings to vote for the appointment of delegates to a general conference.
No elector would refuse to support a candidate on such grounds, though many
might think the conference would end in smoke. As the result of the conference
might be unsatisfactory, another way of attaining our object deserves consideration. We could appeal to that central authority which already exists. Our Parliaments can forward a petition to the Crown, and there is not the least doubt that
such a petition, if supported by all of these colonies, would be most favourably
entertained by Her Majesty's advisers. The Imperial Government, even without
the receipt of a petition, can facilitate the Federation of Australasia by forming
in these colonies a central authority composed of the several governors, and
entrusting to that authority power to decide all cases of appeal against legal
decisions, which are, under the present system, referred to the House of Lords
from these colonies. This council of Governors might also be entrusted with still
more important powers, and authorized to sanction such bills as are reserved for
Her Majesty's assent.
   This central council would, in fact, represent the Colonial Office, and as the
Governors are better acquainted with these colonies than some of the officials in
that office, the colonists would be perfectly satisfied, and the officials in England
spared a certain amount of trouble. The chief advantage, however, which would
be derived by the adoption of this suggestion consists in accustoming the colonists to the existence in Australasia of a central Government, which, in course
of time, must become more representative of these countries, and be entrusted
with more power by the various colonial Parliaments.
   Should, however, the former scheme prove successful, and the delegates
appointed by our Parliaments adopt some plan for electing a chamber composed
of representatives elected by each colony, it would be necessary to pass constitution bills. These bills would not only provide for the election in each province of
the representatives in the central council, but also confer certain powers on this
new chamber. The greater the powers conferred on this central authority the
more representative should it be; and to secure a thoroughly representative
and popular body we are compelled to leave the selection of its members to the

taxpayers. By this it is not meant that the taxpayers in each colony should be called upon *en masse* to make the selection, but that the selection should be left to members of Parliament who are appointed by the taxpayers, and are better able than the great body of electors to judge of a man's fitness for such a high position.

One of the first questions which would have to be settled prior to the formation of this central Parliament, is the number of members each colony should have the right to elect. To take population as a basis is by many considered as injudicious, and there are, doubtless, several weighty objections to it. Victorians, however, would be inclined to grumble if either Western Australia or Tasmania returned as many representatives as they did; yet the advancement of the interests of Western Australia is of as much importance to us as the advancement of those of Victoria. The question of representation has been so frequently discussed by the ablest minds of the age, and is of so far too great a magnitude to be dealt with in a brief essay, that, without pronouncing any opinion as to what is the best system, we here leave it, merely surmising that electors in these colonies will mostly prefer some arrangement which is based on population.

Concerning the powers which should be entrusted to a central authority, we may place in a prominent position, (1) those which concern naval and military matters; (2) the right to charge each colony its due proportion of the cost of maintaining these forces; and (3) authority to recommend the construction of works of intercolonial importance; as well as (4) uniformity in our laws; together with (5) power to veto all bills in which the interests of these colonies, as a whole, or the rest of the British Empire, may chance to be injuriously affected.

It would be folly to expect much from a newly constituted body, but as we became accustomed to its existence, and learned to regard it with feelings of respect and affection, we should gradually become content to surrender some of our selfish notions for the benefit of the common good. Though there are no dangers threatening us which would force us to unite, yet the abilities Australians have shown in organization and self-government, and their natural generosity of disposition, render the task of bringing about Federation more easy than strangers may fancy.

That there is an unmistakable desire to increase our own importance in the eyes of the world which we must lack as separate colonies, will be generally admitted; but we have waited for our politicians to lead the way, and our politicians will not make a start. Not only, however, are we aware that an United Australasia would rank as one of the powers of the world, but we feel that we shall deserve the gratitude of the next generation, if we seize the present opportunity to secure an United Australasia as a heritage for our descendants.

HENRY PARKES

Sir Henry Parkes (1815–96), English-born, self-educated, a politician, poet and writer, emigrated to Sydney in 1839. He was elected to the Legislative Council in 1848, where he supported the push to abolish transportation of British convicts. Premier of New South Wales four times, he was knighted in 1877. Parkes was a talented administrator, and actively promoted Australia's importance to the Empire. [ADB]

from 'Our growing Australian Empire', *Nineteenth Century*, vol. 15, 1884, pp. 138–49.

… Here we have an imperfect picture of the Young England growing up in Australasia, which, in all the best characteristics of the race, is more English than Old England herself. What it is at the end of 1883 it will not be at the end of 1884; but an English people of larger growth, newer aspirations, more extended enterprises, and stouter vigour. And so on year by year, the progress of this Young England will be more and more accelerated. We turn at once to the statesmen who sway the destiny of the Empire, and curiously ask, What will they do with it? It is certain that the present relations, the present modes of treatment, and especially the unconscious estimate of the colonies as a subordinate portion, a convenient appendage, of the Empire, cannot go on for ever. Whatever it may be, change must come. The young man, full of hope and emulation, cannot continue to play his part before the world in the boy's jacket. If it be urged, as I have heard it urged, that there is no feeling of the inferiority of the colonies in the minds of Englishmen at home, I turn to Professor Seeley's thoughtful book on 'The Expansion of England.' He is not a colonist, nor does he move in circles where the colonial view is likely to be contracted, and he tells us plainly that the feeling constantly crops out in the daily speech of the English people. 'We constantly betray by our modes of speech,' he writes, 'that we do not reckon our colonies as really belonging to us. Thus, if we are asked what the English population is, it does not occur to us to reckon in the population of Canada and Australia.' If we are not reckoned as English people, and yet not as foreign people, what kind of status must we occupy in the British-Isles-limited English mind? If we are neither flesh nor fowl, are we regarded as good red herring?

I do not belong to those who attribute to the Liberal party in England a settled desire for the disintegration of the Empire, or a lopping-off of some of its far-away outshoots. We must recollect that an essential part of the political creed of English Liberals is a watchful care for the English taxpayer, the enforcement of economy in the public expenditure. Every vote in Parliament, and every word of advocacy out of doors, must be made to harmonise with these professions of

Liberal policy. It may be expected, therefore, that all proposals to create new offices, and to extend the territorial limits of the Empire, will be viewed with scrutiny and caution, not to say unreserved objection, by the Liberals. The justification for a new advance, or for the maintenance of the old lines, must be made palpably clear to them before it receives their sanction. But I can call to mind no public utterance of any leader of the Liberal party which, fairly examined in connection with his public life, would lead to the conclusion that he is indifferent, any more than his fellow subjects outside the ranks of his party, to the maintenance of the Empire in all its colossal proportions. I believe I am justified in saying that the great Englishman at the head of the Government is fervently anxious to preserve for Her Majesty's successors the free and united Empire over which she herself reigns. As I have no evidence to support any charge of this kind, I do not complain of the conduct of any individual statesman. On the contrary, it must be admitted, and it is acknowledged with gratitude, that the Australian colonies owe a large part of the liberties which they at present enjoy to the wisdom of Liberal statesmen. Still less can it be reasonably charged against the English public that there is any design to inculcate a feeling of indifference towards the colonies. What is alleged and what is keenly felt, is that the English people in the colonies are insensibly regarded as holding some kind of secondary place in the relations of the Empire, as not 'belonging to' the English people at home in the same sense as one part of the nation belongs to all other parts in the United Kingdom. If this prevailing tendency not to 'reckon' us as Englishmen arises from habits of thought and the causal interchange of sentiment in daily life, it only makes the national slight the more pointed and galling. If it is part of the growth of the contemporary mind, silently assented to by governing men and people alike in the mother country, the prospect of a true consanguineous and enduring relationship is next to hopeless.

Amongst the population which I have tried to describe as fast taking form in Australia, the rude sentiments of independence will not lack indigenous nourishment. The thought, expressed or unexpressed, will be, 'If England has difficulty in reckoning us as Englishmen, we are all the prouder of being Australians.' Some form of national pride must take root, and spread itself wide and deep in the soil, and it must inevitably be one of two forms—either truly British, as sharing on equal terms in all the glory of the Empire, or separately and purely Australian, creating a peculiar glory all its own. There will be no possibility of contentment with the status of a Dependency in the Imperial system. In another ten years there will be an addition to the population of Australasia of two millions or nearly, and the boundless resources of the wide territory will be developed to an extent beyond the power of the imagination to foreshadow. The sense of having achieved will stimulate the passion for higher achievement. The successful in adventure and enterprise will want other rewards than the mere accumulation of wealth. The awakening ambitions of the gifted and heroic will need fitting spheres for their honourable gratification. There will be room for all on the common field of a great and united Empire. Or possibly, by some untoward turn of events, a field may be found under the flag of a new Commonwealth.

I believe most thoughtful men in the public life of Australia are in favour of the British path of destiny. But it may be doubted whether any of the schemes for political change which from time to time have been propounded would help us much in that direction. The representation of the colonies in the Imperial Parliament, which has been more than once proposed, would be abortive from the first, and end in creating new jealousies and discontents. Any number of members for Australia that could in the nature of things be entitled to sit in the House of Commons would have no appreciable weight in the decisions of that body, while their admission would be in conflict with the principle that no member should be charged with the advocacy of special interests. This seems to me fatal to any such scheme, without touching upon the difficulty of sending properly qualified men to Westminster from the other side of the globe, and keeping them correctly informed of the progress of matters at so great a distance. The scheme for introducing into British Cabinet a Minister in some way specially designated by the colonies would, I think, fail from kindred causes of failure, to say nothing of it being inconsistent with the free selection of colleagues by the person charged with the formation of a Government.

In meeting the needs arising out of the steady and rapid growth of the colonies some organic change in the constituted form of the Imperial Government must be faced. The constitution of our fathers must be made to fit the great Empire for which it certainly was not in the first place designed. What was suitable to the time of William and Mary, and gave embodiment to the notion of Dependencies which then prevailed, is no longer applicable to the vast proportions of the Empire and the spirit of freedom which has been rooted and is actively stirring in the more distant parts. I naturally treat the whole question from an Australian standpoint, and my reasonings and suggestions can only incidentally or inferentially have any bearing upon India, or Canada, or Africa. But if we can get at a true principle in relation to Australia, its application to all, under necessary modifications, will not be involved in much uncertainty.

In Australia the Liberal statesmen of England have with their own hands sown the seed of freedom and independent authority. They must have foreseen the fruit which the seed would bear. Yet very much the same routine treatment as followed upon the first introduction of Parliamentary Government twenty-seven years ago is pursued at the present day, without any apparent reference to the amazing growth of all the elements of political power which has taken place in the colonies since their emancipation from Downing Street bureaucracy. Even in the act which many persons regard as the most important in the Imperial connection—that of filling the office of Governor—it would be extremely difficult to trace any increasing anxiety, as the colonies advance in the work of self-government, to select the representative of the Crown from men of larger constitutional knowledge and experience. But it would not be at all difficult to point out persons who have received that high appointment in the later years who were less fitted to discharge its functions than Governors in the earlier years of Responsible Government. This would hardly deserve notice if it did not lead to the popular impression—and such impressions sink deep in the popular mind, and are not easily removed—that the office is occasionally made a convenience to influential persons at the seat of the Imperial Government rather than the means of strengthening the constitutional relations of the Empire.

Before venturing upon any suggestions of my own as to changes in the Imperial connection, it does not seem out of place to glance at what would probably happen if Australia at any time in the near future separated from England; an event which, whatever surface-loyalists may say to the contrary, is unquestionably not out of the range of possibilities within the next generation. This is no imaginary ground; for there are persons in Australia, and in most of the Australian Legislatures, who avowedly or tacitly favour the idea of separation. If Australia were independent, say towards the close of the century, with five or six millions of inhabitants, she would speedily and beyond all question rise to the position of a great power. Distance from other Powers would alone be to her the element of immense strength. She has already learnt to rely upon herself for the means of armed defence. Unitedly she could pour upon any point large bodies of enthusiastic defenders, without being under the necessity of burdening herself with standing armies. She could easily create a navy adequate to her wants. Within her own shores she would possess all that is imperatively necessary to keep the machinery of civilised society going with the minimum of privation and inconvenience. In the possible case of being cut off from the rest of the world—a very remote probability—she could, better than any other country on the face of the globe, sustain herself. So much for her capabilities. In the event of her national independence, whatever form of government she assumed, she would in all moral certainty receive the cordial recognition of the great Powers. If not sympathy with new-born freedom, jealousy of England would prompt that recognition. Undoubtedly in such an event Australia would put on a new attraction to foreign nations, and possibly to England herself, so perverse is the intellect in discovering too late the value of what is lost. New population and new capital, fresh streams of brain and muscle, and material power, would flow in upon her; and while she rose in the estimation of foreign nations, her own prosperous citizens would abide with her, as they do not now abide, and help to do her honour. There would be no fear for the career of Australia as an independent nation. But in my view she would miss her higher destiny, her rightful share in what may be a more glorious rule than mankind has ever yet seen.

The English people in Europe, in America, in Africa, in Asia, in Australasia, are surely destined for a mission beyond the work which has consumed the energies of nations throughout the buried centuries. If they held together in the generations before us in one world-embracing empire, maintaining and propagating the principles of justice, freedom, and peace, what blessings might arise from their united power to beautify and invigorate the world! To share in the pacific grandeur of a rule transcending all other forms of dominion, and superior to all other governing powers in capability of improving the condition of mankind, would be better, nobler, more elevating for young Australia than separate national existence, though it were the freest and most prosperous. Under the flag of the United English People, the work of human progress might well go on till the poet's dream melted into the reality of the statesman's achievement—

Till the war-drum throbb'd no longer, and the battle-flags were furl'd
In the Parliament of man, the federation of the world.

To bear an honoured part in a consummation so glorious, to be included in a confederation so all-powerful and so beneficent, is what my feeble voice would claim for Australia. And this amazing destiny lies clear before the English people, waiting to be entered upon, and easy of accomplishment. England, in her day of narrow purposes, has done many things more difficult than placing herself at the head of the civilised world in the present age.

But to take the colonies with her in this work of world-empire, they must be made part of England herself. The very nomenclature of colonies must be dropped out of existence. In large measure the Australian group have outgrown the condition of colonies. To all intents and purposes they are young States. They govern themselves, they are prepared to defend themselves if occasion should arise, they have led the way in political changes where England herself has followed. Why should they not be designated in future the British States of Australia? In this designation the British feeling and the Australian feeling would habitually and perpetually blend. The term colony means nothing; the term British-Australian State would mean everything. Let the Imperial Government formally invite the present colonies to enter into a federation under some such name as is here suggested, which would signify a closer and higher relationship with the parent State, and in which the sentiments of British pride and Australian patriotism would commingle in one glow of loyalty. 'What signifies a name?' may be asked by men who are ever talking of the integrity of the Empire. 'It is only a matter of form,' said the ease-loving monarch, and evoked the memorable reply of the wiser counsellor, 'Your Majesty is only a matter of form!' Momentous issues have been decided by a sentiment; feelings that live in immortal deeds have been called forth by a name. But if this be so, it is not less true that an absurd name has the opposite effect, and puts a damp on everything. The impediments to federation, and there are impediments, would one by one give way. The union would come almost as matter of course, though the basis of federation would probably be imperfect at the beginning. There might, for example, be conflicting tariffs left out of the provisions of agreement, to be brought into harmony afterwards. But all the more thoughtful men engaged in political life in Australia have thought out in one form or other the question of federation.

As soon as we have an Australian federation in any form, let a Council of Australia, to sit in London, be created on some basis of Australian representation which would afford a fair prospect of securing Australian confidence in its proceedings. This body should be charged with all business between the Australian Governments and Her Majesty's Imperial Government, while the functions of Governor should be limited as much as possible to the class of functions which are discharged by the Sovereign in the present working of the Constitution, and to those State ceremonies which are as necessary, and have their high uses as much in Australia as in England. In treaties with foreign nations why should not Australia, so far as Australian interests may be affected, be at least consulted through her Representative Council? And why should not Englishmen in Australia be on an equal footing with Englishmen within the United Kingdom as recipients of marks of the Royal favour. It is not a question of the value of honours. If we were starting afresh, with a clear field before us, it might be fairly open to doubt whether it would be wise to originate any system of honours. But the question now is, 'Why should Her Majesty's subjects in Australia be treated differently from Her Majesty's subjects at home?' and this has to be considered in view of welding together harmoniously and durably all parts of the Empire. If it be replied, as I think I have heard it stated, that there really is no difference shown in this respect at present, my reply is based on a very notable fact. In South Australia, in Victoria, in New South Wales, as in other colonies, we have men of high character and large fortune who have rendered important services to their Sovereign and country, and who deservedly enjoy the respect of their fellow citizens. In what single instance has any one of these men been thought of for the honours of the Peerage, while men, unquestionably inferior to them within the United Kingdom, not unfrequently receive that high consideration from the Crown?

I throw out these suggestions without reserve or hesitation, not as forming any matured plan, but as pointing to the direction in which well-considered changes must take place, if the 'integrity of the Empire,' which is so often and so lightly on men's lips, is to be preserved. And I claim to have done some little to foster a British spirit and to keep together the elements of British progress in Australia. Whatever may be thought at the present moment, the question raised will very soon present itself with an irresistible demand for solution. ...

ARCHIBALD WILLIAM STIRLING _____

Archibald Stirling (c.1856–1923) was a solicitor and some-time journalist whose works include The Never Never Land: a Ride in North Queensland *(1884). [WI]*

_____ *from* 'The Political Outlook in Queensland', *Fortnightly Review*, vol. 44, 1888, pp. 721–7.

... In Queensland, as in New South Wales, of which Queensland once formed a part, legislation is carried on through a nominee upper chamber, and a representative assembly elected by universal suffrage, and consisting of seventy-two members. For the sake of brevity I shall assume that the functions of these two bodies correspond with the functions of the Houses of Parliament in this country. The Crown is represented by a governor, who is paid out of the revenues of the colony a sum of £5,000 a year. In Queensland, as in the rest of the Australian colonies, the line of demarcation in party politics was for many years between the squatting and anti-squatting elements; that is to say, between the vested interests of the large graziers and the capitalists who were connected with them on the one hand, and the mass of the community on the other. By degrees the squatters became merged into what, for want of a better name, was called the 'Conservative' party, while their opponents claimed for themselves the title of 'Liberals.'

It is necessary to go back a few years in order that the present position may be made intelligible. I will not, however, trespass upon the reader's patience beyond the year 1883. At that time the Conservative party had been in power under Sir Thomas McIlwraith for five years, and at the general election, which took place in the winter, two questions of capital importance were presented to the country; one the policy of building railways on the land-grant system, the other the cultivation of sugar by imported and regulated black or other coloured labour. Through a variety of causes, not the least of which was the squatters' objections to land-grant railways, this election proved most disastrous to the Conservative party, and Sir Samuel Griffiths, with a strong Parliamentary following, came into power.

Unfortunately for the country no less than for his party, Sir Samuel had not within his following men of the ability requisite to form a strong administration, or if such men existed the Premier did not select them. From its inception the Liberal Ministry of 1883 was what is called in Australia 'a one-man Government.' Griffiths was the Ministry. The various departments were presided over by Griffiths, diluted with very badly-digested 'Henry George,' as in the case of the Minister for Lands, or Sir Samuel, mixed with milk and water, as in the case of the Attorney-General. By pledging the Government to oppose black labour, the sugar industry, with five millions of invested capital, was destroyed; by vain attempts in the supposed direction of land-nationalisation, one of the main sources of revenue was practically extinguished; by uncompromising hostility to northern separation several constituencies were lost; and finally, by the proposal of a land-tax, property owners everywhere became alarmed, and the ablest of the Premier's colleagues was driven from the Ministry. In short, by a system of 'meddle and muddle,' the all-powerful Government of 1883 went to the country in the early part of this year as discredited and as certain of defeat as the English Liberal administration in 1874. The opportunity had come, the issue of the fight merely depended on whether the Conservative leader was capable of taking full advantage of the occasion.

Sir Thomas McIlwraith grasped the situation, and elected to carry the fight into the very camp of the enemy. He announced his candidature of Sir Samuel's own constituency of North Britain, which had for years been a stronghold of Liberalism, and on the 16th of March he opened the campaign by addressing the largest meeting ever held in the capital.

With merciless logic he exposed the blunders and shortcomings of the Administration, he outbid his opponents on Chinese exclusion, he pronounced boldly for fostering local industries by means of protective duties, while he denounced the proposed Australian Naval Defence Bill, which had been agreed to on behalf of the colony by Sir Samuel Griffiths at the Imperial Conference, and passed into law in the other colonies, as a sacrifice of the country to English interests. The defence proposal he characterised as the payment of tribute by a free colony, and he raised for the first time the cry of 'Australia for the Australians,' from which the National party took its rise, and in a few short weeks swept the country from end to end. At first, I hardly think that the importance of this part of Sir Thomas McIlwraith's speech was appreciated. As, however, the candidates began to feel their way before the various electorates, the 'National' cry rang louder and louder, until before the elections were over the Conservative party had ceased to exist, and from its ashes had sprung up a new and stronger combination, which now not only calls itself, but is called by its opponents 'the National party.'

From one end of Queensland to the other the supporters of Sir Thomas McIlwraith caught at the idea; everywhere the 'Imperialistic' (*i.e.* English) leanings of Sir Samuel Griffiths were a favourite theme of satire and attack. If election literature is any guide to the most effective popular cries, it was the rapid and almost unexpected development of the National movement which contributed in the largest degree to the victory. As Cromwell used the intoxication of religious enthusiasm to stimulate the ardour of his soldiers, as the Royalists in every country have found it necessary to encourage the sentiment of loyalty in their followers, so Sir Thomas McIlwraith developed and made use of the national feeling in Queensland, and gained for himself and his party the greatest victory known in colonial politics. ...

... The result of the general election in Queensland has been to seat in power a Ministry backed by a large majority in the popular chamber, the main planks of whose platform are, reform of the land law by the encouragement of private ownership, total exclusion of the Chinese, the reorganization of the national finances by the adoption of protection, opposition to the Australian Naval Defence Bill, and the welding together of the Australian colonies, at first into a confederation, and then into an independent nation. ...

ANON. ───────────────────────────────

──────────────────────────── 'Australia and the Empire', *Review of
Reviews*, vol. 2, 1890, p. 461.

MAJOR-GEN. STRANGE, in the *United Service Magazine* for November, declares that of all the disunited states of Greater Britain, Australasia appears to be the most disunited. Major-General Strange has travelled extensively in Australasia, and has listened to debates in every legislature in the colonies and has spoken in New Zealand on the question of Imperial Federation. He thinks that the chief cause of the reaction against Imperial Federation in Australia is, first, the abandonment of Northern New Guinea to the Germans, and secondly, the dispatch of French Residents to New Caledonia. The only remedy against the occurrence of such difficulties would be the insistence by the colonies of a voice in the foreign policy of the empire. If Australia were to cut the painter, her present population would be the richest and most defenceless people in the world, having no army, navy, arsenals, or ammunition sufficient for a week's fighting. Germany, he thinks, will inevitably annex Holland, and from Java and New Guinea would be strongly tempted to advance upon unprotected Australia. The new generation is much less patriotic, and the only chance of uniting the empire is while the old colonists still live:—

> History is not one of the subjects taught in the States School of Victoria, and but little of it in the other colonies. When speaking on this subject to a wealthy and cultivated Australian, a graduate at Oxford, I was told, 'They did not desire their young people to waste time over the histories of played-out old peoples, but to make history for themselves.' I got no clear answer to my query, 'What sort of history do you suppose will be made by a people who are not only ignorant of the history of the great race from which they sprang, but of all other races?'
>
> I ask the reader to picture to himself the mind of a young person, almost devoid of historic knowledge, living in a far-off colony, where nature assumes a somewhat monotonous aspect, where there are no historic associations. As our appreciation of general literature is mainly due to such historic knowledge, is it surprising that the young Australian of both sexes, though musical, is not an imaginative or reading person? Upon these practical but unimaginative people depend the future relations of their country to ours. The old colonist is passing away, and is succeeded by his sons, who talk as if they, and not their fathers, had built up the marvellous growth of the Antipodes. ...

EDWARD NICHOLAS COVENTRY BRADDON

Sir Edward Braddon (1829–1904), English-born civil servant and politician, and brother of Mary Braddon the popular sensation novelist, went to India in 1847, then to Tasmania in 1878. Elected to the Tasmanian Parliament in 1879, he was subsequently appointed agent-general in London (1891– 93), knighted, and returned to active politics in the colony. He became Premier (1894–99), supported Federation, and was a member of the Federal Council of Australasia (1888, 1895–99). He produced a range of periodical articles and several books, including Life in India (1872) *and* Thirty Years of Shikar (1895). [ADB]

from 'The Federation Movement in Australasia', *Nineteenth Century*, vol. 40, 1896, pp. 156–72.

Throughout the provinces of Australia, in the Garden Island, Tasmania, and in a lesser degree over the Britain of the South, New Zealand, the idea of a Federated Australasia finds general acceptance. Leaders of men, and they who follow not too blindly, concur in the view that this Federation of the seven constitutionally governed colonies in the Austral seas, together with Fiji, British New Guinea, and any other British territories in the South and West Pacific, must eventually be achieved; and he who is an enthusiast in the cause, not yet daunted by delays and

backslidings on the part of Federationists, asks when, and under what conditions, and by whose agency this splendid dream will be realised. At the National
Australasian Convention held in Sydney in 1891, the late Sir Henry Parkes, then
Prime Minister of New South Wales, spoke confidently of Federation being
accomplished in two years. But those two years came and went, and yet another
two years, without any nearer approach to the 'one nation, one destiny' that had
been so confidently predicted by that statesman. And when in January 1895 the
six Premiers of Australia and Tasmania met in conference in Hobart, to formulate
some plan by which Federation could be urged forward, Sir Henry Parkes, then
a private member of the New South Wales Assembly (and soon to become a
private citizen, bereft of even his M.P.-ship), spoke in scornful terms of those
statesmen who were seeking to achieve that which he had vainly dreamt of as the
immediate result of his initiative.

Who will be the instruments that shall lead the peoples to the destined goal?
None of those, I venture to predict, who occupy the recognised position of
leaders while the petty, personal jealousies and rivalries of fallen statesmen or
discredited politicians intervene to frustrate action—not by these and not at all
shall this great end be attained, until the peoples who should be led become the
leaders, and the *vox populi* demands that the thing shall be done without further
babble. And even if the popular guides could be brought to such a wholesome
frame of mind as would induce them to welcome any instrument efficient for
their purpose, and hail the accomplishment of Federation while standing humbly
aside, self-effaced in their disinterested loyalty—even then Federation, as I see it,
must be the act of the people, only to be brought about when the people are
educated to this lofty but quite practicable ideal.

And when will the people recognise that herein their prosperity, their strength,
and their security lie? When patriotic men shall teach to some purpose instead of
leading in purblind fashion only to attain a present object, and when communities shall take a national instead of a parochial view of affairs, and recognise that
no nation can be great wherein the individual interest is preferred to the general;
that no nation can be wealthy when the common fund is depleted to support
exotic industries; that no nation can be powerful where a scattered people, broken
up into semi-hostile clans, have no united purpose of defence.

It is sometimes said that the Australasian Colonies will only become one under
the shadow of the sword. But what sort of Federation would that be which came
of a sudden panic—the haphazard creation of a threatened invasion—even if the
invader gave such notice of his coming as would admit of any manner of union?
Or what would be the prospect of an effective Federation after a foreign foe had
raided and plundered and left an Australasia crippled as to population, wealth,
and commerce, and thrown back in the path of progress by half a century? If

Federation is to be of practical advantage for the next generation or two, it should be effected now in a time of peace, when statesmen and people can, and they will, give their minds to this great subject.

Australasia (excluding British New Guinea and Fiji) is, except as to population, in advance of the Dominion of Canada; it has greater national resources; it has a larger volume of trade; and (leaving out of consideration the few thousands of aboriginals in Australia, and the Maoris, who number about 40,000) has a population homogeneous as the Canadians are not even now. The Federation of the provinces of the Dominion was effected although Englishmen and Frenchmen had to unite in the common *bund*; although the French language and French laws and customs remained, as indeed, to a great extent, they still endure. Federation is moving on in South Africa, where English and Dutch occupy towards each other much the same position as the English and French in Canada. But in Australasia, where only one tongue is known, whether it be spoken by men of British descent or by nationalised Germans or Swedes or other Europeans, and but one code of laws or manners or customs prevails, Federation is made more difficult by its very simplicity; and men who should be brothers are kept asunder by border Custom-houses that are as inappropriate as would be the raising of an octroi barrier at the entrance to every Australasian city or town.

The idea of a Federated Australasia is no new thing in the Austral Colonies. It may be said to be coeval with the creation of responsible government, for when the colony of New South Wales had her constitution under consideration, one of her statesmen—Mr. E. Deas Thomson—urged the necessity of a central Parliament that should be empowered to deal exclusively with some eight subjects that he specified. Federation was advocated by another and a very distinguished statesman (Wentworth) of New South Wales, while yet that colony was in its infancy. In 1867 it was considered and strongly recommended by a Select Committee of the Victorian Legislative Assembly; and in 1881 a conference was held in Sydney at which a Federal Council Bill, framed by Sir Henry Parkes, was adopted, but without any practical result, inasmuch as neither the Government of Sir Henry Parkes nor any other Government took any action whatever to give effect to it. The creation of a Federal Council as the first tangible step towards a fuller Federation was the work of the convention that met in Sydney two years later. It should be added, as further proof of the early conception of the Federal idea, that the Constitution Bill passed by the British Parliament in 1849 contained a provision whereby the colonies of Australia might enjoy a uniform tariff regulated by a central body.

... Briefly stated, the more important provisions of the Federation Enabling Bill are as follows: Each colony shall elect ten representatives, such election to be on the Assembly franchise and for the colony as one constituency. No person to vote more than once at the same election. When such elections shall have been held in three or more colonies, a meeting of the convention shall be convened for a time and place agreed to by the Governors of such colonies. The convention, having framed and approved the constitution, shall adjourn for a period of not less than sixty or more than 120 days. On the reassembling of the convention, the constitution shall be considered with any amendments that may be proposed, and finally adopted. So soon as practicable after the close of the proceedings of the convention, the question of the acceptance or rejection of the constitution shall be submitted to the vote 'Yes' or 'No' of the Assembly electors in each colony. When the electors of three colonies have accepted the Constitution, both Houses of Parliament may adopt addresses to the Queen praying that the same may be passed into law by the Imperial Parliament; and these addresses being agreed to, the same shall be transmitted to the Queen with a certified copy of the constitution. The Bill gives no power to the Colonial Parliaments to amend the Constitution; they may suggest amendments for the consideration of the congress when it shall assemble finally; so may the press direct attention to possible amendments; but the bill to be submitted to the people shall be one and the same for every colony.

Such is the measure which may be expected to settle for these colonies at an early date whether they shall enjoy a common nationhood or remain isolated provinces. Already public interest has been aroused on this vital question, already candidates for the honourable and responsible position of representatives at the congress are in the field, and before the year 1896 runs out the meeting of the convention may have taken place or be immediately impending.

Meanwhile, those who are earnest in the cause, and who have studied Federation, have imposed upon them the obligation of instructing the people who are to be the ultimate arbiters in this great issue. The men engaged in industries heretofore fostered as exotics by the artificial means of heavy inter-colonial tariffs will need to be taught something of the advantages that come with free trade; and by this teaching may be surmounted the greatest obstacle that presents itself to such a complete union as will abolish those inter-provincial Custom-houses that now hamper trade and divert industrial effort and capital into unnatural channels. The advantages of that union in improved credit, consolidated strength, and enlargement of Australasia's power in the comity of nations will doubtless be taught. And to a people of such a high average of intelligence as that which distinguishes the inhabitants of these colonies the lesson may come home that the individual interest is subordinate to the general interest, and cannot but be shaped by it for good or evil as it (the general interest) prospers or declines.

To the smaller colonies, such as Tasmania, it should be obvious that they cannot stand out of a Federation into which the larger colonies have entered.

Newfoundland is an object-lesson in point. Those smaller colonies are, therefore, well advised that they should take their part in the convention and help to mould the constitution under which, sooner or later, they must come to exist. And it has been already pointed out that this constitution should be considered in a time of peace when hostility, or threatening of hostility, from without interferes in no way with the deliberations of those who frame it. Mr. Deakin, at the Melbourne Conference of 1890, spoke very eloquently upon this head. Others have so spoken from time to time; and always the argument has been with these that it is urgently required of us to settle this great question when it may be viewed and debated in all its aspects calmly, and not delay a settlement until a foreign enemy shall force us to join in an ill-considered union.

But delay may be regarded as dangerous for a reason which has nothing to do with invasion or menace by a foreign foe. It is possible—though I trust not probable—that, with the passing of years, colonies that now experience only insignificant feelings of mutual jealousy may become more and more estranged, may develop racial and hostile instincts fatal to the beautiful idea of 'one nation, one destiny,' with the result that, in addition to Custom-houses along the border of a province, there may be outposts of armed men ready at the word of command to fly at the throats of their brothers on the other side of the boundary. *Absit omen!* May it come about within the next two years, as seems at this moment possible, that Victorians, New South Welshmen, South Australians, and Queenslanders shall be distinguished as such no longer, but be all of them Australasians, under one flag and one central Government!

One lesson there is that happily the people do not need to have imparted to them—that is, loyalty to the mother country. A candidate for the position of representative of Victoria ventured to talk to his audience about a possible separation from England, and at the next meeting of the Australian Natives' Association it was clearly indicated to that candidate that his expressed views about separation met with their cordial disapproval. The Federation Enabling Bill itself discountenances this idea, for it provides for the enactment of the new constitution by the Imperial Parliament with the assent of the Crown.

CLARKE HUSTON IRWIN ⸻

See biographical note on p. 66.

This extract is from a seven-part series which includes: 'Aspects of Social Life', pp. 183–7; 'Politics and Public Men', pp. 256–60; 'The Education Systems', pp. 320–3; 'Churches and Mission Work', pp. 392–7; 'Literature', pp. 520–2; 'The English Language in Australia', pp. 652–5.

⸻ *from* 'Australian Sketches. Politics
and Public Men', *Leisure Hour*,
vol. 47, 1898, pp. 256–60.

… In the proceedings of the Federal Convention, which met at Adelaide in 1896, a long step has been taken in the direction of a federated Australia, Queensland being the only Australian colony that was unrepresented at the Convention. The proposals of the Convention have still to be considered in detail by the Parliaments of the respective colonies, but there is good reason to expect that, in the main, they will be adopted.

On one point the action of the Convention is greatly to be regretted. Petitions were sent in from New South Wales, Victoria, and South Australia, signed by many thousands, praying that the authority of the Deity should be recognised in the preamble of the new Constitution, and that provision should be made for the sessions of the Parliament to be opened with prayer. But the Convention negatived a proposition to insert the words 'under Divine guidance.'

It is said that this very secular position taken up by the Convention is due to the action of Cardinal Moran in seeking election as a member of the Federal Convention, and that its members were afraid of clerical interference. It is to be hoped that even yet the Christian people of the colonies may show themselves strong enough to get some recognition of religion in the Constitution of the Commonwealth. …

… Politics in Australia are very much like politics in other, English-speaking countries. There have been, no doubt, cases of log-rolling. Personal influence has sometimes interfered unworthily, as, for example, in matters of railway administration. Party feeling occasionally runs high, and sometimes the feuds and battle-cries of 'old country' parties are needlessly perpetuated in the new land. But, on the whole, the tone of Australian politics is upward rather than downward. I well remember, during the time of financial panic in Victoria, when the Government was hard pushed to meet its obligations to British creditors, one erratic member of the Legislative Assembly ventured to suggest 'repudiation.' But his dishonourable suggestion was vehemently repudiated by his fellow-members, and I do not think he found a single supporter. British honour is still, and is likely to remain, the dominating force in Australian public life.

FURTHER READING

The choice of pieces for this anthology was very difficult, and these are some that might have been included.

Adams, Francis, 'The Labour Movement in Australia', *Fortnightly Review*, n.s. vol. 50, 1891, pp. 181–95.
—— 'Social Life in Australia', *Fortnightly Review*, n.s. vol. 50, 1891, pp. 392–407, 539–53.
'Some Australian Men of Mark', *Fortnightly Review*, n.s. vol. 51, 1892, pp. 194–212.
—— 'Two Australian Writers', *Fortnightly Review*, n.s. vol. 52, 1892, pp. 352–65.
Adams, Robert Dudley, 'Letter from New South Wales', *Fraser's Magazine for Town and Country*, vol. 92, 1875, pp. 726–41.
Adderley, Charles Bowyer, 'Penal Servitude', *Nineteenth Century*, vol. 7, 1880, pp. 795–807.
'Affairs of the Colonies', *Annual Register*, 1849, pp. 102–23.
Aflalo, F. G., 'Some Practical Travel Hints for Our Boys: The Trip to Australia', *Boy's Own Paper*, vol. 20, 1897–98, pp. 782–3, 795, 813–14, 821–2.
Amos, Sheldon, 'Democratic Government in Victoria', *Westminster Review*, vol. 89, 1868, pp. 480–523.
Andrews, Alexander, 'Western Australia's Advance', *Simmonds's Colonial Magazine and Foreign Miscellany*, vol. 3, 1844, pp. 38–40.
—— 'Diet and Dainties of Australian Aborigines', *Bentley's Miscellany*, vol. 51, 1862, pp. 544–9.
'Answer to Lines "On Leaving Home"', *Home Circle*, vol. 2, 1850, p. 120.
'Answers to Correspondents: Australia wishes to go to Australia', *Working Man's Friend, and Family Instructor*, n.s. vol. 1, 1852, p. 304.
'Australia', *People's and Howitt's Journal*, vol. 2, 1850, p. 12.
'Australia Re-visited after Fifty Years', *Leisure Hour*, vol. 39, 1890, pp. 572–3.
'Australian California', *Eliza Cook's Journal*, vol. 6, 1851–52, pp. 282–5.
'The Australian Colonies', *Westminster Review*, vol. 100, 1878, pp. 311–47.
'Australian Colonies or Republic?', *Fraser's Magazine*, vol. 37, 1848, pp. 566–78.

'An Australian Emigrant's Letter', *Eliza Cook's Journal*, vol. 3, 1850, pp. 180–2.

'Australian Exploring Expedition', *Sharpe's London Magazine*, vol. 2, 1846, pp. 269–70.

'Australian File', *Leisure Hour*, vol. 2, 1853, pp. 340–3.

'An Australian Home', *Bow Bells*, vol. 1, 1863, p. 768.

'Australian Life. Prospects for Emigrants', *Howitt's Journal*, vol. 3, 1848, pp. 384–8.

'Australian Ophir', *Eliza Cook's Journal*, vol. 7, 1852, pp. 214–17.

'Australian Superstitions. From Richard Howitt's *Australia Felix*', *London Journal and Weekly Recorder of Literature, Science and Art*, vol. 1, 1845, p.190.

'"Australian Weather". From Mundy's *Our Antipodes*', *Eliza Cook's Journal*, vol. 8, 1852–53, p. 16.

'Australians' Cricket Tour', *Boy's Own Paper*, vol. 3, 1880–81, pp. 121–3.

'Australia's Metropolis and its Environs', *Tait's Edinburgh Magazine*, n.s. vol. 24, 1857, pp. 526–8.

Bakewell, R. H., 'The Loyalty of the Colonies: a Dialogue between a Globe-trotter and a Colonist', *Nineteenth Century*, vol. 28, 1890, pp. 191–200.

Barmby, Goodwyn, 'The English Emigrant' (poem), *Family Economist*, n.s. vol. 1, 1854, p. 57.

Barry, Alfred, 'The Loyalty of the Colonies', *Nineteenth Century*, vol. 28, 1890, pp. 801–11.

Bayley, Thomas Haynes, 'The Female Convict Ship' (poem), *Mirror of Literature, Amusement and Instruction*, vol. 22, 1833, p. 363.

Beadon, Robert J., 'Australasian Federation', *Westminster Review*, vol. 131, 1889, pp. 537–44.

'Beagle's Discoveries in Australia', *Fraser's Magazine*, vol. 34, 1846, pp. 105–17.

Bingham, Peregrine, 'On Emigration', *Westminster Review*, vol. 3, 1825, pp. 448–87.

'Bird's-Eye View of Australia', *Literary World*, vol. 1, 1839, pp. 391–4.

'Black and Red Ants of Australia', *Saturday Magazine*, vol. 11, 1837, p. 79.

Bowles, Thomas Gibson, 'Give and Take with the Colonies. Union of the Empire by Tariff', *Fortnightly Review*, n.s. vol. 220, 1885, pp. 679–88.

Brabazon, Reginald, 'A Britisher's impressions of America and Australia', *Nineteenth Century*, vol. 33, 1893, pp. 493–514.

Brassey, Thomas Allnutt, 'Water in the Australian Saharas', *Nineteenth Century*, vol. 28, 1890, pp. 425–34.

—— 'Australian Federation', *Nineteenth Century*, vol. 45, 1899, pp. 548–57.

'Brighter Britain', *Review of Reviews*, vol. 1, 1890, p. 468.

'British Emigrant Colonies: 1—New South Wales', *Tait's Edinburgh Magazine*, n.s. vol. 1, 1834, pp. 401–19.

Buckland, Anne Walbank, 'Goldfields Ancient and Modern', *Westminster Review*, vol. 120, 1883, pp. 378–408.

Cambridge, Ada, 'A Chaperon', *Windsor Magazine*, vol. 1, 1895, pp. 363–72.

—— 'Episodes in a Domestic Life', *Woman at Home. Annie S. Swan's Magazine*, vol. 5, 1895–96, pp. 491–501, 652–62.

—— 'Deposed', *Woman at Home. Annie S. Swan's Magazine*, vol. 5, 1895–96, pp. 52–9.

Campbell, Colin T., 'Hints for Actual and Intending Colonists', *Simmonds's Colonial Magazine and Foreign Miscellany*, vol. 2, 1844, pp. 417–19.

—— 'The Extent and Capabilities of our Colonies', *Simmonds's Colonial Magazine and Foreign Miscellany*, vol. 2, 1844, pp. 233–4.

Campbell, J. D. S., 'A Suggestion for Emigrants', *Nineteenth Century*, vol. 25, 1889, pp. 608–14.

Campbell, J. T., 'An Account of an Excursion into the Interior of New South Wales Performed by Governor Macquarie', *Colonial Journal*, vol. 1, 1816, pp. 69–76.

Capper, John, 'Off to the Diggings', *Household Words*, vol. 5, 1852, pp. 405–10.

Capper, John & W. H. Wills, 'First Stage to Australia', *Household Words*, vol. 8, 1853, pp. 42–5.

Caroline, Jane, 'The Sempstress' Farewell' (poem), *People's and Howitt's Journal*, vol. 2, 1850, p. 26.

Champion, H. H., 'The Crushing Defeat of Trade Unionism in Australia', *Nineteenth Century*, vol. 29, 1891, pp. 225–37.

Chapman, Henry Samuel, 'Emigration; Comparative Prospects of Our New Colonies [Canada, Australia and New Zealand]', *London and Westminster Review*, vol. 35, 1841, pp. 131–87.

—— 'Colonial Emigration [and population]', *Dublin Review*, vol. 22, 1847, pp. 388–408.

—— (prob) 'South Australia', *Dublin Review*, vol. 6, 1839, pp. 449–66.

—— (prob) 'Progress of Australian Discovery', *Dublin Review*, vol. 13, 1842, pp. 74–100.

Chapman, John, 'Our Colonial Empire', *Westminster Review*, vol. 93, 1870, pp. 1–37.

'Character of a Good Colonist', *Colonist*, vol. 1, 1848, pp. 29–31.

Chisholm, Caroline & Richard H. Horne, 'Pictures of Life in Australia', *Household Words*, vol. 1, 1850, pp. 307–10.

'Choice of a Colony—Avoid Foreign Countries', *Colonist*, vol. 1, 1848, pp. 13–15.

Christison, Robert, 'Independent Section. United Australia and Imperial Federation', *Westminster Review*, vol. 130, 1888, pp. 335–48.

'City of the Antipodes', *Eliza Cook's Journal*, vol. 7, 1852, pp. 200–3.

'Colonial Progress', *People's and Howitt's Journal*, vol. 2, 1850, p. 6.

'Colonies', *Fraser's Magazine*, vol. 6, 1832, pp. 437–45.

'Colonies and Colonization', *Home Circle*, vol. 1, 1849, pp. 90–1.

'Colonies and Colonization', *Westminster Review*, vol. 131, 1889, pp. 13–25.

'Colonization', *Magazine of Domestic Economy*, n.s. vol. 1, 1843, pp. 500–4.

'Condition of the Poor in Different Countries. I. China, New South Wales, Canada', *Saturday Magazine*, vol. 3, 1833, pp. 53–4.

'"Convict's Farewell", from review of Barry Cornwall's *English Songs and Other Poems*', *Tait's Edinburgh Magazine*, vol. 1, 1832, pp. 645–6.

Cook, Eliza, 'On Seeing Some Agricultural Emigrants Embark' (poem), *Eliza Cook's Journal*, vol. 7, 1852, p. 416.

'Copper Mines of South Australia', *Family Economist*, n.s. vol. 2, 1854, pp. 38–9.

Craig, Isa, 'Emigration As a Preventative Agency', *English Woman's Journal*, vol. 2, 1859, pp. 289–97.

Crawfurd, John, 'New South Australian Colony', *Westminster Review*, vol. 21, 1834, pp. 441–76.

—— 'South Australian Colony', *Westminster Review*, vol. 23, 1835, pp. 213–39.

Crofton, F., 'English Convicts: What should be done with them', *Westminster Review*, vol. 70, 1863, p. 1032.

'Cumberland, New South Wales', *Mirror of Literature, Amusement and Instruction*, vol. 15, 1830, pp. 360–1.

'Delights of Melbourne. By An Emigrant', *Family Economist*, n.s. vol. 3, 1855, pp. 175–6.

'Diggings' (poem), *Working Man's Friend, and Family Instructor*, vol. 1, 1850, p. 30.

'Discoveries in Australia', *Sharpe's London Magazine*, vol. 2, 1846, pp. 295–8.

'Disposal and Control of our Criminal Classes', *Saint Pauls*, vol. 3, 1868–69, pp. 604–7.

Donovan, T. M., 'Industrial Expansion in Queensland', *Westminster Review*, vol. 147, 1897, pp. 245–59.

—— 'Queensland Politics and Federation', *Westminster Review*, vol. 152, 1899, pp. 155–65.

Doudney, Sarah, 'Exiled' (poem), *Leisure Hour*, vol. 29, 1880, p. 664.

'Dr. Rolph on Systematic Emigration and Colonization', *Simmonds's Colonial Magazine and Foreign Miscellany*, vol. 2, 1844, pp. 342–50, 420–35.

Du Cane, Sir Edmund Frederick, 'The Convict System in the Colonies', *Bentley's Miscellany*, vol. 51, 1862, pp. 513–27.

Duthie, D. Wallace, 'The Remittance Man [in the colonies]', *Nineteenth Century*, vol. 46, 1899, pp. 827–32.

'Education in the Colonies and in India', *Eliza Cook's Journal*, vol. 7, 1852, pp. 124–5.

Egan, Pierce, 'The Emigrant' (song; music by John Barnett), *Home Circle*, vol. 2, 1850, pp. 264–5.

Elliot, Henry, 'Australia Fifty Years Ago', *Nineteenth Century*, vol. 26, 1889, pp. 754–75.

'Emigrant Governesses', *London Review*, vol. 4, 1862, pp. 346–7.

'The Emigrant in Port Phillip', *Eliza Cook's Journal*, vol. 1, 1849, pp. 193–5.

'Emigrant-Ship Matrons', *English Woman's Journal*, vol. 5, 1860, pp. 24–36.

'The Emigrant's Complaint' (poem), signed L., *Howitt's Journal*, vol. 1, 1847, p. 324.

'Emigrants' Home and Government Station at Birkenhead', *Working Man's Friend, and Family Instructor*, n.s. vol. 1, 1852, p. 302.

'Emigration', *Chambers' Edinburgh Journal*, vol. 1, 1832, p. 149.

'Emigration', *Chambers' Edinburgh Journal*, vol. 2, 1833, pp. 395–6.

'Emigration [Annals of Industry]', *People's Journal*, vol. 2, 1847, p. 1.

'Emigration [Weekly Record]', *Howitt's Journal*, vol. 2, 1847, p. 1.

'Emigration', *People's and Howitt's Journal*, vol. 7, 1851, p. 4.

'Emigration', *People's and Howitt's Journal*, vol. 7, 1851, pp. 375–7.

'Emigration and the Sexes', *Tait's Edinburgh Magazine*, n.s. vol. 25, 1858, pp. 509–15.

'Emigration for the Million', signed Gershom, *People's and Howitt's Journal*, vol. 7, 1851, p. 31.

'Emigration to Australia', *Working Man's Friend, and Family Instructor*, n.s. vol. 3, 1853, p. 95.

'Emigration to South Australia', *Chambers' Edinburgh Journal*, vol. 7, 1838, p. 229.

'Employment of Women', *Dublin Review*, vol. 52, 1862, pp. 1–44.

'Employment of Young Women', *Eliza Cook's Journal*, vol. 2, 1850, pp. 145–7.

'England and her Colonies' (poem), from Southey's 'Poet's Pilgrimage to Waterloo', *Colonial Journal*, vol. 3, 1816, pp. 11–14.

'English Farmers in Western Australia, Commonly Called the Swan River Settlement', *Saturday Magazine*, vol. 9, 1836, pp. 218–19.

'Enlarged Plan of Emigration', *People's and Howitt's Journal*, vol. 7, 1851, p. 29.

Evans, Mary Sanger, 'Domestic Servants in Australia: a Rejoinder [to Rowe]', *Westminster Review*, vol. 136, 1891, pp. 46–53.

'Expedition into Central Australia', *Sharpe's London Magazine*, vol. 9, 1849, pp. 249–51.

'Expense of our Colonies', *People's and Howitt's Journal*, vol. 7, 1851, p. 26.

'Far West', *Eliza Cook's Journal*, vol. 1, 1849, pp. 401–3.

'The Federation of the British Empire: Thoughts for the Queen's Jubilee on Imperial Federation', *Westminster Review*, vol. 128, 1887, pp. 484–94.

Feilding, William Henry Adelbert, 'What Shall I do with My Son? Part A.', *Nineteenth Century*, vol. 13, 1883, pp. 578–86.

—— 'Whither shall I send My Son? Part B', *Nineteenth Century*, vol. 14, 1883, pp. 65–77.

—— 'Imperial Migration and Settlement', *National Review*, vol. 8, 1887, pp. 777–95.

'Female Emigration', *London Review*, vol. 5, 1862, pp. 97–8.

'Female Emigration to the Colonies', *Reynold's Miscellany*, n.s. vol. 28, 1863, pp. 349–50.

Finch–Hatton, Harold, 'North Queensland Separation', *National Review*, vol. 6, 1886, pp. 796–809.

—— 'The Collapse in Australia', *National Review*, vol. 21, 1893, pp. 436–48.

'First Bushrangers in Australia Felix', *People's and Howitt's Journal*, vol. 7, 1851, pp. 367–9.

'First Railway in Australia', *People's and Howitt's Journal*, vol. 2, 1850, p. 39.

Forbes, Archibald, 'The Present and Future of the Australasian colonies', *Nineteenth Century*, vol. 14, 1883, pp. 720–32.

Fortescue, J. W., 'Guileless Australia: a Rejoinder', *Nineteenth Century*, vol. 30, 1891, pp. 430–43.

Froude, J. A., 'England and her Colonies', *Fraser's Magazine*, vol. 81, 1870, pp. 1–16.

—— 'Reciprocal Duties of State and Subject', *Fraser's Magazine*, vol. 81, 1870, pp. 285–301.

'The Future of Emigration: Colonial Lands', *Westminster Review*, vol. 131, 1889, pp. 167–76.

Garrett, Edward, 'The Family Council. The Boys' Start in Life', *Quiver*, vol. 16, 1881, pp. 180–3.

'Gigantic Trees in Van Diemen's Land', *Saturday Magazine*, vol. 4, 1834, p. 248.

Gillies, Mary Leman, 'A Passage of Domestic History in Van Diemen's Land', *People's Journal*, vol. 1, 1846, pp. 289–92.

Goble, G. F., '*Hints to Intending Gold Diggers and Buyers*' (review), *Athenaeum*, 7 January 1854, p. 18.

'Gold. A Reverie', *Eliza Cook's Journal*, vol. 11, 1854, pp. 85–6.

'Gold and Emigration', *Fraser's Magazine*, vol. 46, 1852, pp. 127–38.

'Gold! Gold!', *Eliza Cook's Journal*, vol. 7, 1852, pp. 33–5.

'The Golden Colony', review of *The History of the Colony of Victoria* by Thomas McCombie, *Tait's Edinburgh Magazine*, n.s. vol. 26, 1859, pp. 481–8.

Govett, William Romaine, 'Sketches of New South Wales', *Saturday Magazine*, vol. 8, 1836, pp. 177–9, 201–4, 217–19, 241–3; vol. 9, 1836, pp. 17–20, 57–9, 97–9, 156–8, 165–7, 183–4, 190–2, 222–4, 239–40, 249–50; vol. 10, 1837, pp. 7–8, 122–4, 133–4, 226–8; vol. 11, 1837, 78–9, 94–6.

'Great Britain and Her Colonies', *Fraser's Magazine*, n.s. vol. 13, 1876, pp. 269–82.

Greg, W. R., 'Our Colonies', *North British Review*, vol. 36, 1862, pp. 535–60.

'The Growth of Colonial England: Australia and New Zealand', *Westminster Review*, vol. 124, 1885, pp. 412–43.

Gwynne, Francis & W. H. Wills, 'Two Letters from Australia', *Household Words*, vol. 1, 1850, pp. 475–80.

H., E. W., 'The City of Sydney, New South Wales', *Tegg's Magazine of Knowledge and Amusement*, vol. 1, 1884, pp. 74–7.

Hamilton, R. G. C., 'Lending Money to Australia', *Nineteenth Century*, vol. 32, 1892, pp. 194–202.

Harkness, Margaret Elise, 'A Week on a Labor Settlement [in Australia]', *Fortnightly Review*, vol. 62, 1894, pp. 206–13.

Herbert, Henry Howard Molyneux, 'Australia in 1888', *Fortnightly Review*, vol. 51, 1889, pp. 420–43.

Heseltine, J. P., 'The Scramble for Gold. No. 2', *Nineteenth Century*, vol. 35, 1894, pp. 73–5.

'"Hints to Australian Emigrants" by Peter Cunningham' (review), *Monthly Review*, vol. 156, 1841, pp. 438–9.

Hogg, James, 'Emigration', *Chambers' Edinburgh Journal*, vol. 2, 1833, pp. 124–5.

Horne, Richard H., 'Convicts in the Gold Regions', *Household Words*, vol. 8, 1853, pp. 49–54.

Hornung, S. W., 'The Luckiest Man in the Colony', *Strand Magazine*, vol. 1, 1891, pp. 422–8.

Horton, R. W., 'On Emigration', *Mirror of Literature, Amusement and Instruction*, vol. 15, 1830, p. 174.

Howitt, William, 'The Old and New Squatter', *Household Words*, vol. 12, 1855, pp. 433–41, 471–8.

—— 'Gardens and Birds at Melbourne', *Family Economist*, n.s. vol. 8, 1860, p. 243.

Howitt, William & Richard Howitt, 'Letters on Emigration to New South Wales, etc.', *Tait's Edinburgh Magazine*, vol. 8, 1841, pp. 270–2.

Huxley, Henrietta, 'The Gold Diggings at Bathurst in 1851', *Nineteenth Century*, vol. 45, 1899, pp. 962–72.

Hyndman, H. M., 'The Australian Colonies and Confederation', *Fraser's Magazine*, n.s. vol. 14, 1876, pp. 641–52.

—— 'Something Better than Emigration: a Reply', *Nineteenth Century*, vol. 16, 1884, pp. 991–8.

'Important Information for Emigrants', *Simmonds's Colonial Magazine and Foreign Miscellany*, vol. 2, 1844, pp. 297–311.

'An Incident of Emigrant Life. From Rowcroft's *Tales of the Colonies*, 1845', *Sharpe's London Magazine*, vol. 1, 1845–46, pp. 294–8.

'Incidents of Australian Travel. First Paper', *Leisure Hour*, vol. 2, 1853, pp. 673–6.

'Incidents of Australian Travel. Second Paper', *Leisure Hour*, vol. 2, 1853, pp. 689–91.

Innes, Frederick Maitland, 'Convict system of Van Diemen's Land', *Monthly Chronicle*, vol. 5, 1840, pp. 431–49.

—— 'Transportation', *Monthly Chronicle*, vol. 6, 1840, pp. 159–62.

'Interesting Discovery near Bathurst, New South Wales', *Simmonds's Colonial Magazine and Foreign Miscellany*, vol. 1, 1844, pp. 197–202.

Jewsbury, Geraldine, '*The Emigrant's Home; or How to Settle: a Story of Australian Life, for all Classes, at Home and in the Colonies.* by W. H. G. Kingston' (review), *Athenaeum*, 10 May 1856, p. 584.

'John Turnbull's *A Voyage Around the World*' (review), *Anti-Jacobin Review and Magazine*, vol. 2, 1805, pp. 148–53.

Johnston, R. M., 'The Attack on the Credit of Australasia', *Nineteenth Century*, vol. 31, 1892, pp. 606–22.

Johnstone, Christian Isobel, 'British Emigrant Colonies: New South Wales', *Tait's Edinburgh Magazine*, vol. 5, 1834, pp. 401–19.

—— 'Howitt's *Colonization and Christianity*' (review), *Tait's Edinburgh Magazine*, vol. 9, 1838, pp. 527–34.

—— 'The New Colony of South Australia, the Penal Colonies', *Tait's Edinburgh Magazine*, vol. 9, 1838, pp. 776–89.

—— 'Three Years' Practical Experience of a Settler in New South Wales' (review), *Tait's Edinburgh Magazine*, vol. 5, 1838, pp. 399–400.

——'Australian Emigration', *Tait's Edinburgh Magazine*, vol. 10, 1839, pp. 168–76.

—— 'The Colony of Western Australasia' (review), *Tait's Edinburgh Magazine*, vol. 6, 1839, p. 822.

—— 'The Manager of the South Australia Company', *Tait's Edinburgh Magazine*, vol. 10, 1839, pp. 135–6.

—— 'Hood's *Australia and the East*' (review), *Tait's Edinburgh Magazine*, vol. 14, 1843, pp. 586–99.

—— 'Quaker missions to Australia', *Tait's Edinburgh Magazine*, vol. 14, 1843, pp. 218–24.

'Journey from the Snowy River Diggings to Neligan. Communicated by a Digger', *Leisure Hour*, vol. 10, 1861, pp. 251–3.

Jukes, Joseph Beete, 'Australia and its Gold Diggings', *Dublin University Magazine*, vol. 39, 1852, pp. 607–25.

—— 'New South Wales and Tasmania', *Dublin University Magazine*, vol. 41, 1853, pp. 453–72.

'Kangaroo and Young' (illustration), *Children's Friend*, vol. 13, 1873, p. 61.

'Kangaroo-Land', *Saturday Review*, vol. 14, 1862, pp. 54–5.

Kenealy, Arabella, 'A New View of the Surplus of Women', *Westminster Review*, vol. 136, 1891, pp. 465–75.

Kingston, William H. G., 'How the Unemployed May Better their Condition', *Colonist*, vol. 1, 1848, pp. 3–6.

Kirkland, Mrs C. M., 'Bush Life', *Working Man's Friend, and Family Instructor*, vol. 2, 1850, pp. 41–4.

Lancelott, J., '*Australia As It Is: Its Settlements, Farms, and Goldfields*' (review), *Eliza Cook's Journal*, vol. 8, 1852–53, pp. 268–71.

Lang, A., 'Mr. Max Muller's Philosophy of Mythology', *Fraser's Magazine for Town and Country*, n.s. vol. 24, 1881, pp. 166–87.

Lang, John, 'Lucy Cooper (An Australian Tale)', *Sharpe's London Magazine*, vol. 1, 1845–46, pp. 114–17, 132–5, 147–51, 179–82, 197–200, 212–15, 227–30.

—— 'Tracks in the Bush', *Household Words*, vol. 16, 1857, pp. 93–6.

—— 'Recollections of Botany Bay', *Welcome Guest*, vol. 1, 1858, pp. 246–8, 476–9, 566–7.

Lang, W., 'Journal of a Voyage to Port Phillip', *Simmonds's Colonial Magazine and Foreign Miscellany*, vol. 3, 1844, pp. 243–58, 436–50.

Langton, Edward, 'Colonial Custom-Houses. A Reply from Victoria', *Fraser's Magazine*, n.s. vol. 18, 1878, pp. 482–9.

'Laurel and Cypress: a Chapter in the History of Australian Exploration', *Fraser's Magazine*, vol. 66, 1862, pp. 726–41.

'Letter from a Convict in Australia to a Brother in England', *Cornhill Magazine*, vol. 13, 1866, pp. 489–512.

'Letter from a Port Phillip Emigrant', *Eliza Cook's Journal*, vol. 5, 1851, pp 238–9.

'Letter from Sydney', *Athenaeum*, 4 November 1829, pp. 685–7.

'Letter from Sydney. New Theory of Colonization', *Edinburgh Review*, vol. 71, 1840, pp. 517–21.

'Letter in Response to Article on Van Dieman's Land', *Mirror of Literature, Amusement and Instruction*, vol. 1, 1823, pp. 212–13.

'Lieut. Col. Collins. *An Account of the English Colony in New South Wales*' (review), *Anti-Jacobin Review and Magazine*, vol. 13, 1802, pp. 66–7.

'Life in New South Wales. By a Working Hand', *Howitt's Journal*, vol. 2, 1847, pp. 74–8.

'Life in the Bush', *Eliza Cook's Journal*, vol. 8, 1853, pp. 230–2.

'Lines on Leaving Home' (poem), *Home Circle*, vol. 1, 1849, p. 296.

'Literary Notice. *Settlers and Convicts; or, Recollections of Sixteen Years' Labour in the Australian Backwoods. By an Emigrant Mechanic*' (review), *Howitt's Journal*, vol. 2, 1847, pp. 44–6.

'Literary Register. *A Voice from Australia* by Hannah Villiers Boyd. London: Partridge & Co. pp. 100', *Tait's Edinburgh Magazine*, n.s. vol. 23, 1856, pp. 575–6.

'Literary Register. *Life in Victoria; or, Victoria in 1853, and Victoria in 1858* by William Kelly', *Tait's Edinburgh Magazine*, n.s. vol. 26, 1859, pp. 367–8.

Lockett, Jeannie, 'Female Labour in Australia: an Appeal for Help', *Nineteenth Century*, vol. 18, 1885, pp. 651–6.

—— 'The Labour Question in Australia: from an Australian Point of View', *Westminster Review*, vol. 132, 1889, pp. 617–23.

'Lord Grey, and his Plans of Colonisation', *Fraser's Magazine*, vol. 35, 1847, pp. 738–49.

Lowe, E., 'Australian Governors and their Ideals', *Westminster Review*, vol. 141, 1894, pp. 553–8.

McCoan, J. C., 'Seven Weeks in Australia', *Westminster Review*, vol. 129, 1888, pp. 52–76.

McCombie, Thomas, 'Australian Sketches', *Tait's Edinburgh Magazine*, n.s. vol. 23, 1856, pp. 78–84, 739–44; vol. 24, 1857, pp. 104–8, 626–30; vol. 25, 1858, pp. 9–13, 493–9; 521–3; vol. 26, 1859, pp. 457–64.

Macdonell, John, 'Imperial Federation and Some Neglected Colonial Ties', *Nineteenth Century*, vol. 47, 1900, pp. 855–65.

Macfie, Matthew, '"The Great West" of Australia', *Westminster Review*, vol. 137, 1892, pp. 481–97.

'Management and Disposal of our Criminal Population', *Edinburgh Review*, vol. 100, 1854, pp. 582–9.

Mann, F. C. T., 'Through the Jenolan Caves of New South Wales, Australia', *Westminster Review*, vol. 143, 1895, pp. 426–34.

Marryat, Miss, 'Friends in Australia', *Household Words*, vol. 19, 1859, pp. 584–8.

Martineau, Harriet, 'The Convict System In England and Ireland', *Edinburgh Review*, vol. 117, 1863, pp. 241–68.

'Mary's Visit to the Gold Fields', *Family Economist*, n.s. vol. 2, 1854, pp. 124–8.

Mayo, Isabella Fyvie, 'The Other Side of the World', *Girl's Own Paper*, vol. 3, 1881, pp. 145–8, 257–9, 289–91.

'Melbourne Exhibition', *Leisure Hour*, vol. 29, 1880, pp. 469–70.

Melville, R. D., 'Aspects of Empire and Colonization: Past and Present', *Westminster Review*, vol. 150, 1898, pp. 363–76.

Melville, S., 'The Mastiff Guard. A Reminiscence of Van Diemen's Land', *Welcome Guest*, vol. 4, 1860, pp. 158–60.

Meredith, Louisa Ann, 'Aborigines of New South Wales', *Hogg's Weekly Instructor*, vol. 1, 1845, p. 63.

—— 'A Van Diemen's Land Tragedy', *Bow Bells*, vol. 1, 1863, p. 439.

—— 'Van Diemen's Land', *Bow Bells*, vol. 1, 1863, p. 648.

'The Metropolis of Australia', *Tait's Edinburgh Magazine*, n.s. vol. 23, 1856, pp. 42–4.

'Mining in Australia', *People's and Howitt's Journal*, vol. 2, 1850, p. 27.

'Mirage in Australia', *Eliza Cook's Journal*, vol. 8, 1853, p. 336.

'Mission of Ticket-of-Leave Men', *St. James's Magazine*, vol. 6, 1863, pp. 163–5.

Mitchell, Edmund, 'The Dead Finish', *Temple Bar*, vol. 117, 1899, pp. 261–9.

'Mitchell's Second and Third Expeditions', *Blackwood's Edinburgh Magazine*, vol. 45, 1839, pp. 113–29.

Molesworth, William, 'New South Wales', *London Review*, vol. 1, 1835, pp. 25–47.

Montgomery, Henry Hutchinson, 'A Voyage Round the World' (poem), *Saturday Magazine*, vol. 7, 1835, p. 55.

—— 'A Mutton Bird Island', *New Review*, vol. 7, 1892, pp. 227–35.

'A Month in the Bush in Australia', *Magazine of Domestic Economy*, vol. 3, 1838, p. 344.

Moon, Sir Ernest Robert, 'Aspects of Australian Life', *Blackwood's Magazine*, vol. 143, 1888, pp. 351–65.

Moon, J. G., 'News From Our Digger: Log Line from the "Chalmers"', *Tait's Edinburgh Magazine*, vol. 24, 1853, pp. 291–7.

Morley, Joseph & Henry Morley, 'Bad Luck at Bendigo', *Household Words*, vol. 8, 1853, pp. 133–9.

Morris, Edward Ellis, 'On Sending Out to Australia', *Longmans Magazine*, vol. 2, 1883, pp. 173–83.

—— 'The Problem of the Kangaroo', *Macmillan's Magazine*, vol. 76, 1897, pp. 221–9.

—— 'Captain Cook's First Log in the Royal Navy; a New Discovery', *Cornhill Magazine*, vol. 80, 1899, pp. 519–32.

'Mother's Farewell to her Emigrant Daughter' (poem), *Eliza Cook's Journal*, vol. 8, 1852–53, p. 336.

Moule, Henry, 'Emigration in the Nineteenth Century', *Home and Foreign Review*, vol. 3, 1863, pp. 472–96.

'Mrs Chisholm', *Eliza Cook's Journal*, vol. 6, 1851–52, pp. 149–51.

'The Natives of Swan-River', *Saturday Magazine*, vol. 8, 1836, pp. 29–30.

'Natural History of Mistakes. XV—A Few "Emigration" Mistakes' (series), *Eliza Cook's Journal*, vol. 9, 1853, pp. 29–30.

'New South Wales' (review), *Blackwood's Edinburgh Magazine,* vol. 44, 1838, pp. 690–716.

'New South Wales: Colonial Immigration—the Bounty System and its Frauds', *Fraser's Magazine*, vol. 28, 1843, pp. 426–41.

'New Year's Family Party. John to Jonathan' (cartoon), *Judy, or the London Serio-Comic Journal*, vol. 18, 1875, pp. 117–18.

'Newspaper Press in Australia', *Mirror of Literature, Amusement and Instruction*, vol. 36, 1840, p. 368.

'Newspaper Press of Victoria', *Leisure Hour*, vol. 3, 1854, pp. 606–7.

Newton, R., 'Facts about Queensland', *Westminster Review*, vol. 15, 1896, pp. 568–74.

'Night in Tasmania', *Leisure Hour*, vol. 2, 1853, pp. 122–5, 139–42.

'Night in the Bush', *Leisure Hour*, vol. 9, 1860, p. 545.

Niven, Robert, 'Squatters, Proprietors in Victoria', *Fraser's Magazine*, vol. 99, 1879, pp. 511–18.

'Notes of a Residence in Van Diemen's Land', *Simmonds's Colonial Magazine and Foreign Miscellany*, vol. 2, 1844, pp. 170–3.

'Notes of a Ten Years' Residence in New South Wales', *Hogg's Weekly Instructor*, vol. 5, 1850, pp. 129–33.

'Notes on Australia', *Leisure Hour*, vol. 1, 1852, pp. 688.

'The Old World And The New', *Fraser's Magazine*, vol. 51, 1855, pp. 291–306.

Ollier, Edmund, 'The Ballad of the Gold-Digger', *Household Words*, vol. 7, 1853, pp. 61–3.

O'Neill, John, 'Not at home [emigration and immigration]', *Nineteenth Century*, vol. 20, 1886, pp. 553–64.

'On the Choice of a Profession', *Magazine of Domestic Economy*, vol. 3, 1838, pp. 237–40.

'On the Necessity for Emigration', *Magazine of Domestic Economy*, vol. 5, 1840, pp. 144–6.

Orpen, Joseph Millerd, 'Emigrant Education', *Nineteenth Century*, vol. 44, 1898, pp. 427–36.

Oss, S. F. van, 'The Westralian Mining "Boom"', *Nineteenth Century*, vol. 40, 1896, pp. 711–20.

'Our Colonies: Which, and Where are They?', *Simmonds's Colonial Magazine and Foreign Miscellany*, vol. 1, 1844, pp. 1–16.

'Our Convicts', *Eliza Cook's Journal*, vol. 10, 1853–54, pp. 49–50.

'Our Note Book. "Cannibals"', *Boy's Own Paper*, vol. 13, 1890–91, p. 159.

Owen, Rev. J. B., 'Life in Australia', *Leisure Hour*, vol. 2, 1853, pp. 214–15, 231–4, 253–5, 280–3.

'Page of Emigration Facts—Australia', *Family Economist*, vol. 5, 1852, pp. 210–11.

Parker, [Edward Stone?], 'The Settlement of Swan River', *Bow Bells*, vol. 1, 1863, p. 768.

Parsons, John Langdon, 'The Northern Territory of South Australia', *National Review*, vol. 3, 1884, pp. 78–88.

Pfoundes, C. S. W., 'In Correspondence. "Australia and Annexation"', *National Review*, vol. 7, 1886, pp. 712–14.

'Pic-Nic in Australia', *Leisure Hour*, vol. 2, 1853, pp. 826–7.

'Poetry and Prose of Francis Adams', *Saturday Review*, vol. 78, 1894, p. 75.

'Political and Social Prospects of the Australian Colonies', *Fraser's Magazine*, vol. 57, 1858, pp. 659–70.

Porter, J., 'Australia; Past, Present and Future', *Simmonds's Colonial Magazine and Foreign Miscellany*, vol. 3, 1844, pp. 358–63, 375–99.

'Professions in the Colonies', *Boy's Own Paper*, vol. 13, 1890–91, pp. 591–2.

'Progress of the World, "Australia and the Empire"', *Review of Reviews*, vol. 2, 1890, p. 461.

'Progress of the World, "Western Australia"', *Review of Reviews*, vol. 1, 1890, p. 179.

'Public Exhibitions: "Mr. G. Peck's Model of Hobart Town"', *Mirror of Literature, Amusement and Instruction*, vol. 36, 1840, p. 138.

Pulsford, Edward, 'An Australian Lesson [in Trade]', *Nineteenth Century*, vol. 24, 1888, pp. 393–409.

'Queensland', *Children's Friend*, vol. 32, 1892, pp. 173–5.

'Recent Intelligence Respecting the Aborigines of King George's Sound, Western Australia', *Saturday Magazine*, vol. 25, 1844, pp. 43–4, 55–6, 71–2.

'Reconnoitering Voyages and Travels, with Adventures in South Australia' (review), *Literary World*, vol. 1, 1839, pp. 299–302.

Reid, G. H., 'The Commonwealth of Australia', *Nineteenth Century*, vol. 30, 1891, pp. 145–53.

'Report on Emigration', *Literary World*, vol. 3, 1840, pp. 181–3.

'Representative Government in Our Colonies', *Westminster Review*, vol. 125, 1886, pp. 50–70.

'Response by Letter to Swan River Article', *Mirror of Literature, Amusement and Instruction*, vol. 15, 1830, p. 365.

'Return of Emigrants from the United Kingdom in 1841', *Simmonds's Colonial Magazine and Foreign Miscellany*, vol. 1, 1844, p. 180.

Richards, Thomas, 'Van Diemen's Land [and prison discipline]', *Westminster Review*, vol. 21, 1834, pp. 18–52.

Rinder, Samuel, 'Four-legged Australians', *Household Words*, vol. 7, 1853, pp. 208–14.

—— 'Australian Carriers', *Household Words*, vol. 11, 1855, pp. 420–7.

Rose–Soley, A. J., '"New Australia" [in Paraguay]: Communistic Work at the Antipodes', *Westminster Review*, vol. 140, 1893, pp. 523–7.

—— 'An Australian Watering-Place', *Westminster Review*, vol. 142, 1894, pp. 546–57.

Ross, Adelaide, 'Life in the Colonies', *Girl's Own Paper*, vol. 12, 1890, p. 487.

Roth, Henry Ling, 'Cataloguing an Empire', *Westminster Review*, vol. 145, 1896, pp. 140–2.

Rowe, C. J., 'Housekeeping Troubles in the Australian Colonies', *Westminster Review*, vol. 134, 1890, pp. 509–14.

Rye, Maria, 'On Assisted Emigration', *English Woman's Journal*, vol. 5, 1860, pp. 235–40, 326–35.

Saunders, John (ed.), 'Autobiography Of A Thief', *People's and Howitt's Journal*, vol. 7, 1851, pp. 177–80, 191–4, 202–4, 233–4, 267–9, 286–8, 304–6, 323–5, 348–50, 361–3.

'Second Page of Emigration Facts—Australia', *Family Economist*, vol. 5, 1852, pp. 232–3.

'Second Report from the Select Committee on South Australia', *Edinburgh Review*, vol. 75, 1842, pp. 140–5.

'Short Description of the British Colonies with a Map', *Colonist*, vol. 1, 1848, pp. 7–18.

Sidney, Samuel, 'An Australian Ploughman's Story', *Household Words*, vol. 1, 1850, pp. 39–43.

—— 'Christmas Day in the Bush', *Household Words*, vol. 2, 1850, pp. 309–10.

—— 'Better Ties than Red Tape Ties', *Household Words*, vol. 4, 1852, pp. 529–34.

—— 'What to Take to Australia', *Household Words*, vol. 5, 1852, pp. 364–6.

Smeaton, Oliphant, 'Curious Legends among the Australian Aborigines', *Westminster Review*, vol. 150, 1898, pp. 276–81.

Smith, Sydney, 'Oxley's Tour in Botany Bay' (review), *Edinburgh Review*, vol. 34, 1820, pp. 422–30.

—— 'Botany Bay', *Edinburgh Review*, vol. 38, 1823, pp. 85–104.

—— 'New South Wales', *Edinburgh Review*, vol. 47, 1823, pp. 87–99.

Smith, William Jardine, 'The Imperial Connection from an Australian Colonist's Point of View', *Fraser's Magazine*, vol. 84, 1871, pp. 384–402.

—— 'Empire or No Empire?', *Fraser's Magazine*, vol. 86, 1872, pp. 667–85.

—— 'Australian Federation and Imperial Union. By a Colonist', *Fraser's Magazine*, n.s. vol. 16, 1877, pp. 526–39.

'Snowy River Gold-Field, New South Wales. Communicated by a Digger', *Leisure Hour*, vol. 10, 1861, pp. 204–6.

'Something about Emigration', *Family Economist*, vol. 6, 1853, pp. 61–4.

Southern, Henry, 'Cunningham's New South Wales', *Westminster Review*, vol. 8, 1827, pp. 219–44.

Spedding, James, 'South Australia', *Contemporary Review*, vol. 75, 1842, pp. 140–62.

'Spirit of the Public Journals. The Natives of New South Wales', *Mirror of Literature, Amusement and Instruction*, vol. 2, 1823, pp. 411–13.

St. John, Percy B., 'The Gold-Man. A Legend of the Dry Diggings', *Eliza Cook's Journal*, vol. 5, 1851, pp. 17–20.

'State-Directed Colonization', *Westminster Review*, vol. 128, 1887, pp. 71–82.

'Statistics of New South Wales', *Simmonds's Colonial Magazine and Foreign Miscellany*, vol. 1, 1844, pp. 214–18.

Stewart, G. C., 'A Day's Excursion in Van Diemen's Land', *People's and Howitt's Journal*, vol. 2, 1850, pp. 150–1.

'Stokes's Discoveries in Australia', *Foreign Quarterly Review*, vol. 37, 1846, pp. 257–80.

'Stray Notes on Australia and the Diggings', *Leisure Hour*, vol. 1, 1852, pp. 640.

'Stud-framed Farm-House for Emigrants', *Mirror of Literature, Amusement and Instruction*, vol. 35, 1840, pp. 229–30.

'Suicide on the Ocean', *Eliza Cook's Journal*, vol. 2, 1850, p. 95.

Sulman, T., 'A Trip to New South Wales', *Children's Friend*, vol. 32, 1892, pp. 93–5.

Sutcliffe, Constance, 'Landing of the Primrose' (poem), *Ainsworth's Magazine*, vol. 1, 1842, pp. 303–4.

'Swan River', *Mirror of Literature, Amusement and Instruction*, vol. 15, 1830, pp. 33–6, 78–80.

'Swan River', *Mirror of Literature, Amusement and Instruction*, vol. 21, 1833, pp. 221–2.

'Swan River Newspaper', *Mirror of Literature, Amusement and Instruction*, vol. 16, 1830, pp. 429–30.

'Sydney in September', *Temple Bar*, vol. 90, 1890, pp. 111–17.

'Sydney, New South Wales', *Mirror of Literature, Amusement and Instruction*, vol. 4, 1824, pp. 305–6.

'Sydney, New South Wales', *Mirror of Literature, Amusement and Instruction*, vol. 21, 1833, pp. 257–9.

Thompson, Stephen, 'Young Australia [second generation]', *Westminster Review*, vol. 128, 1887, pp. 548–59.

'*Three Ages of the Colonies; or Concerning their Past, Present, and to Come*' (review), *Anti-Jacobin Review and Magazine*, vol. 12, 1802, pp. 476–82.

Threlkeld, L. E., 'An Australian Grammar. I–III', *Saturday Magazine*, vol. 8, 1836, p. 6; vol. 9, 1836, pp. 237–8; vol. 10, 1837, pp. 14–15.

Tooke, W. Eyton, 'Emigration Report', *Westminster Review*, vol. 6, 1826, pp. 342–73.

Torrens, W. M., 'Transplanting to the Colonies', *Nineteenth Century*, vol. 9, 1881, pp. 536–46.

'Treasure-finding and Wool-gathering', *Family Economist*, n.s. vol. 3, 1855, pp. 186–8.

'Trip to Australia', *Working Man's Friend, and Family Instructor*, n.s. vol. 3, 1853, pp. 170–1.

Tuke, J. H., 'With the Emigrants', *Nineteenth Century*, vol. 12, 1882, pp. 134–60.

—— 'State Aid to Emigrants: a Reply to Lord Brabazon', *Nineteenth Century*, vol. 17, 1885, pp. 280–96.

'Under Discussion. Some Aspects of Emigration', *Leisure Hour*, vol. 40, 1891, pp. 124–9.

'Van Diemen's Land', *Ainsworth's Magazine*, vol. 15, 1849, pp. 535–6.

'Van Diemen's Land', *Saturday Magazine*, vol. 1, 1832, pp. 35–6.

'Varieties. The Antipodes', *Girl's Own Paper*, vol. 1, 1880, p. 32.

'Victoria', William Westgarth's *Victoria: late Australia Felix, or Port Philip District of New South Wales*' (review), *Dublin University Magazine*, vol. 43, 1854, pp. 192–204.

'Victoria, or Port Philip', *Eliza Cook's Journal*, vol. 7, 1852, pp. 273–5.

'Victorian Gold-Diggings', *Eliza Cook's Journal*, vol. 7, 1852, pp. 316–18.

Vincent, Frank, 'Australian Jim Walker', *Household Words*, vol. 17, 1858, pp. 500–4.

—— 'Coo-ee', *Household Words*, vol. 17, 1858, pp. 232–6.

Vincent, Frank & Henry Morley, 'John Chinaman in Australia', *Household Words*, vol. 17, 1858, pp. 416–20.

'A Visit to Australia and its Gold Regions', *Home Friend*, vol. 1, 1852, pp. 461–8, 487–92, 529–34.

Vogel, Sir Julius, 'New Guinea and Annexation', *Fortnightly Review*, n.s. vol. 199, 1883, pp. 251–62.

—— 'Is it Open to the Colonies to Secede?', *Nineteenth Century*, vol. 26, 1889, pp. 897–911.

—— 'A Zollverein of the British Dominions', *Nineteenth Century*, vol. 32, 1892, pp. 498–508.

—— 'Bank Panic in Australia', *Fortnightly Review*, vol. 59, 1893, pp. 753–61.

—— 'Government Life Insurance: how not to do it', *Fortnightly Review*, vol. 56, 1894, pp. 225–41.

—— 'The Scramble for Gold. No.1', *Nineteenth Century*, vol. 35, 1894, pp. 58–72.

—— 'Greater Britain and the Queen's Long Reign', *Nineteenth Century*, vol. 41, 1897, pp. 343–51.

—— 'Prospect of Australian Federation', *Contemporary Review*, vol. 74, 1898, pp. 275–9.

'A Voice from Australia being a Genuine Letter from an Emigrant, verbatim et literatim', *Working Man's Friend, and Family Instructor*, n.s. vol. 2, 1852, p. 261.

'Voyage to Australia', *Leisure Hour*, vol. 1, 1852, pp. 615–19.

'Voyage to Van Diemen's Land.—Parts I, II', *Dublin University Magazine*, vol. 43, 1854, pp. 9–20, 275–82.

Waddy, P. R., 'Our Open Column. The University of Sydney', *Boy's Own Paper*, vol. 13, 1890–91, p. 719.

'Western Australia', *Westminster Review*, vol. 129, 1888, pp. 163–73.

'What Are We To Expect?', *Fraser's Magazine*, vol. 35, 1847, pp. 244–52.

'What Will the Government Do?', *Fraser's Magazine*, vol. 36, 1847, pp. 743–50.

White, Arthur Silva, 'Australia as a Strategic Base', *Nineteenth Century*, vol. 39, 1896, pp. 457–64.

Whyte-Melville, George, 'The Old World and the New', *Fraser's Magazine*, vol. 51, 1855, pp. 291–306.

Willoughby, Howard, '"The Seamy Side of Australia": a Reply from the Colonies', *Nineteenth Century*, vol. 30, 1891, pp. 292–302.

Wills, W. H., 'Safety for Female Emigrants', *Household Words*, vol. 3, 1851, p. 228.

Wilson, Alexander Johnstone, 'British Trade. No. X. Australia and New Zealand', *Fraser's Magazine*, n.s. vol. 15, 1877, pp. 701–2.

Wilson, E. D. J., 'The Colonial Empire of England', *Dark Blue*, vol. 1, 1871, pp. 770–80.

'Women's Employments. Prospects for Women Emigrants', *Woman at Home. Annie S. Swan's Magazine*, vol. 2, 1894, pp. 470–1.

'A Word to Intending Emigrants', *Chambers' Edinburgh Journal*, vol. 3, 1834, pp. 63–4.

Worthington, J. W., 'South Australia', *Foreign Quarterly Review*, vol. 25, 1840, pp. 374–93.

'A Yarn about an Emigrant Ship', *Leigh Hunt's Journal*, vol. 1, 1850–51, pp. 206–8.

Yorke, A. C., 'The Jackeroo', *Nineteenth Century*, vol. 45, 1899, pp. 833–40.

INDEX